OVERLORD'S EAGLES

OVERLORD'S EAGLES

*Operations of the
United States Army Air Forces
in the Invasion of Normandy
in World War II*

by JOHN J. SULLIVAN

McFarland & Company, Inc., Publishers
Jefferson, North Carolina, and London

The present work is a reprint of the illustrated case bound edition of Overlord's Eagles: Operations of the United States Army Air Forces in the Invasion of Normandy in World War II, *first published in 1997 by McFarland.*

LIBRARY OF CONGRESS CATALOGUING-IN-PUBLICATION DATA

Sullivan, John J., 1925–
    Overlord's eagles : operations of the United States Army Air Forces in the invasion of Normandy in World War II / by John J. Sullivan.
        p.   cm.
    Includes bibliographical references.

    ISBN 0-7864-2338-2 (softcover : 50# alkaline paper)

    1. World War, 1939–1945 — Campaigns — France — Normandy. 2. World War, 1939–1945 — Aerial operations, American. 3. United States. Army Air Forces — History — World War, 1939–1945. 4. Normandy (France) — History, Military. I. Title.
D756.5.N6S85   2005   97-1650
940.54'2142 — dc21

British Library cataloguing data are available

©1997 John J. Sullivan. All rights reserved

No part of this book may be reproduced or transmitted in any form or by any means, electronic or mechanical, including photocopying or recording, or by any information storage and retrieval system, without permission in writing from the publisher.

Front cover photograph: *Top to bottom:* P-38 Lightning, P-51 Mustang and P-47 Thunderbolt. (U.S. Air Force Photo Collection [USAF Neg. No. 52585 AC], courtesy of National Air and Space Museum, Smithsonian Institution.)

Manufactured in the United States of America

McFarland & Company, Inc., Publishers
  Box 611, Jefferson, North Carolina 28640
    www.mcfarlandpub.com

To Clara Tomisman Sullivan

Table of Contents

Lists of Tables, Diagrams, Maps   ix
List of Photographs   xi
Preface   xiii
Introduction   1

I. Air Preparations for Invasion

1. Overlord's Air Command   2
2. Eighth Air Force Operations, 1942–43   19
3. Eighth Air Force Fighter Problems   29
4. The Allied Expeditionary Air Forces   52
5. USSTAF's Campaign to Weaken the German Air Force   59
6. The Plan to Bomb French and Belgian Rail Centers   69
7. Opposition to the Transportation Plan   73
8. Air Preparations to Support Invasion Forces   83

II. Air Operations in Support of Overlord

9. Attacks on Rail Centers, Oil Plants, and V-Weapons Before D-Day   93
10. Attacks on Bridges and Airfields Before D-Day   107
11. Air Support for the Landings in Normandy   115
12. Close Air Support for Invasion Forces   123
13. Counter-Invasion and Resistance Operations   130
14. Air Support for the Allied Breakout from Normandy   135
15. Reorganization of Eisenhower's Air Command   147

III. Evaluations of Overlord's Air Campaigns

16. Surveys of the Transportation Campaign and Interdiction — 153
17. German Opinions of Allied Air Campaigns — 165
18. Evaluations of Allied Air Offensives: Oil, V-Weapons, Aircraft, Road Junctions, Carpet Bombing — 169
19. Postwar Debates About Allied Air Campaigns — 175

Epilogue — 177
Notes — 181
Glossary — 199
Bibliography — 201
Index — 205

List of Tables, Diagrams and Maps

Tables

AWPD-42 Recommended Air Strength	20
Estimated GAF Strength in May 1944	90
Effort Expended on the Transportation Campaign	99
Sortie Totals for U.S. Aircraft	104
Ninth Air Force Operations, June 1944	122
IX TAC Results, D-Day to December	126
Freight Traffic, January–July 1944	164
Selected Attacks on French Rail Bridges	164
Flight Hours of Pilots in Training	171

Diagrams

Organization for Overload	17
Ninth Air Force, June 1, 1944	84
Ninth Tactical Air Command	124
AAF Evaluation Board Bridge Diagram	162

Maps

River Seine Bridge Targets	110
Normandy Lodgment Area	116
The Seine-Loire Line of Interdiction	120
Operation Cobra	138

List of Photographs

Air commanders in North Africa	6
General Carl Spaatz receiving medal from General Dwight D. Eisenhower	7
General H. H. Arnold in an observation airplane	8
General Ira Eaker and reporters	10
General Dwight D. Eisenhower and his air commanders	16
B-17 leaving target at Marienburg	25
P-38 Lightning, P-51 Mustang, P-47 Thunderbolt	37
P-51 Mustang dive-bombing	39
Tommy Hitchcock in World War I	41
The first Merlin Mustang	42
General Frank O'D. Hunter and Robert A. Lovett	45
Harry Hopkins and J. Gilbert Winant	48
General Dwight D. Eisenhower and Major James Howard	50
B-26 medium bombers attacking target in France	57
B-24 Liberators attacking target at Tours	63
Colonel Donald J. M. Blakeslee	67
Colonel Glenn Duncan and Generals	86
Devastation in St. Lô	97
Marshaling yard at Rouen after bombing	100
First Lieutenant John T. Godfrey	105
A bridge at Vernon	108
Bombed aircraft factory near Bettenhausen	114
Rubble in St. Sauveur	119
Cut railroad bridge at Tours	121
General Elwood Quesada pumping gasoline	125
Train under attack by 363rd Fighter Group	129
Generals Omar Bradley, Leonard Gerow, Dwight D. Eisenhower, and J. Lawton Collins	141
Soldiers after Cobra's carpet bombing	142
Generals George S. Patton, Jr., and Otto Weyland	144

Devastated marshalling yard at Paris/Juvisy 154
Collapsed bridge at Pontaubault 159
Destroyed railroad bridge at Mantes-Gassicourt 159
Bombed bridge at Rouen 160

Preface

Operation Overlord and its most hazardous phase, the Normandy Invasion, have been described in thousands of books, articles, motion pictures and television dramas. It is strange, then, that Overlord's air campaigns have received little scrutiny by writers and historians. It cannot be due to any intrinsic dullness in the subject, for many stirring books describe air fighting—books about air engagements in World War I and the Battle of Britain, for example. Perhaps Overlord's air battles were overshadowed by its ground actions. Everyone remembers Field Marshal Bernard L. Montgomery and General George S. Patton, Jr., but few can identify General Carl A. Spaatz or Air Chief Marshal Sir Trafford Leigh-Mallory, the men who directed Overlord's most crucial air offensives.

Most historians who have written about Overlord's air campaigns, however briefly, have neglected or misinterpreted major developments. The P-51 Mustang fighter changed the character of the air war in 1944, but no one has explained the critical part played in the airplane's career by Tommy Hitchcock. General H. H. Arnold, chief of the Army Air Forces [AAF], dismisses Hitchcock with a few lines in his autobiography: "When I went overseas in the spring of 1941, Tommy Hitchcock and Mr. Winant talked to me about the P-51, although they didn't know much about it at that time."[1]

Arnold has the date wrong. It was 1942 when Hitchcock collared him at the U.S. Embassy in London to promote the Mustang. But much more serious is the implication that Hitchcock's part in the Mustang story was trivial. Actually, the efforts of Hitchcock and his friends, Ambassador John G. Winant and Assistant Secretary of War for Air Robert A. Lovett, to convince the Army Air Forces to order P-51s resulted in Mustangs being available to send to the U.K. in time to take part in the crucial air battles of 1944. Arnold admitted later that "we could have had the long-range P-51 in Europe rather sooner than we did. That we did not have it sooner was the Air Force's own fault." That it did arrive in the nick of time was largely the result of Hitchcock's efforts. Arnold also disparaged with faint praise the crucial contributions of the British to the development of the Mustang. The great fighter came into production because of British initiative, and its superiority was due in large part to Rolls-Royce engines. It first went into combat with the Royal Air Force.

Autobiographies like Arnold's exert a powerful influence on histories of Overlord, but they are almost inevitably one-sided and self-serving. Books written by Air Marshal Sir Arthur Tedder, General Eisenhower and General Omar Bradley contributed to the unbalanced, erroneous public perceptions of major events in Overlord. General Bradley's distorted account of the carpet bombing that began Operation Cobra was widely accepted and repeated. Cobra was a major event; it broke open the front in Normandy and led to

Allied victory in the Battle of France, but no historian reported its carpet bombing accurately.

The unbalanced picture of Overlord painted by existing memoirs and autobiographies is further exaggerated by the failure of some major Overlord commanders to write their own. Generals Eaker and Spaatz refrained from doing so; Air Marshal Leigh-Mallory died in an aircraft crash during the war. Fortunately, these commanders left extensive collections of documents that can be invaluable to students of Overlord. In recent years most of this material has had secrecy classifications removed.

Undoubtedly, the most important air operation that writers have neglected or misconstrued was the bombing of French and Belgian rail centers. This major Overlord campaign took place prior to D-Day. It siphoned off a tremendous amount of Allied air resources from the battles for air supremacy; it caused enormous suffering and destruction in France and Belgium. Eisenhower and Tedder claimed that it was both effective and crucial to the success of Overlord. Actually, it was neither. No one has described this campaign thoroughly and objectively. Solly Zuckerman's studies in 1944–45 suffered from a shortage of personnel and from his obsession to justify a campaign that he himself planned. His memoirs confused the picture even more. The official AAF history warned of the inadequate nature of reports on the subject with the statement: "Long after D-Day, there remained the sobering question as to whether the results of the plan were commensurate with the cost in air effort and the ruin inflicted on French and Belgian cities." Several investigations in 1944–45 answered this question, but the reports were given secrecy classifications and filed away.

Writers and historians have also neglected both Air Chief Marshal Sir Trafford Leigh-Mallory and the organization he led, the Allied Expeditionary Air Forces [AEAF]. The official history of the Army Air Forces urges scholars to examine the "unhappy history of AEAF ... the least successful venture of the entire war with a combined Anglo-American command," but historians have not taken up the challenge.[2] Leigh-Mallory did not survive the war and was thus unable to rebut the many negative assessments of his record. Needless to say, he was somewhat shortchanged: he directed air operations that crucially helped the invasion to succeed; he originated the proposal for the carpet bombing near St. Lô and directed the operation. This assault pierced the front in Normandy and led to Allied victory in the Battle of France. He deserves much more attention than he has received.

This book developed from research in primary sources—letters, reports, memorandums, diaries and the like. It is fitting then to express gratitude to the dedicated archivists who helped the author so generously. Unfortunately, there are too many to list here but three great archives were indispensable: the Manuscript Division of the Library of Congress, the British Public Records Office, and the United States Air Force Historical Research Agency.

Introduction

The Normandy Invasion started on June 6, 1944. It was the most hazardous phase of Operation Overlord — the Allied drive aimed at the heart of Germany and the destruction of her armed forces. Powerful armies gathered in England to execute Overlord. Allied leaders knew that a failure of this operation would have catastrophic consequences, perhaps assuring the survival of Nazi Germany.

Overlord's amphibious assault would attempt to establish a beachhead in Normandy extending from the mouth of the Orne River, north of Caen, to the east coast of the Cotentin Peninsula, twenty miles northwest of Bayeux. In the first critical weeks of the operation, only a small part of the Allied force could be deployed in France. If German forces launched a powerful attack against the disorganized troops on the beaches, they could repel the invasion by wiping out its ragged leading edge.

German anti-invasion forces would have a trump card to play: the excellent European railroad system could move troops, equipment and supplies rapidly to an invasion sector. By exploiting the capability of railroads to move great loads swiftly to virtually any part of France, the Germans could, at critical points, deploy forces strong enough to overwhelm the invaders.

The Allies counted on their formidable air power to neutralize the enemy's transportation advantage. In the months before D-Day, British and American air forces would attack transportation facilities — especially railroads — ceaselessly.

Air superiority in the west was an absolute prerequisite for the invasion. To wear down the German Air Force before D-Day, Allied air forces would engage it in battle at every opportunity. After D-Day tactical air forces would provide close, continuous support for Allied armies. As Overlord's chief planner warned: "The successful outcome of the operation is, therefore, dependent in very large measure on the action of our air forces."

Although Allied planners acknowledged the importance of air power to Overlord, they argued for months about specific ways to employ it. The question debated most heatedly involved employment of strategic air forces. General Eisenhower approved the proposal of his deputy, Air Chief Marshal Sir Arthur Tedder, to employ them to attack French and Belgian railroad centers prior to D-Day. Tedder believed that this campaign would critically disrupt the rail transportation available to anti-invasion forces.

General Eisenhower's top U.S. air commander, Lieutenant General Carl A. Spaatz, warned him repeatedly that there was a far more important objective for Allied air forces than the disruption of the European railway system, important as that was. The German Air Force had to be overwhelmed before D-Day, Spaatz explained. If this were not accomplished, the invasion itself would be unacceptably hazardous. Eisenhower accepted Spaatz's contention, and, in the first quarter of 1944, Allied air forces carried out Operation Pointblank. In battles provoked by this operation, Allied air forces won air superiority; it was largely an achievement of the U.S. Army Air Forces.

On D-Day, Allied tactical air forces took center stage. They "saved the day" at Omaha Beach and provided excellent, close air support for Allied armies in the final campaigns leading to Germany's defeat. German commanders later described the formidable impact of the tactical air forces as the key to Allied victory in the invasion of northwest Europe.

Overlord began officially in early 1943 when Allied leaders appointed a British officer to direct planning for the invasion. Substantial parts of the early plans, however, had to be revised after General Eisenhower took command of the operation. It is with President Roosevelt's momentous decision to appoint General Eisenhower to command Overlord that chapter one begins.

Part I
Air Preparations for Invasion

Chapter 1

Overlord's Air Command

On December 7, 1943, President Roosevelt's airplane landed at an airfield near Tunis. General Dwight D. Eisenhower waited to greet his chief. As they rode to Eisenhower's headquarters, Roosevelt said, "Well, Ike, you are going to command Overlord."[1] The code name referred to the forthcoming invasion of northwest Europe. Overlord's assault phase would be the largest, most hazardous amphibious attack in history. From bases in the United Kingdom, Allied forces would first establish a lodgment area in Normandy, then undertake operations aimed at the heart of Germany and the destruction of her armed forces.[2] As Overlord's supreme commander, Eisenhower would report directly to the Combined Chiefs of Staff [CCS].

The success of Overlord would depend heavily on Allied air power. Substantial reduction of German air strength on the western front, especially of fighter forces, was an absolute prerequisite for the invasion. Air supremacy over the invasion area was essential in order to give soldiers wading through the surf onto hostile beaches a reasonable chance to establish a secure beachhead.

Eisenhower needed no reminder of the importance of air support in amphibious operations. During the Italian campaign, forces under his command had narrowly escaped annihilation on the beaches at Salerno. German aircraft from nearby airfields had pummeled his troops, while Allied aircraft had had to operate from Sicily with a tactical radius too short to give them more than a few minutes over the beachhead.[3] At several critical times in the North African and Italian campaigns, Eisenhower had asked for air reinforcements from the U.K. but had been turned down.[4] These rejections left a bitter memory and stiffened his resolve to insist on strong air support for Overlord.

As he prepared to establish the Supreme Headquarters of the Allied Expeditionary Force (SHAEF) in the U.K., Eisenhower faced a multitude of difficult decisions — none more important than the selection of his chief subordinates. Constraints inherent in relations between Allied nations mandated that British officers be named to the top positions under Eisenhower. A Royal Air Force (RAF) officer, Air Chief Marshal Sir Arthur Tedder, became deputy supreme commander. He had commanded air forces in the Mediterranean theater. Eisenhower welcomed Tedder's appointment. He explained to General George C. Marshall, U.S. Army chief of staff, that too few air commanders had operational experience coordinating air and ground forces: "Air Chief Marshal Tedder is not only expert in these matters but has such a high standing in the British air forces that the readiness of the C.A.S. [RAF chief of staff] to place, during critical junctures of the land campaign, every last airplane in England under ... the Air Commander will be enhanced."[5]

Command of Overlord's ground, sea and air forces also went to British officers.

Air commanders in North Africa: Air Vice Marshal Arthur Coningham, Air Chief Marshal Arthur Tedder, General Carl Spaatz and James H. Doolittle. (Courtesy of the Library of Congress.)

General Bernard L. Montgomery would command ground forces during the amphibious assault phase. Admiral Bertram Ramsey would command naval forces. Air Chief Marshal Trafford Leigh-Mallory had been at work for many months directing air planning for Overlord. He later received the appointment to command the Allied Expeditionary Air Forces (AEAF).

To command units of the U.S. Army Air Forces (AAF) assigned to Overlord, Eisenhower wanted Lieutenant General Carl A. Spaatz, who had been on his team in the North African and Italian campaigns. Spaatz's position in Overlord would reflect the semi-autonomous status of the AAF. He would be Eisenhower's top American air commander, but he would also have responsibilities that transcended Overlord. He would command the U.S. strategic air forces (USSTAF). In this capacity he reported directly to General H.H. Arnold, chief of the AAF, who was a member of both the U.S. Joint Chiefs of Staff (JCS) and the CCS. Spaatz would receive directives regarding the strategic air war from Air Chief Marshal Charles Portal, a British member of the CCS. Eisenhower fully expected that deliberations about employment of air forces would be quarrelsome. An incipient conflict between air and ground officers had simmered for decades. It grew out of their failure to understand or accept each other's contentions. Eisenhower kept his reservations about airmen subdued for the most part and earned the respect and confidence of Arnold and Spaatz.

General Dwight D. Eisenhower pins an Oak Leaf Cluster to General Carl Spaatz's Distinguished Service Medal. (U.S. Air Force Photo Collection [USAF Neg. No. 55067 AC], courtesy of National Air and Space Museum, Smithsonian Institution.

These three American Army officers, whose decisions did so much to shape the campaigns that made Overlord a success, were all West Pointers. Arnold graduated from the U.S. Military Academy in 1907, Spaatz in 1914 and Eisenhower in 1915. Arnold became a pioneer Army aviator. While stationed at Governor's Island in New York City's harbor, he witnessed a flight by Wilbur Wright in one of the world's first powered aircraft. Arnold

General Henry H. Arnold in a small observation airplane during a visit to the Italian theater of operations. His pilot is Major J. T. Walker. (U.S. Air Force photograph)

became fascinated by flight, joined the fledgling Army air service and took flying lessons from the Wright brothers.[6]

Spaatz served in the infantry for a brief period, then transferred to the Army's air service. He piloted some of the Army's first airplanes as part of General Pershing's campaign on the Mexican border. Spaatz directed pilot training at a flying school in France during World War I while Eisenhower and Arnold performed critical jobs in the U.S. Spaatz managed to get into air combat long enough to shoot down several German aircraft.[7] An airman who knew Spaatz well said that he "never commanded a unit that did not turn out tops."[8] Spaatz served as a military observer in France and England in 1940. He was there during the Battle of Britain and sent home reports criticizing both German and British performance, although he did recommend that the U.S. continue to support the British by sending supplies and equipment.[9]

Eisenhower and Spaatz came from similar backgrounds — country villages, German-American families, West Point and life in the lean peacetime Army with its sparse resources and slow advancement. Both men held the rank of major for many years. Spaatz's wife remembered that "Tooey was a major forever, longer than anybody in history."[10]

The career paths of Arnold and Spaatz crossed many times. At the start of World War II, Arnold was chief of the Army Air Corps; he regarded Spaatz as the Air Corps' best operational commander. Both men learned to adjust to the prejudice against the Air Corps that was rife in the Army. In the prewar era many Army officers considered airmen to be little more than daredevils who wasted Army funds on antics that would contribute little to the Army's performance in battle. Throughout World War II, the AAF remained a subordinate part of an army controlled by ground officers. Eisenhower's respect for the AAF increased steadily, but he never fully trusted the judgment of air commanders; too often, in his opinion, they wanted to execute missions not closely related to critical ground operations. Often, the air operations that ground officers perceived as frivolous or unimportant were those AAF commanders considered vital. Airmen believed that their arm had capabilities extending far beyond support for ground troops. They used the word "strategic" to identify operations designed to deliver significant, even war-winning, blows against an enemy.

Eisenhower's deputy, Air Chief Marshal Tedder, understood air-ground enmity well. The RAF, though now an independent service, had likewise encountered opposition from ground and naval personnel. During the early period of his service with Americans, Tedder wrote to Portal that Eisenhower and his chief of staff, Major General Walter B. Smith, were "instinctively antagonistic" to air force autonomy: they found it "difficult to understand that every General has not a divine right to command his own private air forces, and incidentally a divine inspiration by which he knows better than anyone else how those air forces should be employed."[11]

Tedder, like many of his British colleagues, had grave reservations about the competence of American officers. British leaders accepted the need for an American supreme commander — preferably little more than a coordinator — but wanted his chief subordinates, the men who would actually direct operations, to be British.[12]

The selection of Spaatz to direct Eisenhower's American air forces ignited opposition. Tedder asked Portal to sidetrack Spaatz. Tedder, who was obviously trying to strengthen his own position in Overlord, also tried to separate Eisenhower and Smith. The intrigue reached a high level when Portal asked Prime Minister Churchill to help. Churchill tried to influence Roosevelt to block Spaatz's appointment to Overlord but had to report failure: "I have already given the President the hint most strongly in the sense you desire but I can do no more."[13] Spaatz and Smith survived the back-stabbing British conspiracy. Eisenhower gave them unyielding support.

Tedder had a full quota of the arrogance that characterized so many British officers. Although he skillfully concealed his contempt for the Americans, it frequently found expression in his letters. Early in his association with Eisenhower, he described the situation to Portal: "There are many things one sees which are wrong and criminally uneconomical, but it would be worse than useless to go at it like a bull in a china shop. The only way in which we can get things really tidied up is by showing the Americans the right way to do things and letting them see where they are wrong and then letting them propose and put into effect the necessary remedies."[14]

Spaatz's appointment to Overlord led to a fracas in the AAF, too. Lieutenant General Ira Eaker commanded Eighth Air Force, the strategic air force operating out of the U.K. Spaatz wanted him replaced by Major General James H. Doolittle, who had served under Spaatz in the Mediterranean theater. Eaker protested strongly against the proposed switch. Eighth Air Force was now a powerful air force and he hated to leave it when, after a long, painful growth, it was able to make a decisive contribution to victory. But Spaatz and Arnold agreed that Eaker should direct Allied air operations in the Mediterranean theater. Fifteenth Air Force would begin strategic operations there, and Eaker's experience

Brigadier General Ira Eaker and reporters. (U.S. Air Force Photo Collection [USAF Neg. No. 22500 AC], courtesy of National Air and Space Museum, Smithsonian Institution.)

would be invaluable to it. Eaker had a knack for working smoothly with the British, and this talent would be highly useful in his new job. Spaatz was certainly aware, too, that changes would have to be made in Eighth Air Force practices and that they could be made more expeditiously with a new leadership team. Eaker had become somewhat resistant to change. He was known to resent suggestions that some Eighth Air Force policies needed to be changed. A letter he wrote to a friend at AAF headquarters contains complaints of a kind he expressed many times:

> I rely greatly on you ... to keep a great deal of the fanciful, theoretical, idealistic and impractical out of directives. I realize that we are not unique in the burden of criticism we have to bear from distant critics. ... I only hope it does not get so bad that it will develop an acrimonious situation. I am prepared for this, however. ... we shall not take it lying down.[15]

In reaction to Eaker's protest, Arnold appeared to waver, or so it seemed to Spaatz. Arnold had to placate General Marshall who objected to some of Eisenhower's personnel requests. Marshall informed the supreme commander that it was wrong "to gut the Mediterranean headquarters and leadership." Marshall informed Eisenhower that he was "disturbed over the pressure of Tedder and Spaatz to move Eaker to the Mediterranean because Eaker did not appear at all particularly suited for that theater: and I am forced to the conclusion that their attitude is selfish and not purely objective."[16]

Marshall was President Roosevelt's chief military advisor, as well as chairman of the

JCS, and was extremely influential. His comments caused great concern in Eisenhower's staff, but Spaatz did not yield. He made it clear that he did not want the Overlord job if Eaker remained in command of Eighth Air Force. The final decision was Eisenhower's and Eisenhower wanted Spaatz. The records do not show explicitly that Eisenhower lacked confidence in Eaker, but it is certain that he remembered the times when Eaker had opposed transfers of Eighth Air Force units to the Mediterranean where they were desperately needed. Spaatz recorded his appreciation of Eisenhower's support: "My original estimation of Eisenhower's fairness has been strengthened by the way in which he is taking this, and the way he is standing by me in my decisions. General Eisenhower ... is firm in his decisions and I consider him one of the finest men I know."[17] Spaatz's respect for Eisenhower was reciprocated. The supreme commander later wrote: "On every succeeding day of almost three years of active war I had new reasons for thanking the gods of war and the War Department for giving me 'Tooey' Spaatz."[18]

During the eighteen months they had worked together in the North African and Italian campaigns, Eisenhower had learned to appreciate Spaatz in spite of certain reservations he had about the airman's style. Spaatz disliked writing and public speaking. He avoided desk work.[19] Eisenhower often complained about loose AAF discipline. He warned Spaatz: "Frankly, I think our air forces have been behind in this matter. I am struck by the number of times I walk across flying fields to be classically ignored by officers, to say nothing of enlisted men."[20] Like most ground officers, Eisenhower believed that airmen were promoted too rapidly. He grumbled about Spaatz "constantly urging more promotions for his subordinates and seeking special favors [such as] ... a liquor ration...." After almost a year of working together, Eisenhower wrote a fitness report on Spaatz which was favorable but not without criticism. He was not certain that Spaatz was "tough enough and hard enough personally to meet the full requirements of his high position. ... [but] he does not seek personal glory or publicity, and he is a most loyal and hardworking subordinate."[21]

Spaatz's staff came in for frequent criticism. Eisenhower believed that Spaatz had "apparently picked officers more for their ... comradeship and friendliness than for their abilities as businesslike, tough operators."[22]

Spaatz accepted such complaints in stride. He had served for thirty years in an army where ground officers griped endlessly about alleged Air Corps deficiencies such as slackness in military courtesy. Airmen believed that ground crews working on intricate aircraft maintenance should not be distracted by nonessential, spit-and-polish courtesies. As regards Spaatz's staff, there certainly was a severe shortage of staff officers in the AAF due to its explosive growth. Arnold himself received complaints from Marshall for poor staff work: Arnold "had a very immature staff," Marshall wrote, "[composed of] antique staff officers or passé airmen ... busy taking stands ... about promotions."[23] Marshall's bias can be perceived in this comment. He believed that too many air officers had avoided staff jobs so that they could retain their flight pay, a bonus that many ground officers considered to be unmerited.

Spaatz must have been somewhat amused by Eisenhower's attitude about discipline. He knew that the supreme commander had stood 125th out of 162 in his class at West Point with respect to discipline.[24]

Eisenhower was more receptive to air-war doctrine than many ground officers. Early in his military career he had recognized the importance of aviation in military operations and had taken flying lessons. He logged over 350 hours of flight time. Under the combined tutelages of Tedder, of Spaatz and of combat, Eisenhower's education in air war continued. He conceded that air forces should be unified under a single commander in a theater of operations, not parceled out to army units in penny packets and subordinated to ground officers.

Spaatz, too, modified his prewar ideas of air power as a result of battle experience. He explained to Arnold: "When the battle situation requires it all units, including medium and heavy bombardment, must support the ground operations. Air support of the ground forces, on the other hand, cannot be made effective in the face of air supremacy, superiority, and under certain conditions, even parity on the part of the enemy's air forces. It follows from this that in order for the army to advance, the air battle must first be won."[25] These convictions guided Spaatz throughout the war. They became part of AAF doctrine.

Spaatz set up headquarters in the U.K. close to SHAEF so that he could work closely with Eisenhower and Tedder. Eisenhower disliked city life and soon found a cottage in the country with a garden, a putting green and fields for his dog to run in — the kind of setting the man from Kansas liked. On some evenings Spaatz came over and played his guitar. Eisenhower enjoyed a game of bridge. Spaatz preferred poker; he needed little sleep, and the poker games often continued on into the morning hours.[26] American commanders in the U.K. needed good British drivers to cope with the confusing driving conditions. Kay Summersby, an attractive, spunky Irish girl, became Eisenhower's driver. She knew Spaatz well and judged him to be a "serious man, serious to the point of grimness, and certainly the hardest-working man in the whole U.S. Army Air Force."[27]

Two powerful strategic air forces, RAF Bomber Command, commanded by Air Chief Marshal Sir Arthur Harris, and Eighth Air Force, now commanded by Doolittle, operated from the U.K. Their mission was to carry out strategic bombing, that is, to destroy Germany's industrial means and its will to wage war. Eisenhower expected the strategic air force commanders to resist coming under his authority. He alerted Tedder that "there will be some trouble in securing necessary approval for integration of all air forces that will be essential to success of Overlord. I expect that use of these air forces for the necessary preparatory phase will be particularly resisted. To support our position it is essential that a complete outline plan for use of all available aircraft during this phase be ready as soon as possible."[28] It is clear that Eisenhower expected Tedder to be his chief advisor on air operations and, in fact, to direct air planning for SHAEF, although this would normally be Leigh-Mallory's responsibility as AEAF commander. It was one of the ambiguous areas in his command arrangements that Eisenhower would have to clarify. Eisenhower began discussions about air matters, determined to bring as many air forces as possible under his control as soon as possible.

Arnold and Spaatz agreed that air forces in a theater of operations should be under the authority of a supreme commander so they could be employed most effectively. They believed in unity of command. Arnold's faith in this principle was so great that he tried to establish a single unified command for all Allied air forces in the U.K. and the Mediterranean theater. Failing to win over the British to this proposal, Arnold convinced the JCS to establish USSTAF with Spaatz in command. In this position Spaatz had authority over both Eighth Air Force in the U.K. and Fifteenth Air Force in the Mediterranean theater. He would coordinate their strategic operations against Germany. As USSTAF's commander, Spaatz received directives, not from Eisenhower, but from Portal; Eisenhower expected to change this soon.

Spaatz also exercised administrative control over the U.S. Ninth Air Force which would be built up in the U.K. to provide close support for Allied ground forces during the invasion. Arnold considered Spaatz his chief commander in the European theater; he counted on Spaatz to prevent a dog fight for personnel and supplies between Eighth, Ninth and Fifteenth Air Forces.

Major General Lewis H. Brereton commanded Ninth Air Force. Brereton, a career Army officer, was a legendary flier. Like Spaatz and many AAF leaders, Brereton had served in the Army's air service in World War I. On one of his reconnaissance missions, he had made the crucial observation that the German army was in retreat. Brereton had commanded air forces under General MacArthur in the Philippines. Later he had commanded AAF units in the Middle East and had directed a costly attack against enemy oil plants in Romania.

Brigadier General Elwood Quesada commanded Ninth Air Force fighters. He had served with Spaatz in the Mediterranean theater. Brigadier General Samuel E. Anderson commanded Ninth Air Force bombers (light and medium).

Spaatz had wide-ranging responsibilities and needed tact and patience to be effective. Fortunately he was respected throughout the AAF and had unwavering support from Arnold. He worried little about titles or chains of command; he advised his staff not to waste time trying to illustrate his authority with diagrams. Also he knew he could work with Tedder and Eaker. Although Spaatz did not want Eaker as Eighth Air Force commander, this did not damage their ability to work together. The two were old friends and associates, having worked together on many projects in peace and in war. In the Twenties Eaker as well as Quesada had served on a team directed by Spaatz which had conducted a pioneer aviation experiment in refueling aircraft in flight.

USSTAF's primary mission, defined by Allied leaders at the Casablanca conference, was to bring about "the progressive destruction and dislocation of the German military, industrial and economic system, and the undermining of the morale of the German people to a point where their capacity for armed resistance is fatally weakened." Since this directive also applied to RAF Bomber Command, the campaign to implement it received the name "Combined Bombing Offensive" (CBO). Allied air operations to carry out the CBO bore the codename Pointblank. The AAF believed that before bombing could devastate German industry the German fighter force would have to be overwhelmed. Thus the German Air Force (GAF) and Germany's aircraft industry became "intermediate objectives of the highest priority."[29]

Many airmen perceived air superiority to be a prelude to an all-out strategic bombing offensive designed to bring about a collapse of the German war machine. Eisenhower, most of his staff and most ground forces commanders, however, thought of it as a prerequisite for the invasion of northwest Europe. This difference in outlook caused dissension, but Spaatz kept the heat down by persuading Eisenhower that a strategic bombing offensive was the best way to bring the GAF to battle and thereby to destroy its fighter force. Eisenhower agreed with the objective without accepting all the AAF's strategic bombing doctrine.

In December 1943, Arnold reviewed the results of the CBO and found them distinctly unsatisfactory. Only four German industries — aircraft, anti-friction bearings, oil and rubber — were (1) vital to Germany's war effort, (2) vulnerable to aerial bombardment, and (3) capable of being destroyed by existing Allied air forces. But only 20 percent of the bombs dropped by the AAF on German targets in the preceding four months had been directed at one of these industries. Arnold wanted this proportion increased; he relied on Spaatz to make it happen.[30]

Spaatz realized that the time remaining to achieve Pointblank objectives was short; he expected that USSTAF would soon be obligated to provide direct support for Overlord.

In one of his first directives, he warned: "In view ... of the steady increase in German fighter strength, which if unchecked may render us unable to fulfill the tasks allotted to us by the Combined Chiefs of Staff, the priority objective will be 'The Destruction of the German Air Force.'"[31]

Strategic bombing loomed large in Spaatz's thoughts, but Overlord preoccupied Eisenhower. Specific air programs had to be developed to coordinate efforts to execute these two major operations. As the supreme commander recorded in his diary, "the air problem has been one requiring a great deal of patience and negotiation."[32] This comment showed that Eisenhower had acquired the British habit of understatement.

Perhaps the most prickly problem facing Eisenhower was the ambiguous status of his air commander, Air Chief Marshal Leigh-Mallory. In the early planning stages of Overlord, a need had existed for an expert on fighter operations, and Leigh-Mallory got the assignment. He had commanded fighters in the Battle of Britain and also had experience directing air support for ground operations. The planning job made him a likely candidate to command AEAF, and he received that appointment before Eisenhower became supreme commander of Overlord.

General Smith, who was in England to prepare the way for Eisenhower, reported that "appointment of Tedder as deputy Allied commander without portfolio and Mallory as [air] commander in chief will make a difficult situation. I personally believe that Tedder should be the real air commander and your advisor on air matters, which Mallory now considers himself. I don't think there is a place for both of them."[33] In the coming months relations between Tedder and Leigh-Mallory grew increasingly strained even though both were RAF officers.

Eisenhower communicated his strong feelings about his air command to Marshall: "I hear that Tedder, who I have assumed to be my chief air man is really intended to be an officer without portfolio, and that a man named Mallory is to be my chief air man ... this tendency to freeze organization so that a commander may not ... use trusted and superior subordinates in their proper spheres disturbs me very much indeed."[34] These were uncommonly strong words for Eisenhower to use in a message to Marshall, and they show the depth of his feelings on the subject. He would eventually reshape his air command, but it would take months of effort.[22]

Leigh-Mallory went to bat on Eisenhower's team with two strikes against him. From AEAF's inception Arnold felt distinctly antagonistic to it. He insisted that the AEAF commander would be merely a general operational coordinator for U.S. air forces assigned to it. Arnold's antipathy to AEAF also made him reluctant to assign competent staff officers to it. This lack of AAF support, plus Leigh-Mallory's preference for British officers, insured that AEAF became an RAF-dominated organization.

Prime Minister Churchill kept close watch on Allied command appointments. Surprisingly, he agreed with Eisenhower about SHAEF's muddled air command. He informed Portal: "I do not feel Leigh-Mallory compares with Tedder in experience or capacity and I had not contemplated that he would have all the assigned air under his command. I do not know that Tedder is any great authority on war in general. ...He has however proved himself a master in the use of the air force and this is the task I hoped he would have assigned to him by the Supreme Commander."[35]

Churchill and his chief advisors respected Eisenhower as a coordinator but did give him a high rating as a commander. They believed that British officers could always be found to fill important positions and that by virtue of their training, experience and native abilities they were superior to any Americans who might be considered for the jobs.

High-level arguments about Eisenhower's air forces, their commanders — including RAF Bomber Command's head, Air Chief Marshal Sir Arthur Harris — and their employment in Overlord dragged on for months. Eisenhower's diary summarizes them:

> After long discussions and negotiations it developed that the British did not trust Leigh-Mallory to be the directing head of my Air Forces. This came as somewhat of a surprise to me since I understood he had been especially selected by the British themselves for this post. I found, on the other hand, that they did trust Tedder and I immediately announced ... that Tedder would be the directing head of all my Air Forces, with Leigh-Mallory, Spaatz and Harris operating on a coordinate plane. I definitely proposed that the turning over of Spaatz' and Harris' Air Forces to me should be made consequent upon the approval by Portal and myself of a general air preparation plan which would take into account all of the objectives of Pointblank so far as they were consistent with our great need for preparing for Overlord.[36]

The agreement alluded to, when eventually adopted, introduced greater cohesion into Eisenhower's air organization, and it satisfied his demand that the air forces come under his control. It reduced Leigh-Mallory's authority sharply and widened Tedder's. Portal agreed that Tedder should be given authority to direct SHAEF's air operations. Tedder had been doing that job *ex officio* for some time. He was preparing an overall plan for employment of air forces in Overlord and had authority to call upon Leigh-Mallory, Spaatz and Harris for assistance.[37]

Eisenhower now had an air command organization more to his liking but major decisions had to be made about employment of strategic air forces. He would have to convince Spaatz and Harris to support whatever plan SHAEF proposed. Tedder expected that it would be difficult to win over the strong-minded air force commanders. Harris expressed his feelings about Overlord forcefully in a message to Portal: "It is clear that the best and indeed the only efficient support which Bomber Command can give to Overlord is the intensification of attacks on suitable industrial centers in Germany." In short, he wanted RAF Bomber Command to continue doing what it had been doing for several years. He objected to the use of his heavy bombers to attack such targets as gun emplacements or beach defenses and labeled it an "irremediable error" that would divert "our best weapon from the military function for which it has been equipped and trained to tasks which it cannot effectively carry out."[38]

It was vintage Harris rhetoric. The official history of Bomber Command states that Harris "made a habit of seeing only one side of a question and then exaggerating it. He had a tendency to confuse advice with interference, criticism with sabotage and evidence with propaganda. He resisted innovations and he was seldom open to persuasion."[39]

Portal exercised extraordinary patience in dealing with Harris. He explained that Bomber Command would have to come under SHAEF's authority but that support for Overlord did not necessarily mean close or even direct support. There was still a chance, according to Portal, that SHAEF would agree that attacks on German cities helped Overlord.[40]

Churchill, who usually backed Harris, astounded Eisenhower by declaring that he had never intended that Bomber Command would be turned over to the supreme commander. It could be assigned to assist Overlord for brief periods, but it had other crucial, long-term goals. This was unacceptable to Eisenhower, and he made it clear that he would resign his command if the CCS agreed with Churchill on this issue.[41]

Portal and Eisenhower eventually hammered out an agreement on the strategic air forces and other air matters. It gave the supreme commander most of what he wanted from

Eisenhower (second from right) and his air commanders on the observation tower of an airfield in England: Quesada, Brereton, Coningham, Spaatz, Eisenhower, Leigh-Mallory. (U.S. Air Force Photo Collection [Neg. No. 51406 AC], courtesy of National Air and Space Museum, Smithsonian Institution.)

the air forces. By early March several major kinks in the air chain of command had been straightened. Tedder would direct all SHAEF's air operations. Under him "on a coordinate plane" would be Leigh-Mallory, Harris and Spaatz. The strategic air forces would come under SHAEF's control at some as yet unspecified date prior to D-Day. After Allied invasion forces were securely established on the continent, the CCS would review the status of the strategic air forces. Eisenhower felt confident that he would get Spaatz's full cooperation; Spaatz was pleased that he did not have to take orders from Leigh-Mallory.

General Spaatz warned his staff not to try to diagram Overlord's tangled lines of command. Diagram 1 is adapted from a valiant effort made by General Hansell for his book, *The Air Plan That Defeated Hitler*. Although useful, it fails to show that:

1. Spaatz had administrative and logistical control over Ninth Air Force and, in fact, exercised firm authority over it in general;
2. Montgomery's command of First Army would be temporary; and
3. Fifteenth Air Force was a unit in the Mediterranean Allied Air Forces commanded by General Eaker.

Diagram 1: Organization for Overlord

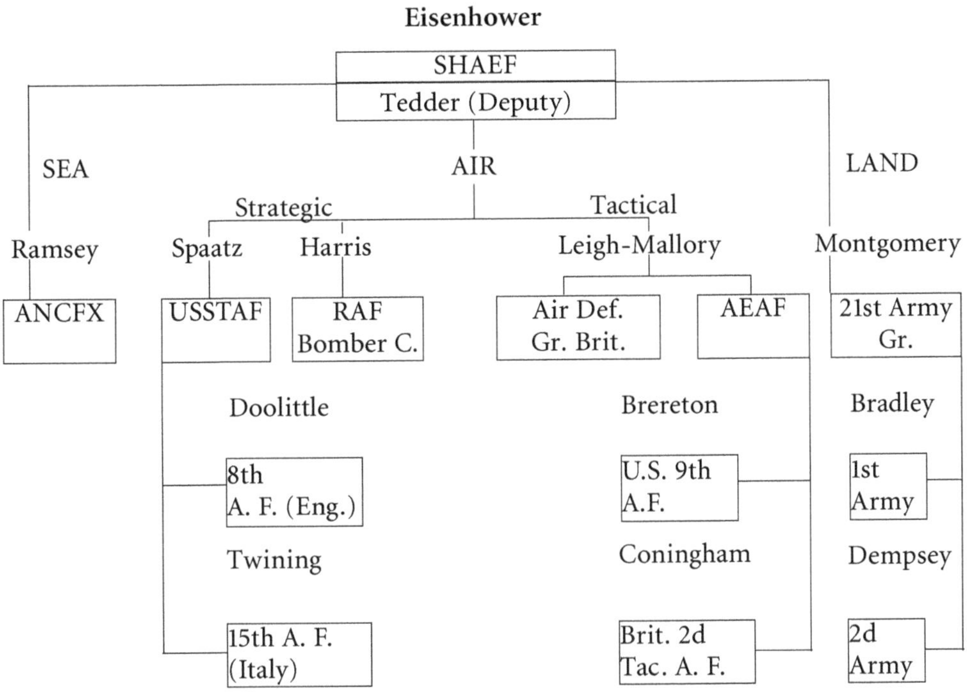

```
                        Eisenhower
                          SHAEF
                       Tedder (Deputy)
        ┌─────────────────┼─────────────────┐
       SEA               AIR               LAND
                  Strategic    Tactical
                               Leigh-Mallory
     Ramsey     Spaatz  Harris                  Montgomery
     ┌────┐    ┌─────┐ ┌──────┐   ┌────────┐┌────┐ ┌────────┐
     │ANCFX│   │USSTAF│ │ RAF  │  │Air Def.││AEAF│ │21st Army│
     └────┘    └─────┘ │Bomber C.│ │Gr. Brit.│└────┘│  Gr.   │
                       └──────┘   └────────┘      └────────┘
                Doolittle              Brereton        Bradley
                ┌────────┐            ┌──────┐       ┌──────┐
                │  8th   │            │U.S. 9th│     │ 1st  │
                │A.F.(Eng.)│          │ A.F.  │      │ Army │
                └────────┘            └──────┘       └──────┘
                Twining                Coningham      Dempsey
                ┌────────┐            ┌──────┐       ┌──────┐
                │15th A.F.│           │Brit. 2d│     │ 2d   │
                │ (Italy) │           │Tac. A.F.│    │ Army │
                └────────┘            └──────┘       └──────┘
```

Several provisions of the Eisenhower-Portal agreement later caused dissension. One gave the British the option to retake direction of RAF forces if the U.K. were threatened. Another involved the effective date of the agreement. Eisenhower assumed that it became effective immediately, but in fact the CCS had to approve it before it became effective.[42]

The agreement committed the strategic air forces to participate in Overlord under SHAEF's direction, but the ways and means remained to be determined. Tedder was responsible for this and encountered enormous difficulty achieving the cooperation of Spaatz and Harris. He informed Portal that the "two strategic air forces are determined not to play. Spaatz has made it abundantly clear that he will not accept orders, or even co-ordination from Leigh-Mallory...." Harris frequently produced technical, operational reasons for dismissing SHAEF's proposals. Tedder expressed confidence in Portal's ability to "bring Harris to heel, but I do not think that SPAATZ or Eisenhower will accept a position in which the Americans will take my orders and the British will not."[43]

Spaatz and Harris were never "brought to heel," but Tedder was a match for them in stubbornness. Eventually they had to yield to the supreme commander's authority.

While the Eisenhower-Portal agreement awaited the CCS's approval, criticism of it came from another commander, one who exerted a powerful influence on Allied decisions. General Marshall objected to words like "direction" and "supervision" to describe the supreme commander's authority. Such words conformed to the British conception of Eisenhower's role, but not Marshall's. He wanted a commander to command. Eisenhower, less concerned with semantics, explained that he would be given full authority over the air forces "whether they were engaged on close in targets or in deep penetrations for the destruction of the German Air Force...."[44] Later he recorded: "I was told the word 'direction' was acceptable to both sides of the house. Amen!"[45]

The AAF strategic air force that felt a reluctance to join Eisenhower's team was an established organization with long-range goals that Spaatz feared might be jeopardized by coming under SHAEF's authority. To understand his concern, and to appreciate its validity, it will be useful to review briefly the history of Eighth Air Force in the years before it became associated with Overlord.

Chapter 2

Eighth Air Force Operations, 1942–43

The U.S. Eighth Air Force was one of the strategic air forces that SHAEF wanted to support Overlord. Operating from the U.K. since early 1942, it had attempted to put strategic-bombing principles into practice. The effort was a learning exercise with trial-and-error characteristics. The long-range objective of Eighth Air Force was to soften up Germany by assaulting its industrial base, thereby making an invasion of northwest Europe feasible or even, as some hoped, unnecessary. The AAF believed that it would have to weaken the GAF before it could direct its full power against German industry.

In the decades before World War II, the Army Air Corps, forerunner of the AAF, had adopted strategic bombing principles. It had claimed for itself a mission that could be decisive in the event of war—destruction of an enemy's vital industrial plants by bombing. Given the means to accomplish such a mission, the AAF would acquire a status on a level with that of the Army and the Navy.

In 1941, a short time before the Japanese attack on Pearl Harbor, President Roosevelt approved an air-war plan, AWPD-1, which called for a massive buildup of the AAF to counter the air power of potential enemies. During its subsequent explosive growth, the AAF shaped its policies concerning personnel, equipment, tactics and war objectives in accordance with its commitment to strategic bombing. AWPD-1 included a provision for the execution of an "unremitting and sustained air offensive against Germany." Planners estimated that strategic air forces could be created, moved overseas, formed into efficient striking forces and readied for major operations in about a year and a half. AWPD-1 forecast that 2,164,916 men and 68,416 aircraft would be needed to accomplish U.S. air-war objectives. After the U.S. entered the war, the Air War Plans Division (AWPD) modified AWPD-1 to meet the requirements of a global war on two major fronts—Europe and the Pacific.[1]

Since 1938, when Hitler used the threat of air attacks to help him win a great diplomatic victory at Munich, Roosevelt had championed the development of U.S. air forces. In August, 1942, after six months of conflict and many defeats, President Roosevelt asked the War Department to estimate the number and types of combat aircraft which "should be produced in this country for the Army and our allies in 1943 in order to have complete air ascendance over the enemy." In compliance with the President's request, AAF drafted AWPD-42. It recommended a buildup of U.S. air strength in the U.K. to reach the levels shown in Table 1.[2]

The basic, strategic rationale of AWPD-42 was almost identical with that of AWPD-1.

Table 1: AWPD-42 Recommended Air Strength

	Groups	Aircraft
Heavy Bomber	42	2,016
Medium Bomber	15	960
Light Bomber	5	320
Fighter	25	2,500

A strategic air offensive against Germany from bases in the U.K. remained a high priority. German aircraft-assembly and aircraft engine plants would be primary objectives. First, GAF fighter defenses would be overcome, then the AAF would attack submarine construction yards, transportation targets, the electric power system and installations producing oil, aluminum and synthetic rubber.

Although Eighth Air Force had not yet given strategic bombing a thorough trial in combat, AWPD-42 expressed complete confidence in it: "It is perfectly feasible to conduct precise bombing operations against selected precision targets from altitudes of 20,000 to 25,000 feet in the face of anti-aircraft artillery and fighter defenses."[3]

In 1942, flocks of heavy bombers—B-17 Flying Fortresses and B-24 Liberators—began flying Atlantic routes to bases in the English countryside. It would take more than a year before their numbers reached planned levels. B-17s were four-engined monoplanes capable of carrying bomb loads of 5000 pounds to targets up to 700 miles from their bases at speeds which varied between 200 and 300 miles per hour. With reduced bombloads or speed, the tactical radius could be increased. [Tactical radius is the maximum distance a plane can fly from its base with a combat load, operate for thirty minutes in a target area and return to base without refueling.] B-17s could operate at altitudes as high as 30,000 feet. They carried at least ten .50-caliber machine guns for defense against enemy fighters and a crew of ten, including pilot, copilot, navigator, bombardier, radioman and gunners. A B-24, also a monoplane, could carry a bombload which varied between 8,800 and 12,800 pounds depending on variables such as speed and distance to target. Its tactical radius with a light bombload of 2,500 pounds was 1,425 miles. It was in demand for anti-submarine patrols. Its armament and crew size were similar to the B-17's.[4]

Arnold sent Eaker to England early in 1942 to supervise the buildup of Eighth Bomber Command in the U.K. Like Eisenhower, Eaker came from a rural part of the heartland of the U.S., growing up in Texas and Oklahoma. When the U.S. declared war on Germany in 1917, all the boys in Eaker's college class volunteered for military service. He became a pilot and a regular Army officer.

Eighth Air Force's growth was slow and irregular. Repeatedly, units scheduled to join it had to be diverted to other theaters, and some groups left the Eighth to bolster air forces elsewhere. Eaker succeeded Spaatz as Eighth Air Force commander when Spaatz joined Eisenhower in North Africa. Spaatz advised Eaker to conduct bombing operations cautiously at first so that heavy losses could be avoided and strategic bombing given a fair trial.

Eaker demonstrated a surprising ability to work smoothly with the British. It was a talent by no means common among American officers. Tact and diplomacy were essential; the neophyte Eighth Air Force depended on the RAF for much of its supplies, equipment, facilities, operational expertise, weather forecasting and intelligence. RAF fighters escorted and protected the Eighth's bombers on many of its early missions. The RAF trained many AAF personnel in its schools.

But on one major policy Eaker would not follow the RAF's lead. He would not accept the British recommendation, offered repeatedly, that the Eighth join the RAF in night-bombing operations. He was warned that it would be suicidal for heavy bombers to fly long distances to and from targets in Germany in daylight. German fighters would annihilate them. On this issue as on so many others, the RAF claimed the superior wisdom of experience. Early in the war it had attempted daylight bombing and had suffered extremely high losses. Patiently, Eaker explained that the AAF believed in daylight, precision bombing. Its equipment was designed for it and its personnel were trained to execute it.[5] Eighth Air Force would employ speed, deception, altitude, tight bomber formations and aerial gunnery to keep losses at acceptable levels. If the AAF failed to execute strategic bombing, a great span of effort — from the initial labor of mines and factories to the heavy bombers ready on Eighth Air Force flight lines — would go to waste. The resources so expended should, then, have been put to other uses, as the AAF's many critics had suggested all along. Eaker and Arnold, however, believed that the AAF's strategic-bombing effort would not fail.

AAF doctrine maintained that the overriding purpose of strategic bombing was to destroy the enemy's critical industries by bombing their vital installations. This could only be done in daylight in clear weather. Of course it was always difficult to bomb targets from twenty thousand feet, but the AAF had confidence in its bombsights. Its bombing accuracy improved steadily. Each bomb group's best bombardiers became lead bombardiers; on a signal from the lead bombardier, eighteen or more aircraft in a box salvoed their bombs simultaneously. Commanders exhorted pilots to fly tight formations, to minimize the dispersion of bomb strikes and to concentrate the bombers' gunfire against enemy fighters.

One of many valuable ideas taken from the RAF was the operational research system. Operational research sections [ORS's] examined operational records closely to discover ways for air crews to perform their tasks better. They used scientific techniques to analyze current problems as well as those likely to arise. ORS's employed civilian scientists who prized their independence and took pride in reporting candidly.

One of the first lessons learned by Eighth Air Force ORS was that bombing accuracy improved as bomber formations tightened and dispersion of bomb strikes lessened. This finding was far from obvious; in fact some bomb group commanders refused to accept it. Nevertheless, data supported its validity: bomb groups that flew tight formations achieved better bombing results.[6]

In the summer of 1942, Eighth Air Force carried out its first bombing operation with American equipment. On August 17, twelve B-17s bombed the railroad yard near Rouen, a historic Norman city on the Seine near the English Channel. RAF fighters escorted the small formation, which included *Yankee Doodle* with General Eaker aboard. All aircraft returned from the mission, and bombing results were encouraging. It was the first of hundreds of missions; Eighth Air Force would one day send out more than one thousand bombers and as many fighters on a single mission.

Eighth Air Force would be only a token force for many months, but its operations would uncover problems and teach vital lessons. Eaker pleaded constantly for personnel and aircraft. Several times during the early period, Arnold had to transfer some of the Eighth's bomber and fighter groups to the Mediterranean theater where Eisenhower's forces needed help. Eaker protested against some of these transfers; and, on more than one occasion, Eisenhower's requests were denied. These latter incidents may have been in the mind of Overlord's commander when he wrote to Marshall: "I am anxious to have

"... a few senior individuals that are experienced in the air support of ground troops. ... it takes men of some vision and broad understanding to do the job right. Otherwise a commander is forever fighting with those air officers who, regardless of the ground situation, want to send big bombers on missions that have nothing to do with the critical effort."[7]

During the second half of 1942, Eighth Air Force restricted operations to attacks on targets in German-occupied territory, rather than in Germany itself. B-17s and B-24s attacked submarine pens on the Bay of Biscay often — so often that the GAF concentrated anti-aircraft guns and fighters near them. Losses were high on some missions, even with RAF fighter escort. The losses were particularly bitter to the airmen, for they knew that their bombs had done little damage to the submarine pens, protected as they were by massive, concrete bulwarks. It was one of the first instances in which AAF units were ordered to bomb targets regardless of how little damage they could do to them. These missions could be justified as learning exercises, but the GAF was learning too. The race to improve tactics and equipment continued throughout the war. Brigadier General Haywood S. Hansell, an Eighth Air Force wing commander, recalled that group commanders' meetings after a mission were a "trial by fire," but these ordeals were necessary if mistakes were to be exposed and corrected.[8]

One of the Eighth's group commanders, Colonel Curtis LeMay, criticized what he perceived to be "stinko" bombing. He had the kind of mind that zeroed in on a problem and chewed at it until it was solved. Other group leaders told him that bombers had to take evasive action during bomb runs to avoid deadly flak. He didn't believe it. "The only point in flying a bomber in this war,..." he later explained, "was to drop bombs where they could do the most harm to the enemy."[9] Aircraft could not bomb accurately if they were flitting about trying to dodge artillery shells. LeMay ordered his pilots to fly straight, smooth bomb runs. He experimented with various formation patterns. His group's performance improved steadily, and other groups adopted his methods.

The AAF's confidence in strategic bombing rested in part on a belief that aerial gunners could repel fighter attacks. When combat experience raised doubts about this assumption, the AAF blamed crew training for the failures. Intense effort went into gunnery training, and Eaker pleaded for gunnery ranges and shotguns so that gunners could improve their skills. The efforts produced little improvement. In fact, some of the techniques taught to gunners relied on false assumptions, but scientists did not discover this until the war was almost over. Training exercises such as firing from a fixed position at a jeep towing a target or blasting away at clay discs with shotguns did not simulate conditions encountered in air fighting. Pilots badgered gunners to lead their targets, but in many situations to do so would guarantee misses. One ORS investigation discovered that 50 percent of machine-gun damage to B-17s was actually caused by fire from other B-17s.[10] Many of the problems facing gunners, such as frostbite and guns failing in frigid temperatures, could be solved, but some remained beyond the physical and intellectual capabilities of humans to solve, given the equipment and knowledge existing at the time.[11]

Another serious problem that plagued Eighth Air Force was even more intractable. Daylight precision bombing from high altitude required clear weather over targets; bombsights were useless if bombardiers could not see aiming points. Weather along the routes and over bases was also important; it took many months for Eighth Air Force to learn to assemble bombers in tight formations and make timely rendezvous with escort fighters in conditions of poor visibility. Weather conditions in Europe bewildered AAF weather forecasters. They came under heavy criticism, but it was far more difficult to predict weather in Europe than in the U.S. Unfavorable weather became a major deterrent to precision bombing.

Eaker's small force experienced heavy losses and frustrating setbacks in 1943, but it sharpened its techniques and tactics and improved its equipment. Lessons learned would help bomb groups that arrived later. Airmen learned to avoid frostbite and to keep equipment functioning in frigid temperatures. Armored clothing reduced the incidence of flak wounds. Better flying suits, oxygen systems and communications gear came into use. Aircraft modification went on continuously in response to combat conditions, although changes made to cope with one problem often worsened others. General Hansell recalled that Eighth Air Force removed bombsights from all but the lead and deputy lead bombers in a box. Machine guns went into the space thus freed. "This was a pretty drastic field modification," Hansell wrote, "but General Eaker endorsed it and the need spoke for itself."[12] GAF fighters had created the need to which Hansell alluded by executing deadly head-on attacks.

All phases of Eighth Air Force operations improved steadily, including intelligence gathering, navigation, bombing, formation flying and photographic reconnaissance. Flying in formation, which was deemed essential for defensive purposes, had drawbacks. The maneuvers required to assemble bombers into precise formations consumed both time and gasoline. This shortened their tactical radius proportionally. Also large clusters of bombers could be located more promptly by German air controllers, who could then readily direct attacks against them. With each raid, GAF intelligence sections found more effective means to bring down Allied bombers. Flak blasted many bombers out of the sky. At times, the GAF mauled Eighth Air Force so badly that it had to curtail operations.

ORS's made significant contributions to operational efficiency, but Eaker did not always applaud their efforts. He warned his staff "that the ORS's have a lot of merit, but ... men, who in their zeal to find something of importance at times will talk out of turn, in an effort to make a name for themselves...."[13] Eaker wanted to bring ORS civilian scientists under military discipline, but he received a cogent warning from a friend at AAF headquarters: "These Operational Research people are, in a sense, prima donnas, or perhaps I should say strong individualists. That is why they are able to do the work that they do. Therefore, any form of regimentation is likely to interfere very much with what they are trying to do."[14]

British criticism of daylight precision bombing disturbed Anglo-American relations. Portal reminded Americans that in 1940 the RAF abandoned daylight bombing because of high losses: "We were thrown back upon the general blasting of industry [at night] by means of big area attacks in which few bombs are wasted."[15] This comment about wasting bombs signals another point of disagreement between the RAF and the AAF. The British argued that no bomb which fell on a German-populated area was wasted. AAF leaders believed that any bombs that did not hit vital industrial equipment were, in fact, wasted in that they accomplished little of value to the Allied cause.

Portal worried about Eighth Air Force getting so deeply involved in an unwise air campaign that it would be unable to extricate itself from it. "The danger seems to be," he wrote, "that if they suffer heavy casualties with 5 or 6 groups they will merely say that the job requires 15 or 20 groups."[16] It was more than a danger: Eaker frequently sent home pleas for a larger force, and the AAF planned to build one.

Churchill complained about Eighth Air Force's meager accomplishments in 1942. It had not dropped a single bomb on Germany, he charged. He questioned whether the effort put into Eighth Air Force was commensurate with its achievements. Strongly influenced by Harris, Churchill suggested that Eighth Air Force would make a far greater contribution to the Allied war effort by joining the RAF in night bombing.[17]

In spite of strict censorship, writers joined the debate about AAF policies. A comprehensive, detailed critique appeared in a book by Allan Michie. The author had obviously received help from RAF staff in developing his arguments. The book was "born" during a visit by Michie to Harris's home. Harris claimed that Germany would quit the war if the AAF joined the RAF in blasting her cities. Michie described the weaknesses in the AAF's daylight-bombing methods and virtually endorsed RAF Bomber Command's area-bombing campaign. He leveled serious charges: the AAF, with its misguided allegiance to daylight bombing, wasted lives and prolonged the war: only a stubborn obsession to defend prewar decisions made AAF leaders cling to tactics that were obviously unsound. Eighth Air Force, according to Michie, should participate in the RAF's night-bombing offensive. In words that might have been written by Harris himself, Michie declared: "The R.A.F. has perfected concentrated mass bombing to a fine art...."[18] The destruction of Germany, "city by city," was merely a problem of getting enough airplanes of the right type to haul the necessary weight of bombs to the targets.

Michie sharply criticized some AAF aircraft types, as the RAF too had done repeatedly. Michie pointed out that B-17s and B-24s carried smaller bomb loads than British heavy bombers. He conceded that American bombers bombed accurately in clear daylight, but "on not more than *twelve* days per year can you expect perfect weather conditions [in northern Europe] for precision bombing...."[19] Michie warned that AAF bombers would suffer heavy losses when they attacked targets in Germany: they would come under attack repeatedly during the long flights to and from targets; hand-operated machine guns would freeze in the frigid temperatures. Even the best-defended bombers were at an "enormous disadvantage against the modern cannon-equipped fighter, which has the advantage in weight of fire, size of target, speed, ability to climb, and maneuverability."[20] Michie blamed American aircraft manufacturers for some of the AAF's problems. They misled the public and Congress with glossy, exaggerated advertising. British and German aircraft engines for fighters were both superior to American engines. He criticized General Motors' Allison engine, which powered several U.S. fighters: its power dropped as altitude increased.

Another book, even more critical of U.S. aviation policies, became a bestseller. Alexander De Seversky's *Victory through Air Power* pulled no punches. Unlike Michie, De Seversky was an aviation expert — military pilot in World War I, consultant to the Army Air Corps, aviation engineer and president of Republic Aviation Company. He was a prolific writer, and his informed articles on aviation often criticized AAF policies. "Knowing, as we do, that certain American aircraft types are inferior to British planes in the same category, why do we continue to build them in ever greater quantities," he inquired.[21] Many of the faults in AAF equipment "must be traced to their source in the backward thinking of the topmost military officialdom."[22] De Seversky did not accept the excuse that a miserly Congress was to blame for America's aviation backwardness. Army Air Corps leaders, not Congress, had set shortsighted procurement specifications, such as those that called for only two guns on fighters and forbid installation of bomb racks on them.

As 1943 began, Churchill continued to criticize Eighth Air Force. He asked Portal about the effectiveness of Eighth Air Force gunnery: "Is there the slightest truth in these American claims [of enemy aircraft shot down]?"[23] Portal responded: "The American claims should be divided by three."[24] Portal did not believe that "with uncontrolled

B-17 leaving a target at Marienburg. (Courtesy of the Library of Congress.)

wobble-guns they can shoot well enough to defend themselves for nearly three hours against fighter attack...."[25]

Arnold warned Eaker about British criticisms: "I sent a cable over recently in which I questioned the accuracy of your estimates of the number of airplanes shot down.... I want to be sure that we are not kidding ourselves. There is too much at stake in this matter of defeating the German Air Force for us to take credit for losses on the German side where credit is not due."[26] Arnold complained that he had been "put on the defensive by both the British and the United States for not having our heavy bombers bombard Germany." He asked a member of his staff to remind Eaker that the RAF had executed seventeen bombing missions against targets in Germany in February, 1943, whereas, during the same month, "we have [not] made more than 2 or 3 bombing raids in any direction with our heavy bombers from England." He reminded Eaker that "our records indicate that there are 173 B-17s and 34 B-24s in the 8th Air Force as of February 24, 1943.... This is quite a sizable force and one that should not be allowed to remain idle on the ground."[27]

Arnold's complaints put pressure on Eaker to emphasize numbers — sorties, bomb tonnage — rather than the amount of damage done to critical German industrial resources.

Eaker often complained about "distant critics" but in early 1943 an indictment of Eighth Air Force came from a source close to home. Two former group commanders wrote a scathing review of its practices. They blamed Eighth Air Force headquarters for encouraging groups to send aircraft on missions despite mechanical problems: "The airplane which proceeds on an operation with guns inoperative or with defective oxygen system, merely to maintain a low abortive rate and avoid adverse criticism of the unit, is potentially a lost airplane."[28] The report questioned the competence of Eaker's staff, some of whom were not AAF career officers. Eaker himself had little prewar experience with bombers.

Eaker and the AAF generally have been blamed for shortsightedness regarding their supposed allegiance to the flawed doctrine of the "self-defending bomber." It is a charge that requires close examination. Certainly Eaker expressed confidence many times in the ability of his bombers to operate effectively without fighter escort. He did not deprecate fighters, but he knew they were in short supply. He did not believe nor want to foster the assumption that his air force was inoperative without them. Nevertheless, he knew — no one knew it better — that a fighter escort cut bomber losses. He protested forcefully when P-38 fighters he had counted on for escort were sent to the North African theater. He informed Spaatz: "I received the sad blow that you had decided to take all of our P-38's. We had the 78th Group ready to accompany our bombers about February 1 [1943].... I think this was the most serious blunder we have made in a long time."[29]

It is true that for a brief period before the war some airmen believed that bombers, with speed and aerial gunnery, could ward off fighter attacks. But this opinion did not survive long. By 1940 it was clear that the fighter was ascendant over the bomber. The RAF clearly demonstrated this fact in the Battle of Britain.

A desire to get appropriations for bombers partly motivated the AAF's confident assessment of the aircrafts' capacities for self-defense. The AAF wanted to avoid having the growth of its strategic-bombing force held back by overspending on fighters. The U.S. Army tended to favor fighters and dive bombers, which they perceived to be valuable for the support of ground forces.

Eaker had to walk a fine line on the issue. His major concern was to keep Eighth Air Force growing. The best way to do this was to show results — or at least to demonstrate that important results would be obtained as soon as the strength of his force reached appropriate levels.

The AAF had to maintain a constant guard against diversions of its aircraft to uses it considered secondary. There was never a shortage of proposals to use heavy bombers for purposes other than strategic bombing. Army commanders griped ceaselessly about a lack of air support and the ineffectiveness, in their opinion, of "bombing some factory in Germany." Navy leaders objected to the extraordinary AAF demands for skilled personnel and scarce resources and pleaded for heavy bombers to hunt submarines, a use that Harris derided as "blowing up codfish." Eaker warned Arnold: "The only thing which may jeopardize our accomplishment of the Combined Bomber Offensive is the diversion of aircraft and crews and failure to receive the force required. The loss of 120 B-24's to Africa depreciated our effort here by approximately 20 to 25%. The threat to move our long-range B-17's to an operation against German naval units would, of course, make it entirely impossible for us to accomplish the Combined Bomber Offensive."[30]

Eaker became a persuasive spokesman for strategic bombing and promoted it brilliantly, although not always with complete candor. He knew that his gunners' claims of enemy aircraft shot down were wildly inflated, but he moved slowly to establish methods to make them more accurate. To adjust gunners' claims too soon would weaken the case for strategic bombing and damage the morale of bomber crews.

Criticism of Eighth Air Force peaked when Churchill called for a review of bombing policies at the Casablanca conference of Allied leaders. He "regretted that so much effort had been put into the daylight bombing, and still thought that a concentration upon night bombing by the Americans would have resulted in a far larger delivery of bombs on Germany...."[31] Churchill, with a staff able to offer persuasive arguments against daylight bombing, posed a serious threat to AAF strategic-bombing plans. One of Marshall's associates at the conference described the British delegation: "They swarmed upon us like locusts, with a plentiful supply of planners.... we were confronted by generations and generations of experience in committee work."[32]

Arnold organized a concerted defense of AAF bombing policies. He directed Eaker to prepare a defense of Eighth Air Force and to come to Casablanca to present it. The president's advisors, Harry Hopkins and Averell Harriman, spoke to the prime minister in support of the AAF. They warned Churchill that if daylight bombing were repudiated, the AAF would concentrate on operations in the Pacific theater. Portal had second thoughts: he advised the British delegation to ease up on their censure of Eighth Air Force. The British secretary of state for air, Sir A. Sinclair, warned Churchill not to criticize the AAF so severely that it would cut its commitment to the U.K.: "We shall have a much better chance of influencing them in the direction of night bombing if they are over here than if they are at home."[33]

Churchill called off his attack. He later claimed that he came to understand "how much had been staked on this venture by the United States and all they felt about it. I decided to back Eaker and his theme, and I turned around completely and withdrew all my opposition to the daylight bombing by the Fortresses."[34]

Churchill's intervention in the bombing controversy had unfortunate consequences. It increased pressure on Eighth Air Force to bomb German targets before it was strong enough to do so effectively with acceptable losses.

The Casablanca conferees produced a directive for Allied air forces that authorized them to execute a strategic air offensive (the "Combined Bomber Offensive") against Germany. The wording of the directive satisfied, more or less, three military groups with sharply divergent views about the air war.

1. The RAF interpreted it as supporting its campaign of area bombing of German cities by night.
2. The AAF interpreted it as a mandate to carry out daylight bombing of German industry.
3. Allied ground commanders perceived it to be authorization for air campaigns to prepare for an invasion of northern Europe.

The CCS designated Portal to direct the Combined Bomber Offensive; codename Pointblank. At about this time one of Arnold's advisory committees issued a report that influenced Eighth Air Force's plans for the offensive. The Committee of Operations Analysts, composed of American industrialists, identified targets crucial to the German war effort that Allied strategic air forces were capable of attacking. Industries producing aircraft, submarines, electric power, transportation, oil, rubber, motor vehicles and ball bearings were recommended objectives.[35]

Soon after the Casablanca conference, Eighth Air Force began to hit targets in Germany. Losses increased sharply as the British had predicted, but Eaker continued to issue optimistic reports. He wrote to a friend at AAF headquarters: "The one thing our heavy bombers have done during the past few months, and don't let anybody ever tell you anything to the contrary — we have knocked the ears off the German day fighters."[36]

Eaker's confidence was severely tested when his bombers penetrated into Germany's air space. In six days of July, 1943, Eighth Air Force lost eighty-eight bombers. Losses at this rate could not be borne for long. Worse was yet to come. On August 17, 1943, after a year of operations, Eighth Air Force sent 376 heavy bombers to attack ball bearing plants at Schweinfurt and aircraft factories at Regensburg. As soon as escort fighters turned back, enemy fighters attacked with skill and fury. Sixty heavy bombers went down, taking with them six hundred highly trained crewmen. Many of the surviving bombers were badly damaged, with dead and wounded crewmen aboard.[37]

On October 14, B-17s attacked ball bearing plants at Schweinfurt again, and again sixty heavy bombers were lost. The GAF coordinated attacks expertly and employed a variety of weapons, including aerial bombs, cannons and rockets. It was clear that GAF tactics and weapons would improve steadily, thereby clouding future prospects for daylight, precision bombing.

On that black day in October 1943 when Eighth Air Force lost sixty bombers, Arnold wrote to Portal complaining about the lack of support given by RAF fighters to Eighth Air Force: "As presently employed it would appear that your thousands of fighters ... are not making use of their full capabilities." Referring to a costly AAF operation, Arnold asked, "Why should not all of our medium bombers and vast numbers of your Spits (equipped with belly tanks and bombs) have smashed the Germans while they were pinned to their refueling airdromes?"[38] This blunt letter may have relieved Arnold's feelings, but it infuriated Portal and provoked a sharp reply which the British minister for air described as a "salutary drubbing" of Arnold. Portal wrote: "The thousands of fighters (to which you refer as being ... in England) so far as the R.A.F. is concerned, total an average figure of 1,464.... The day fighter force has consistently been employed offensively ... mainly in conjunction with medium and light bombers and latterly with your heavy bombers."[39] Arnold had touched sensitive RAF nerves when he pointed out that the range of Spitfires should be extended by modifying them and that they could be used as fighter-bombers. Portal asked Leigh-Mallory also to draft a reply; the AEAF commander wrote the following: "With operation Overlord in mind, our Fighter force has been designed to obtain air superiority over Northern France, for which it is eminently suitable.[40] Portal would not allow the performance of the legendary Spitfire to be lowered by adding gasoline tanks and other paraphernalia in an attempt to make it into a long-range escort fighter or a bomber. But the issue would heat up repeatedly in the months to come.

Eighth Air Force losses in the summer and fall of 1943 demonstrated that the heavy bomber could not effectively defend itself against fighters. Out of desperation Arnold pushed re-equipment of some heavy bombers giving them extra guns and armor; he hoped they would be able to protect their formations. This experiment failed dismally. These overloaded aircraft could not keep pace with the formations they were trying to protect. At this point Arnold was willing to try any promising remedy. He asked Eaker to consider using modified B-26 medium bombers to protect heavy bomber formations. This proposal astounded Eaker; in a letter to a friend, he labeled it the "most surprising one I have yet heard in all my service. There is not the slightest probability that the B-26 can protect anything against fighters. It is itself vulnerable to enemy fighter action."[41]

The demonstrated vulnerability of the heavy bomber raised questions about AAF prewar decisions. Arnold felt defensive about the issue, especially since the RAF had predicted the outcome. It was now clear that the AAF had been at fault in not developing a long-range escort fighter. Some of its prewar planning boards judged such an aircraft to be technically unfeasible, but now, in the summer of 1943, Arnold executed a 180-degree turn and set up a rush program to produce these escorts.[42]

Although the AAF had not anticipated the crucial need for escort fighters, it was able to provide them by late 1943 and 1944 to protect heavy bomber formations. The Allied air forces then won air superiority over the GAF, a victory that made Overlord feasible. To appreciate the scope of this achievement, it will be useful to examine briefly some of the fighter problems encountered by Eighth Air Force and their solutions.

Chapter 3

Eighth Air Force Fighter Problems

Heavy losses of bombers in 1943 galvanized the AAF to conduct a searching review of its strategic-bombing program. Not only were current bomber losses high, but a definite possibility existed that GAF tactics and equipment would become even more deadly in the coming months. A scientific advisor for the War Department warned General Marshall that "ever since our daylight precision bombing started … there was a substantial chance that the enemy might be able to introduce new techniques which would render formation bombing in daytime, unsupported by fighters, unduly costly." The memo cited aerial bombing and rocket fire as potentially devastating to bomber formations. It expressed amazement "that the enemy appears not to have a proximity fuse for rockets at this stage … for we have had them for a long time…."[1]

GAF fighters enjoyed a distinct advantage in that they could operate free of danger from attack when Allied bombers flew beyond the tactical radius of their escort fighters. The GAF could organize waves of fighters to attack bomber formations in the most effective ways. It continuously developed new methods and equipment. The AAF badly needed countermeasures. Fighter cover or night bombing were two possibilities, but the AAF rejected the latter.

AAF fighters began operating from the U.K. in July 1942, when Brigadier General Frank O'D. Hunter, commander of Eighth Fighter Command, set up headquarters there after directing flights of AAF fighters and bombers across the Atlantic. Transfers of groups to other theaters handicapped Eighth Fighter Command during its early career; equipment breakdowns, overcautious tactics and mediocre leadership also weakened it.

Republic Aviation's P-47 Thunderbolt arrived in the U.K. early in 1943 slated to become Eighth Fighter Command's principal weapon. It was a new, unproven aircraft and suffered from many mechanical problems when it started combat operation. Pilot morale was poor at the outset and deteriorated substantially. Eighth Fighter Command's 4th Fighter Group received pilots who had served with the RAF and had transferred to the AAF. Many of them disliked and disparaged the big P-47, so different from the RAF fighters they admired.

In late 1942 the AAF had to transfer aircraft and pilots of the 78th Fighter Group from Eighth Fighter Command to the North African theater. This took from Eaker the P-38 Lightnings, built by Lockheed Aircraft Company, that he had planned to use for long-range bomber escort.[2]

In reply to a message from Arnold asking why Eighth Fighter Command and its P-47s were accomplishing so little, Eaker wrote: "We had to train our pilots on a new type, and work out a lot of maintenance difficulties with a new engine and a new plan.... We think it is going to be all right. The full tactical use of it depends to a considerable degree on how fast you can furnish us with long range tanks."[3] This was one of Eaker's first requests for jettisonable fuel tanks (droptanks). They soon became one of his major headaches.

A great part of the difficulty in getting Eighth Air Force fighters ready for combat resulted from the priority given other needs. As Eaker explained: "We were definitely told that sending the fighter planes to Africa was our first priority, and this has consumed 75% of the full capacity of our depots and maintenance agencies. The second priority was devoted to repairing battle damage to our heavy bombers and making necessary modifications on the replacement bombers arriving, such as installation of the nose-gun and the improvement of gunfire in the lower hemisphere in the B-24s." Eaker expressed optimism but also pointed out deficiencies. He wrote to a friend at AAF headquarters: "All the people in this theater who thought daylight bombing impracticable are now beginning to swing round to our view." But, as Eaker explained, an urgent need existed for "some long range fighter protection with our bombers.... The supply of additional long range P-47 [drop] tanks is therefore of greatest importance so that these planes can go with us for deepest penetrations to German targets."[4]

As has been suggested, AAF prewar doctrine was largely to blame for the shortage of long-range fighters. AAF planners and many aircraft designers then believed that such a fighter was a technical impossibility. A prewar Army Air Corps Pursuit Board concluded that it was "obvious that no fighter airplane can be designed to escort heavy and medium bombardment to their extreme tactical radius of action and there engage in offensive combat with enemy interceptor types on equal terms."[5] This dogmatic assertion rested on the premise that a long-range fighter would have to carry large amounts of ammunition, gasoline and oxygen, as well as extra navigation gear and communications equipment. These burdens would put it at a disadvantage against enemy fighters not so handicapped. It seemed evident that jettisonable gasoline tanks could alleviate the weight problem, but AAF policies did not put a high priority on their development. Churchill asked Portal why the RAF did not use droptanks on its fighters since the Japanese were using them effectively. Portal gave the conventional answer: "Increased range can only be provided at the expense of performance and maneuverability.... The long range fighter whether built specifically as such, or whether given increased range by fitting extra tanks, will be at a disadvantage compared with the short range high performance fighter."[6] Unfortunately, Churchill, who often disputed assumptions of his military advisors, did not challenge this one.

In 1943, despite dogma that declared it to be futile, the AAF conducted a high-priority search for ways to increase the ranges of its fighters. As Eaker had suggested, droptanks offered great promise for making timely extension of the P-47's tactical radius. External gasoline tanks had been used to ferry fighters across the Atlantic.

Pratt and Whitney, air-cooled, radial engines powered P-47s. These engines developed 2,000 horsepower and gave the fighter speeds in excess of 400 miles per hour at 27,000 feet. The P-47 carried eight .50-caliber machine guns—firepower that could destroy a wide range of air and ground targets. One of the Thunderbolt's major weaknesses was its short range: its engine burned gasoline at a prodigious rate. Early models had a tactical radius of less than two hundred miles, depending on such variables as altitude, load and speed. Most of the P-47's strengths and weaknesses derived from its great size and sturdy construction. It was larger than first-line British, Japanese and German fighters. It was said to be an aircraft built around its massive supercharger. Superchargers help aircraft to maintain power at higher altitudes. As altitude increases, air density and oxygen decrease, thinner air offers less resistance to aircraft and thereby tends to allow them greater speeds, but the reduced oxygen intake into carburetors cuts engine power. Superchargers compress air to a density approximating that at sea level before feeding it to engines, but their size and weight exact serious aerodynamic penalties.

The Thunderbolt's rate-of-roll and diving characteristics were excellent, and it could withstand an exceptional amount of damage and keep flying. The large engine limited visibility to the front but furnished some protection to the pilot from bullets and flak. P-47s accelerated and climbed slowly, characteristics that made the British flatly reject them for interception. The P-47's large, four-blade propeller made a big undercarriage necessary. At first, P-47 pilots assumed that to prevail in combat they had to maintain high speed and altitude. They avoided combat below eighteen thousand feet. These prudent tactics limited the fighter's usefulness and made some observers conclude that its pilots were overcautious.

P-47s entered service with Eighth Fighter Command bearing a dubious reputation not improved by pilots who believed that the RAF flew better fighters. During their first few months of operations, P-47s experienced a multitude of exasperating mechanical malfunctions. Radios failed to work properly — they were not properly shielded from ignition emissions. Without dependable radio communication, fighter missions from the U.K. were virtually impossible. Even more worrisome were the frequent engine failures; some of these caused crashes that killed pilots. The AAF had a long case history on the Pratt and Whitney engine in bombers, where it was dependable. In fighters, however, where it had to perform during wrenching aerobatics, it sometimes failed. Engine and aircraft manufacturers sent engineers to England to search for engine flaws and make corrections. They installed engine counterweights and subjected the engines to an accelerated battery of tests. The P-47s flew night and day, "literally wringing out the airplanes," in the words of an Eighth Air Force staff officer.[7] Every P-47 in the U.K. had to have engine modifications in the spring of 1943, and production lines in the U.S. were altered accordingly. A harried matériel officer replied to an abrasive query from Arnold: "We are fully cognizant of the necessity of making the airplane *completely operational* in the eyes of our people in the U.K. ... Pratt and Whitney engine service personnel and Republic service are right there on the job and are going to stay on the job until we get the troubles licked."[8]

Emergency engineering efforts overcame the engine and radio problems, but the shortage of droptanks continued in spite of determined but uncoordinated efforts to erase it. P-47 groups needed droptanks that could be pressurized for use at high altitudes. Without such tanks they could escort bombers only to the frontier of Germany. Bomber crews complained bitterly: GAF fighters waited until the P-47s were forced to turn back to England then launched devastating attacks. General Hunter demanded droptanks; at a commanders' meeting he warned that "he would not assume responsibility for the fact that they did not have them." A supply officer told him that tanks produced in the U.K. seemed promising but that he had "pushed this so hard that the British were getting irritated at our insistence."[9]

In January 1943, Eighth Fighter Command had only one thousand 205-gallon, steel droptanks on hand. Furthermore, pilots preferred a smaller tank, one that could provide just enough fuel to reach fighting altitude as they crossed the "far shore"—the continental coastline where tanks could be jettisoned. P-47 pilots believed that they should not enter skies patrolled by the enemy encumbered by droptanks. Metal tanks of 100-gallon capacity were ordered from British sources, but war production authorities warned that a vast quantity of steel would be required to satisfy requirements, since pilots usually jettisoned droptanks during a mission. British suppliers produced some 108-gallon droptanks made of pressed paper, but these proved to be unsatisfactory. Later, Eighth Fighter Command requested a supply of 150-gallon steel tanks, and British manufacturers promised to supply them. Delay, confusion and name-calling, involving producers in both the U.S. and the U.K., resulted from these volatile orders. One investigation of the fiasco blamed the British. They had "failed utterly to meet delivery commitments." Urgent orders were then placed in the U.S. in August and September 1943.[10]

During the droptank crisis Eaker's overly optimistic progress reports probably confused the supply agencies in the U.S. trying to satisfy his requests. In a letter to the assistant secretary of war for air, he wrote: "Tests were run off yesterday [June 14, 1943] with the paper tank and proved entirely satisfactory. We should ... see our P-47s going with the bombers all the way to the Ruhr...."[11] As it turned out, both mechanics and pilots hated the paper tanks since they could not be pressurized properly for use at high altitudes.

AAF personnel sought scapegoats for the predicament. Eaker wrote an unusually offensive letter to RAF Air Marshal Wilfred Freeman blaming the British for the droptank shortage and consequent bomber losses. Freeman did not accept the rebuke meekly. Eaker received a sharp reply: "I assume that you do not wish ... to blame this ministry for the loss of fifty heavy bombers a month, in view of the fact that your technical staff did not give us full clearance at an earlier date.... It was not until June that an urgent application was made to me for these jettisonable tanks."[12]

The RAF had called attention to the droptank problem six months before Eighth Air Force suffered the heavy losses of August and September. On February 18, 1943, Freeman had alerted the chief of Eighth Air Force Service Command: "The proposal to manufacture dropable fuel tanks for your fighter aircraft in this country has been under discussion for some time and no definite conclusion has yet been reached. I am anxious that the matter should be settled and the necessary arrangements made so that we are not suddenly faced with an overwhelming demand."[13] Freeman suggested that tanks be prefabricated in the U.S., shipped in nested stacks to conserve space, and welded and assembled in the U.K. It was a farsighted suggestion but went unheeded.

In the summer of 1943, Allied supply services did indeed suddenly face an overwhelming demand for droptanks. Confusion bordering on chaos marked the AAF effort to supply them. Bitter recriminations flew between responsible agencies. At one Eighth Air Force meeting, Hunter's representative announced angrily that "Fighter Command would in future take no part in the production or experimentation in any way whatsoever in the P-47 tank project." He told the group that during a recent effort to provide tanks "fuel lines had to be changed and the Fighter Command had never been informed." A supply officer charged that far too many people were involved in the project. Every time a meeting was held another idea was born, which caused another change and more delay.[14]

Whenever Eighth Fighter Command could scrounge some usable droptanks, it penetrated deeper into Germany and gave the GAF some painful surprises. When P-47s escorted bombers to target areas, Luftwaffe losses rose and bomber losses dropped. In August, the 4th and 56th Fighter Groups carried out missions with 75-gallon tanks; these gave P-47s a tactical radius of about 280 miles; 108-gallon tanks increased this to 320 miles.

The search for efficient droptanks was part of a general AAF range-extension program for fighters. Arnold received weekly reports on its progress. In January 1944, he sent a reprimand to Eaker about the droptank situation: "The use of 75-gallon tanks on Thunderbolts (for which it was not intended) results in an unanticipated reduction in a definitely limited supply and thereby endangers the mission of the Mustang which can be flown at present only with the same 75-gallon metal tank."[15] Arnold promised to supply tanks of various sizes for Hunter's fighters. After months of confusion and delay, in the late fall of 1943, P-47 groups began to receive a sufficient number of tanks, mostly 75-gallon, 108-gallon and 150-gallon metal ones.

Eighth Air Force losses and the evidence of incompetence, exemplified in the droptank episode, intensified Arnold's concern about Eaker and his chief subordinates. His doubts inevitably centered on Hunter. In a letter to the theater commander, Arnold wrote: "Information I receive from England is that our fighter pilots are looking for excuses to go to the Savoy.... May this not be the result of having a leader who is not sufficiently aggressive? Has Monk Hunter lost his spirit — his dash? I know he isn't the Monk Hunter I used to know. He seems to be playing safe on most of his missions."[16]

Hunter had been a fighter pilot since World War I, when, as a pursuit pilot in the U.S. Army Air Service, he had shot down eight German aircraft. In peacetime he often worked with Arnold and Spaatz. Once described as "fiercely mustachioed," the spic-and-span Hunter cut a handsome figure. The failures associated with fighter escort for bombers were not all his fault, but some were perceived to be the result of his "playing safe." Bomber crews complained bitterly about the lack of fighter escort. At a bomb group commanders' meeting, Colonel LeMay expressed outrage about fighters leaving bomber formations to accompany other fighters that aborted missions because of mechanical breakdowns.

Arnold received several negative reports on Eighth Fighter Command. One report charged that "fighters are not escorting our heavy bombardment to the full extent of their capabilities. They have been in very little combat, have few operational losses and have knocked down very few enemy aircraft."[17] Arnold's advisors believed that pilots could extend the P-47's range if they were less concerned with their own safety. Reports had come to AAF headquarters charging that pilots in the U.K. climbed to ceiling on droptanks and then dropped them even though about eighty gallons of gas remained unused. Pilots did this, the report stated, because they were "naturally anxious to burn the gas out of the auxiliary tank behind the pilot seat before getting into combat.... While these practices will give the pilot a slightly better chance in combat, they are not essential and considerably reduce the distance over which close support can be rendered to bombardment." These charges tended to substantiate Arnold's suspicion that Hunter was overly conservative. Arnold's staff warned him: "If the P-47 does not actually have the ability to escort on fairly deep penetrations, we have been badly fooled and our planning has been extremely faulty. We have a lot of eggs in that basket. It will be the only American fighter type airplane in the U.K. until December 1943 when 1 group of P-38s will make its appearance."[18]

Reports like this could not be pigeonholed. Arnold asked his staff to draft a message to Eaker expressing his apprehensions about Eighth Fighter Command. His advisors produced the following diatribe:

> Of grave concern to me is the employment of your fighters. I cannot comprehend what value is derived from the frequently reported so-called offensive fighter sweeps in which the enemy is rarely sighted. Except as a means of consuming gasoline

> I see no purpose in this practice. Meanwhile your bombardment goes out and returns unescorted or inadequately escorted to a distance which is definitely short of the ... [P-47's] capabilities. Bombardment is bearing full brunt of enemy fighter attacks and to date have had no real support from American fighters. Apparently Germans know that our escort will leave bombers shortly after reaching the mainland and consequently withhold their attack until the departure of fighters.... What is the reason for the short escort? I hesitate to ascribe it to the range characteristic of the P-47. This airplane has large internal tankage which should enable it to provide escort ... up to a distance of at least three hundred miles. I understand it is a practice in your theater to climb to altitude on the belly tank thus consuming about one hundred twenty gallons of gas and then dropping the tank with remaining eighty gallons of gas even though no combat is imminent.... I understand further that it is a universal practice to cruise at high power while escorting in order to have speed up for combat if encountered. By throttling back and obtaining increased range should not our fighters have ample time to accelerate before actually engaging in combat? German pilots are known to avoid clashes with our fighters and go direct for the bombers. This practice should afford our fighters an advantage. I feel that a vigorous escort can successfully be accomplished if the fighters are less cautious.[19]

This intemperate memo questioned the competence and courage of pilots and leaders of Eighth Fighter Command. Arnold was often blunt and candid, but he decided not to send such a blistering indictment to Eaker officially. Nevertheless, Eaker received a copy unofficially.

Anticipating that he would have to defend Eighth Fighter Command's record, Eaker asked Hunter to prepare a rebuttal of the charges.[20] Hunter gave notice to Eaker that if he received such a document as Arnold had sent officially he would resign and ask for a court-martial. The statement Hunter wrote gave only a hint of the rage he felt. He recalled that "we, ... the people giving it [the P-47] its initial introduction into battle, should do everything possible to build up confidence in it and avoid using it in such a manner as to bring out its weaknesses." He defended fighter sweeps: they trained pilots, tested equipment and built up morale; occasionally, enemy aircraft were engaged. On the crucial issue of bomber escort, Hunter stated that the P-47's short tactical radius of only 180 miles made long-range escort impossible. It was a "new unproven airplane," he wrote, "which initially had many bugs and which still has two great weaknesses, namely poor climb and acceleration...." Hunter defended the practice of pilots flying at fast cruising speeds. Poor acceleration made this necessary since you do not have time to accelerate before combat." Hunter also denied that he or his pilots were overcautious:

> By a stupid, improper, and reckless use of this airplane it could easily have received such a black eye, it would have taken a long time to overcome.... In spite of the P-47's we first received being really not fit for combat, we have pressed forward ... and built up a reputation for the airplane.... This has been done in the big league air theater of the world, against the best the enemy have, with comparatively small forces, and with an airplane which in all round performance is definitely inferior to that of the enemy.[21]

Hunter's staff produced a summary of operational data to bolster his case: 9,709 sorties carried out in little over a year's operations resulted in eighty enemy aircraft destroyed. Fighter sweeps provoked 1,566 GAF sorties which caused "material ... wear and tear on enemy matériel and personnel."[22]

Unofficial though it was, Hunter's rebuttal reached AAF headquarters where it failed to impress Arnold's staff. Arnold's advisory committee insisted that fighters should be operated "in such a fashion as to insure that the maximum combat radius of action possibilities are realized. This should include operation at economical throttle settings and retaining external tank until empty or until forced by enemy attack to drop them. Full advantage should be taken of the possibility of rendezvous over enemy territory."[23]

The manner in which fighters carried out bomber escort duties wasted gasoline. Eighth Bomber Command wanted them to fly close escort patterns, and Eaker approved the tactic. But the P-47's poor acceleration made it unsuitable for close escort. If pilots maintained high speeds to be ready for combat, they had to weave around the bombers to remain in proximity to them. This reduced their intrinsically short tactical radius even more.[24]

Eighth Air Force escort guidelines directed fighter groups to overtake bomber formations passing from rear to front approximately five thousand feet over them, gradually losing altitude to bomber level. Squadrons took station on each flank, and a third remained above the formation. Pilots were instructed to "maneuver generally [weave] maintaining positions ... to ward off hostile fighter attack. Should any flight sight the enemy, the whole flight immediately attacks and tries to engage them before they can launch an attack on the bombers.... No attempt is made by the attacking flight to follow the enemy down once they dive for the deck, but the attack is broken off and the flight regains altitude and position to continue the escort."[25]

Close fighter escort of bombers had other drawbacks than the wasting of gasoline. It was a defensive tactic, one clearly unsuitable for fighters whose effectiveness depended on aggressive, offensive operations. GAF fighter pilots could prepare to attack bomber formations unmolested by AAF fighters. Even when AAF fighters pursued them, the pursuit terminated "once they dive for the deck."

With great reluctance, Eaker accepted replacements for his chief subordinates in late 1943. Brigadier General Frederick Anderson became Eighth Air Force bomber commander. Major General William Kepner replaced Hunter. Arnold's staff regarded Anderson as the AAF's foremost bombardment expert. Soon after his appointment, Anderson wrote to a friend:

> Do not believe for one moment that I am complacent about the many things that are not being done well enough ... some of which are glaringly apparent to me.... One of our deficiencies is our inability to ascend and assemble on top of overcast.... Within a month I expect to be able to do it. Another is bombing at dusk and returning at night. We will be ready to do this the latter part of August. The third, is the question of many pronged attacks on six or eight different targets simultaneously on one day, that is the problem of using the available fighters for escort to the maximum benefit.

Anderson recognized that group commanders were the key to effective operations. They "must not be the contentious type who blames failure on the orders of higher ups.... Those officers of the Air Forces, who have shown throughout the years, weakness or lack of soldierly qualification, should never be permitted to command a Group...." Eighth Bomber Command now had a commander able to recognize its faults and determined to eliminate them.[26]

Major General William Kepner, the new commander of Eighth Fighter Command, had spent his adult life in military service. After a hitch in the Marine Corps, he had joined the Army National Guard and fought with the 4th Infantry Regiment in World War I. At war's end he commanded a battalion. After the war Kepner switched to the Army Air Corps and became a pilot. He was commanding fighters on the West Coast when Arnold picked him to take over Eighth Fighter Command. Kepner came to the U.K. briefed by Arnold to change fighter policies. Hunter told him that 175 miles was the practical tactical radius for fighters. Kepner later recalled his reply and his early impressions of Hunter's Fighters:

> If I had anything to do with it, we would certainly have to go to Berlin.... I think he almost fainted when I told him that. When I came here ... our pilots had very little training in combat. Some of them had shot down a couple of airplanes. Some of them had gotten quite a few, but knew in their hearts that they hadn't done well, could have done better.... It takes about 100 combat hours for a fellow to do that plane he is flying justice, and the sky that he is operating in with the German operating in it too: justice to the plane, to himself, and to the quality of the opponent. Now, they reached that stage somewhere around January [1944]....[27]

Kepner and Anderson had to be patient in changing policies; they did not always get Eaker's support. Soon after joining Eighth Air Force, Kepner remarked at a commanders' meeting that "Eighth Fighter Command's box score was low. Germans wait until the P-47s ran out of gas before attacking." Eaker told him sharply that "it was the primary duty of our fighters to escort bombers whether German fighters were brought down or not."[28] Kepner would have to wait for Eaker to be replaced before that policy could be altered.

Eaker had to accept replacements for his trusted colleagues, but he could not refrain from defending his record to Arnold: "I have never thought that you placed quite the confidence in me officially as an officer, as you did as a friend. I sometimes thought that you were tough on me officially in order to make certain that nobody had a feeling that I got the positions I held through our personal friendship...." With regard to Eighth Bomber Command, Eaker explained: "Anderson had to be brought along very fast to be ready by July 1st. It would have been impossible to have put in anybody else now here prior to that time without taking a great chance, an unwarranted one with that very difficult job. This Bomber Command job of ours is a man-killer." Eaker also defended Hunter's performance: he was "definitely the only man I have had for that job.... He believes he has done the best he could, bearing in mind the conditions here. He still insists that it was absolutely necessary, having new men and a new plane, to break them in gradually.... I have continually urged Hunter to greater boldness in this regard. I must admit, however, that Hunter's system is now paying results. His fighter pilots have high morale; they are enthusiastic about supporting the bombers."[29]

In the fall of 1943, the GAF and bad weather forced Eighth Air Force to interrupt its offensive against targets in Germany. Severe losses in September and October left gaps in personnel and aircraft that had to be filled. Thick cloud cover over Germany precluded precision bombing on many fall and winter days.

Most of the P-47's mechanical problems had been solved. Pilots had learned that they could hold their own against the best GAF fighters. The Thunderbolt's tactical radius had increased with the use of droptanks and cruising practices that improved fuel efficiency, but it still could not reach many of the targets that Eighth Air Force wanted to bomb.

One of the most intractable fighter problems was poor gunnery. Eighth Fighter Command's ultimate objective was to get enemy aircraft lined up in the gunsights of its P-47s. Even after pilots accomplished this difficult feat, they often failed to destroy enemy aircraft. An ORS investigation found that for the period October–December 1943: "Pilots' estimates of range have not improved ... [and their] aiming has not improved significantly. They still fire consistently behind and below the target, and miss completely ... most of the time."[30] More than two-thirds of the enemy aircraft attacked escaped destruction.

P-38 Lightning, P-51 Mustang, P-47 Thunderbolt. (U.S. Air Force Photo Collection [USAF Neg. No. 52585 AC], courtesy of National Air and Space Museum, Smithsonian Institution.)

Arnold decided to send some fighters to Eaker that had greater range than P-47s. He transferred a P-38 group to the U.K. from the Mediterranean theater despite protests from Spaatz and Eisenhower. He alerted another P-38 group in the U.S. to move to the U.K. The P-38 Lightning's impressive record in the Mediterranean and Pacific theaters appeared to contradict the maxim that twin-engined fighters could not prevail against single-engined types. But operating in the "big league" of air warfare, the P-38 encountered a multitude of problems unanticipated by the AAF.

The Lightning was easily recognized. It had conical booms tapering gracefully from twin engines to its tail assembly. The 12-cylinder, supercharged Allison engines turned propellers in opposite directions to reduce torque. The cockpit occupied a pod between the engines. The Lightning was huge compared with British, Japanese and German fighters; early models weighed about 15,000 pounds. Its large fuel tanks stored 300 gallons. Its armament consisted of four .50-caliber machine guns and a 20mm cannon. With 150-gallon droptanks attached to pylons on its wing, a P-38 had a tactical radius of 520 miles under combat conditions. Despite continuous modifications, serious mechanical problems plagued P-38s. A report of P-38 trials by the AAF Proving Ground Command stated that it was the "best production line fighter tested to date with respect to range, endurance, speed, altitude and fire power, but diving speed was severely limited due to tail buffeting." Also, the cockpit became uncomfortably cold at high altitudes. The report expressed doubt that "this aircraft will meet in combat any type of enemy aircraft in which close-in dog fighting will be its best offensive action."[31]

German pilots recognized P-38s instantly. This gave them a significant advantage: pilots are taught that those who are slow to identify enemy aircraft are likely to become their victims. When flown in ways that maximized its strengths the P-38 was formidable—but so were its weaknesses. Pilots considered it suicidal to put it into a vertical dive; it had a slow rate of roll, stiff aileron control and its booms and wing blocked pilots' vision. P-38s could climb rapidly and make tight turns; pilots were advised to turn toward attackers and approach them head-on. Over Germany, far from their bases, stiff with cold, and outnumbered, P-38 pilots fought against fearful odds.

The 55th Fighter Group flew P-38s from the U.K. beginning in late 1943. It suffered heavy losses escorting bombers to targets in Germany. Many pilots were so badly frostbitten on returning to base that they had to be helped out of their cockpits. Usually outnumbered, many did not return. On November 29, 1943, seven P-38s were lost on a bomber escort mission to Bremen. Seventeen pilots had aborted the mission because of mechanical problems; the operations report recorded that "The remaining thirty-eight aircraft were bounced by 40 plus ME 109's attacking from head-on and above; at the same time an additional 40 plus e/a [enemy aircraft] passed through our formations before a majority of our a/c [aircraft] dropped their belly tanks. These e/a continued their attacks very aggressively...."[32]

General Kepner later recalled: "We ... had plenty of trouble with the 38s—difficulty due to the very low temperatures at high altitudes ... engines would quit mechanically due to this cold temperature. Those lads flying P-38s sure deserve plenty of credit for fortitude."[33]

Seventy-six known engine failures occurred on P-38J aircraft during their first few months of operations from the U.K. It was not known how many were lost on operations as a result of engine failures. The situation became so critical that General Doolittle requested a special blend of gasoline to "improve engine operation, reduce engine failures, save pilots and boost the sagging morale of P-38 pilots."[34] Doolittle had been an aviation gas expert for an oil company in peacetime.

With the invasion of northern Europe less than six months away, and air supremacy far from assured, strategic bombers had to force the GAF into battle by attacking targets in Germany. But they needed fighter escort all the way to and from their targets. P-47s and P-38s would continue to give heavy bombers critical support, but Eighth Air Force needed more and better long-range fighters. The airplane that was to satisfy this need was already operating from the U.K. in small numbers: The P-51 Mustang was the legendary fighter that was crucial in winning air superiority over the GAF in 1944, thereby making Overlord's Normandy invasion feasible. The Mustang, like its predecessors in Eighth Fighter Command, experienced exasperating mechanical problems. AAF doctrine, which

A P-51 Mustang of the 361st Fighter Group drops two 500-pound bombs. (U.S. Air Force Photo Collection [USAF Neg. No. 52739 AC], courtesy of National Air and Space Museum, Smithsonian Institution.)

taught that long-range fighters were difficult if not impossible to design, delayed the Mustang's acceptance.

The P-51 Mustang had an additional handicap: its heritage was not 100 percent American. It was a product of both British and American industrial genius. In April 1940, the Anglo-French Purchasing Commission gave North American Aviation (NAA) of Inglewood, California, an order for 320 fighter airplanes. NAA had almost no experience in building fighters, but the British and French needed military aircraft desperately. NAA decided to design a new fighter, rather than merely to copy some existing type. Specifications called for a single-seat monoplane powered by an Allison V-12, in-line, liquid-cooled engine. This type of engine allowed an aerodynamically streamlined frontal area — some of the best German and British fighters had liquid-cooled engines.

With personnel working sixteen hours a day, seven days a week, NAA designed and built a prototype Mustang airframe in less than four months. On October 26, 1940, the first Mustang flew over Inglewood. By April 1941, Mustangs were coming off assembly lines; the first-production Mustang arrived in the U.K. in November 1941 for service with the RAF.

Mustangs carried four to six .50-caliber machine guns. Armor gave pilots some protection and self-sealing fuel tanks reduced the danger of fire. An air scoop located on the underside of the fuselage gave the Mustang a unique profile. NAA believed that its wing, of revolutionary design, was largely responsible for the Mustang's excellent handling characteristics, speed and fuel efficiency.[35]

The Mustang project was started under British auspices, and at first the AAF felt little enthusiasm for it. Indifference was laced with resentment and chauvinism. RAF officers often criticized American aircraft, including the B-17, P-47 and P-38. They frequently reminded Arnold that the British Lancaster bomber could carry a 10,000-pound bomb-load to a target 700 miles away, whereas the B-17 could bear only about half as much weight that far. RAF criticisms stung and certainly produced a definite resentment in the AAF. General Arnold may have recalled these anti–British feelings later, when he admitted that it had been the AAF's own fault that it did not have Mustangs on operations sooner. A few months' more delay in getting Mustangs to the U.K. and they would not have been available in sufficient numbers to play a crucial role in the battles for air supremacy prior to D-Day. Without air superiority over at least western Europe, the invasion would have been postponed, if not canceled, and Nazi Germany might have survived.

Two Mustangs arrived at the RAF aircraft testing center at Duxford, England, in January 1942. Performance trials soon convinced test pilots that the Mustang was "an excellent low and medium altitude fighter and certainly the best American fighter that has so far reached this country."[36] These aircraft evaluators and RAF pilots flying Mustangs on operations praised its flying characteristics, especially its speed, maneuverability and range. But at high altitudes the Allison engine lost power and the airplane's performance diminished. Some pilots asked why it could not be given a better engine. With this option in mind, the commander of the Duxford base contacted a pilot at the Rolls-Royce aircraft-development center and asked him to fly a Mustang. Rolls-Royce manufactured excellent engines that powered some of the RAF's fighters and bombers.

Ronald Harker, a test pilot for Rolls-Royce, flew one of the Mustangs under test at Duxford. Many years later he still remembered the experience vividly:

> The first thing I noticed during the flight was that the indicated speed was some thirty miles per hour more at similar power settings than on a Spitfire! The ailerons were light and gave a rapid rate of roll; this was one of the areas where the Focke-Wulf had an advantage over the Spitfire. The guns, too, were close inboard, which gave a concentrated fire, but most important the internal fuel capacity was three times greater than the Spitfire....[37]

Harker promptly drafted a proposal urging that Rolls-Royce fit three Mustangs with Merlin engines for trials. Harker became one of the earliest Merlin Mustang champions. He campaigned for his proposal with "all the enthusiasm and conviction I could muster." It was not totally clear sailing: Merlin engines were in great demand for other aircraft; little enthusiasm could be expected initially from either the AAF or General Motors (manufacturers of Allison engines) for an airplane built under British auspices and powered by a British engine.[38]

Rolls-Royce Merlins were liquid-cooled engines and had excellent supercharging. In 1940 an American group headed by Secretary of the Treasury Henry Morgenthau arranged to have the Packard Motor Company manufacture Merlins in the U.S. under license. It was a critical move and would have a crucial impact on the career of the Merlin Mustang.[39]

With RAF approval, Rolls-Royce executives ordered Merlin engines installed in a few Mustangs. NAA kept closely informed about the effort and, in fact, soon started a similar project using Packard Merlins. Major Thomas Hitchcock, an AAF officer serving as military attaché in England, kept close tabs both on the Mustangs the RAF was using,

Tommy Hitchcock, a pilot in the French Lafayette Flying Corps, standing in front of his Nieuport airplane in World War I. (U.S. Air Force Photo Collection [Neg. No. 89-12598] courtesy of the National Air and Space Museum, Smithsonian Institution.)

The first Merlin Mustang at the Rolls-Royce experimental-flight test center, Hucknall, England. (Courtesy of the Rolls-Royce Heritage Trust.)

mostly on ground-attack missions, and on the experimental Merlin Mustang. Hitchcock had exceptionally strong credentials for his job. In World War I he had flown fighters for the French in the Lafayette Flying Corps. Instructors at the French pilot-training school at Avord judged Hitchcock to be one of the finest natural pilots the school turned out. Only eighteen at the time, Hitchcock displayed skill and aggressiveness on operations. He shot down two German aircraft before he himself was shot down and captured. With characteristic energy and initiative, he escaped and made his way to Switzerland.

In peacetime Hitchcock worked as an investment banker. He maintained his interest in aviation and flew an airplane from his home on Long Island to a mooring near Wall Street on the East River to get to his office. He was a financial advisor to corporations. Between the world wars he prospected for oil, held an executive position with a coal company and helped to reorganize a shipping line. His job experience made him adept at evaluating air weapons and production methods.

Strong character, experience, training and energy made Hitchcock an efficient military attaché, but he also had influence that enabled him to bypass the Army's bureaucracy and send his reports directly to the highest levels of the War Department, even to the president. Hitchcock's close friend, John G. Winant, ambassador to the U.K., could communicate directly with the White House. Winant, a former governor of New Hampshire, was a trusted associate of both Roosevelt and Harry Hopkins, the president's most influential advisor. Like Hitchcock, Winant had flown fighters in World War I. The two fliers had first met at St. Paul's school in New Hampshire, where Winant was a teacher and Hitchcock, a student.

In the Twenties, Hitchcock became the world's finest polo player. In fact, he was a superstar and media celebrity at a time when only a few athletes could achieve that status. For most of the two decades he played polo, he received the top handicap of ten goals. He captained teams that played British teams for the Westchester Cup. Averell Harriman, another influential presidential advisor, played with Hitchcock on some of the championship U.S. polo teams. Journalists followed Hitchcock's activities closely. Even as an army officer he had little difficulty attracting media attention to his proposals.

Hitchcock had enormous energy and drive; it was said of him that he pursued goals in life with the same reckless intensity that he did on polo fields. Following in the footsteps of his father, who had also been an Army pilot in World War I, he attended Oxford for a brief time in the Twenties. His experience in various fields of endeavor — aviation, finance, sports — and his friends in high government offices gave him the capability to exert tremendous influence on AAF decisions.

The Hitchcocks were wealthy enough to afford fox hunts and polo, but Tommy joined a world of even greater wealth and influence when he married Margaret Mellon, a member of the family that owned one of America's largest banks and many other businesses. Two of Hitchcock's friends from the financial world held high positions in the War Department: Secretary of War Henry Stimson and Assistant Secretary of War for Air Robert A. Lovett. Tommy's friend Averell Harriman carried out special missions for President Roosevelt and became a close friend of Prime Minister Churchill.[40]

Soon after the U.S. entered the War, Hitchcock, aged 42, enlisted in the AAF. Winant helped him get an assignment to the American embassy in London as an air attaché. He became a familiar figure at military airfields, air-testing centers and aircraft factories in the U.K. Hitchcock piloted a Beechcraft assigned to the embassy on many of his trips. When he had the opportunity he flew fighter planes, not only to assess their quality but to sharpen his piloting skills. One of his goals was to become an active fighter pilot. It seemed an impossible dream for he was far over the strict AAF age limit for fighter pilots.

Hitchcock and Winant became vociferous Merlin Mustang proponents. During a visit to the Rolls-Royce aircraft experimental center, Hitchcock flew a Merlin Mustang; he was the first American to do so. Every distinguished visitor to the American embassy received a briefing on the merits of the Mustang. The list included Eleanor Roosevelt and Captain Eddie Rickenbacker, the famous World War I ace; Stimson had sent him to the U.K. to inspect Eighth Air Force. After receiving Rickenbacker's report, Stimson jotted a note: "P-51. Uncanny! Everybody crazy for it — get it into production by April [1943]."[41]

Stimson was wrong. Not everybody was crazy for it. On June 5, 1942, Hitchcock warned his friend, Lovett, that the AAF chief was only lukewarm about the fighter:

> The English testing field at Duxford has sent an extremely favorable report on the Mustang.... The great possibilities of this plane as a fighter for the Americans when equipped with a high altitude engine was brought to the attention of General Arnold by Ambassador Winant and myself when the General was in London a few days ago.... At the time I saw him he was not particularly enthusiastic on the type.... It was somewhat surprising to me to find that we had developed a fighting plane of really exceptional quality and [Arnold] knew so little about it.... It seems likely that the Mustang with the Merlin engine presents us with an opportunity to regain qualitative superiority in the fighter business in the not too distant future providing we push the development with energy.[42]

In Lovett, Hitchcock had approached a man of extraordinary competence. The assistant secretary of war for air was a match for Hitchcock in intelligence, experience and forcefulness. During World War I, Lovett had interrupted his studies at Yale to fly for the U.S. Navy, compiling a distinguished war record. In peacetime, like Hitchcock, he had worked at the highest level of finance on Wall Street; he had been a partner in Brown Brothers, Harriman and Company, where he worked closely with Averell Harriman. Lovett occupied a key position in the War Department with regard to air issues. He involved himself deeply in AAF issues during World War II and intervened in matters that were to have a crucial impact on the war. Lovett joined Hitchcock and Winant in prodding the AAF to increase its orders for P-51 Mustangs; Hitchcock warned him to be alert for anti-Mustang bias in the AAF: "The Mustang had no friend to fight for it at AAF headquarters."

National chauvinism and a steady drumbeat of criticism from the RAF about AAF equipment and practices had fostered the growth of anti-British feelings among American airmen. Moreover, top AAF leaders felt defensive about some of their decisions in the prewar period. The discord made some AAF officers hesitate to express approval for anything British; they risked being labeled as pushovers for propaganda. Even Spaatz, the most objective and pragmatic of individuals, expressed reservations about British claims for the Mustang: "Taking into account the British fondness for their own equipment, it is interesting." These prejudices complicated Hitchcock's work, which primarily involved reporting on British methods and equipment.

Lovett refused to be stonewalled by AAF staff. He sent Hitchcock's report on the Mustang to the commander of the AAF Matériel Command for comment. The reply referred to the "attached letter from Mr. [sic] Hitchcock. We have been thoroughly aware of the Mustang's performance [but] have not considered this performance such that would warrant interference with bomber production in the North American plant.... We are now in the throes of vigorously prosecuting a development of a 61 [Merlin] in the Mustang. We, too, feel that it has great promise as our engineering calculations appear to support the British estimate of its possibility."[43]

Although hardly an accolade, the reply showed that the AAF had at least decided to investigate Merlin Mustangs. On June 15, Lovett wrote to Hitchcock: "I can comfort you with the knowledge that, for several months past, we have been pushing at the P-51 and in about 90 days we ought to see some results."[44]

German victories in 1940–1941 shocked U.S. Army planners and motivated them to scrutinize the methods used by German armies. Arnold came under heavy pressure from Marshall to build up a force of dive bombers — a weapon the Germans had used effectively. AAF doctrine did not favor dive bombers — they were vulnerable to fighters — but Arnold agreed reluctantly to have some Mustangs fitted for dive bombing. Other modest orders for Mustangs followed, and assembly lines remained in production. In June 1942, the AAF placed an order for twelve hundred P-51-A's to be used primarily as low-altitude fighters.

Hitchcock returned to the U.S. in November 1942 to promote the Merlin Mustang cause. He knew of course that the P-51 had to compete with other aircraft for Merlin engines, scarce materials and labor. He arrived in the U.S. with an appointment to see Harry Hopkins at the White House. About this time General Arnold received a note from President Roosevelt: "I am told by an American friend returning from England that the British are very keen about the P-51 and feel they could use Rolls Royce engines in them. Do you know anything about it?"[45] By this time Arnold must have sensed a groundswell of support developing for the P-51. He also knew that Roosevelt and Hopkins were the AAF's greatest friends. He answered the president promptly: "Tests indicate that they [Merlin Mustangs] will be a highly satisfactory pursuit plane for 1943. We think so much of them that we have already given orders for approximately 2200...."[46]

The barriers of egotism and chauvinism were crumbling but tough technical and mechanical problems remained to be solved. The president of NAA, James H. Kindelberger, informed Arnold: "As you probably know, we have an arrangement to expedite 400 of these planes.... As we have told you, we expect this airplane to be the best in the world in every department, including high speed, rate of climb and ceiling.... If everything works out as hoped for, 400 of these planes on the British front might conceivably

Hunter, Lovett, and unidentified AAF officers at an airfield in England in 1943. (U.S. Air Force Photo Collection [USAF Neg. No. 79067 AC] courtesy of National Air and Space Museum, Smithsonian Institution.)

have a decisive effect on important operations."[47] Kindelberger deserves high marks for prophecy, especially since NAA had not yet built a single Merlin Mustang and since Packard Motor Company, the American manufacturer of Merlin engines, was having production difficulties with them.

Hitchcock wangled an assignment to visit aircraft plants to study production methods. Newspaper photographs show him standing beside a Mustang as he had so often posed next to a polo pony. "It will be the best fighter in the world for 1943," he predicted. He didn't tell reporters what he really thought of American fighter production, but he wrote a report for Arnold which spelled it out bluntly: "40% of our present production is in the obsolete P-40. The rate of production of the P-47 increases sharply until it will account for approximately one-fourth of our total fighter output, if measured in numbers, and considerably more than one-fourth when measured in terms of man hours necessary to build the plane.... The planned production of the P-51 seems small considering the importance and excellent performance of the plane."[48]

Hitchcock was protesting against the production numbers game — the idea that quantity of weapons is more important than quality, the reluctance to interrupt assembly lines because to do so reduces output. Infatuation with quantity was encouraging the production of inferior aircraft. Such a policy can lead to disaster. Superior aircraft usually prevail in aerial combat. Charles Lindbergh echoed Hitchcock's complaint. He wrote at about the same time: "I tried my best in 1938 and '39 to get this government to concentrate on aircraft design and research. But I was only partially successful and was criticized severely for suggesting that it was more important to develop the right types of military aircraft than to begin mass production at that time."[49]

Hitchcock returned to London after his tour of aircraft factories. In communication with Hopkins, Lovett and others, he and Winant badgered the AAF to expedite production of Merlin Mustangs.

The Mustang was not Hitchcock's sole interest. He made hundreds of recommendations about air matters. One of them concerned a British gunsight that he judged to be superior to those used by the AAF. When they were eventually installed in American aircraft, they remarkably improved gunnery and had an important impact on operations. Hitchcock invited scientists to visit the U.K. and took them to airfields and factories to study operations. He had a definite scientific bent and liked to base his judgments on data. At a dinner hosted by Winant, attended by most of the high-ranking air officers in the U.K., he distributed a questionnaire asking guests to rate fighter characteristics crucial in combat. He understood that aircraft design involves tradeoffs; if one element, say armor, is increased, another will decrease, speed for example. The RAF officers at the dinner may have wondered why a mere major should be permitted to carry out such an exercise at such a time; the AAF officers, though, understood that Hitchcock had influence that transcended military rank.

Hitchcock worked closely with Hunter on fighter issues. Hunter did not favor modification of P-51s to extend their range. Despite his great need for long-range fighters, he asked Eaker "to do everything possible to cut the weight down and get a really light fighter." He alerted Eaker to efforts underway to install tanks in P-51s to increase gasoline storage capacity from 105 gallons to 190 gallons. Hunter favored the use of droptanks but did not want to see the P-51's basic structure altered. He feared that the proposed alterations would displace the center of gravity and reduce maneuverability. He urged Eaker to make "strong representations ... to the AAF that the built-in gas capacity of this airplane be 115 gallons...."[50]

Hunter's policies on fighter equipment echoed prewar Army Air Corps doctrine. A 1941 Pursuit Board chaired by Spaatz, which included Hunter and Eaker, issued a clear warning against loading a fighter with accessories which "often serve to render the plane less effective in accomplishing its primary mission."[51] Hunter's recommendations must have delayed, if only briefly, the effort to make the P-51 a long-range fighter.

Lovett visited the U.K. in 1943 to inspect AAF units. On his return he sent a statement to Arnold that had an important impact on the outcome of the war: "There is an immediate need for long range fighters," he wrote; "This may be met by proper tanks for P-47s but ultimately P-38s and P-51s will be needed."[52]

Lovett's historic memo spurred Arnold to action. He started a Fighter Range Extension Program and assigned it the highest priority. He informed Lovett that "A study is now being conducted to determine the best long-range fighter.... The test results, with external tanks, for extending the range of pursuit airplanes showed approximately three (3) hours for the P-47, four (4) hours for the P-38 and four (4) hours and forty-five minutes (45) on the P-51B. It appears that the P-51B is the best airplane at present but the P-38 lends itself to further adaptability and may prove later to be the better airplane."[53]

Arnold's allegiance to the P-38, despite an abundance of evidence indicating that its performance did not match that of the best German fighters, showed a stubborn streak in his character that sometimes fostered unwise decisions. But he sent an unambiguous order to his deputy, Major General Barney M. Giles, to carry out an objective review of AAF fighters and give it the highest priority:

> This [Lovett's memo] brings to my mind very clearly the absolute necessity for

building a fighter airplane that can go in and come out with the bombers. Moreover, this fighter has got to go into Germany. Perhaps we can modify some existing type to do the job.... About six months remain before the deep penetration of Germany begins. Within the next six months, you have got to get a fighter that can protect our bombers.... Get to work on this right away because by January '44, I want fighter escort for all our bombers from U.K. into Germany.[54]

Giles did get to work on it right away. He reported to Arnold in early July: "Action is under way designed to provide a fighter type airplane with sufficient duration to accompany bombers during deep penetrations into Germany." Giles's next comment shows how difficult it was for career AAF officers to abandon peacetime dogma: "It must be anticipated that such a fighter airplane will be inferior in combat performance to German interceptor types which will be encountered on these penetrations."[55]

There was evidently little doubt in Giles's mind about which of the three fighters had the greatest potential as a long-range fighter. The commander of the AAF Proving Ground Command informed him that room could be found in P-51s behind the pilot for an 85-gallon gasoline tank.[56] On September 9, 1943, Giles wrote to Spaatz: "In order to increase the range of our escort fighters, we are going to install an 85-gallon leakproof tank in the fuselage of the P-51B and C airplanes. The installation will be incorporated in the production line and modification kits will be made for all P-51B series now in service. This should give the P-51 a practical radius of action of approximately 600 miles."[57]

The P-51's intrinsic gas efficiency and the additional eighty-five gallons would ultimately give it a tactical radius even beyond Giles's estimate; meanwhile, the installation of the tank on production lines and in aircraft in service was bound to cause delays. The tank also weakened the P-51's structure and displaced its center of gravity; AAF test pilots reported that "with the internal fuselage tank filled ... the airplane is so unstable longitudinally that violent pullouts or tight turns must be executed with caution...."[58]

A Mustang project officer revised that assessment. He flew a simulated U.K.-to-Berlin flight over the U.S. and found that the P-51's stability returned after a sufficient amount of fuel was consumed in flight.[59] P-51s operating from the U.K. would normally burn enough gasoline to restore aircraft stability before meeting the enemy.

The Fighter Range Extension Program was well under way by September 1943. To help Eighth Air Force until a sufficient number of long-range Mustangs could be sent to the U.K., Giles combed out P-51s and P-38s from training and reconnaissance squadrons and sent them to Kepner. He aimed to have four P-51 groups and two P-38 groups in the U.K. by January 1, 1944. After that date the force would grow rapidly as production of Mustangs reached six hundred per month.

Giles prodded AAF aircraft procurement officers to expedite the long-range escort program: "It is desired that wherever possible a short cut be taken to eliminate all service tests and delays.... Exert the greatest possible pressure to rush the P-38s and P-51s with this extra built-in gas."[60] Rush jobs usually encounter problems. Modifications of the P-51 were partly responsible for structural failures; aircraft disintegrated in flight. Kepner wrote to Giles: "We are having a little trouble with the wings on the P-51D. They seem to bend enough to crack the paint.... We have had some wings pulled off in high speed dives."[61]

The ninth report on the AAF's Fighter Range Extension Program, January 7, 1944, informed Arnold that personnel at the P-38 modification center at Dallas, Texas, "worked outdoors on the flight line 24 hours a day.... Provision had been made for shipping a combined total of 650 P-38Js and P-51 aircraft to the UK for Eighth Air Force." The AAF

Hopkins and Winant. (Courtesy of Franklin D. Roosevelt Library.)

overcame the droptank shortage; it shipped 41,000 droptanks of 75-gallon capacity in December 1943.⁶²

Giles and his team did a remarkable job on the fighter-range extension project, but not without setbacks. One of the greatest resulted from the complexity of the P-51 modification. "[It] has proven to be much more complicated and extensive than was originally estimated by North American," a matériel division officer informed Giles; "Instead of 450 man-hours ... the initial mock-ups have required 1200 man-hours."[63]

General Haywood Hansell returned to the U.S. in the summer of 1943 to work on a revision of U.S. air plans. He gave the AAF headquarters staff an authoritative picture of Eighth Air Force's problems and operations. "German fighters are very determined, very skillful, and unless you knock them down, they will come in and make costly attacks," he explained. At about the time Hansell spoke, GAF fighters were continuing to inflict heavy losses on Eighth Air Force. "Rockets constitute a very real hazard," he warned. "Another is heavy caliber cannon. On at least one occasion they have stood out of range of our effective fire from the rear quarter and knocked down four B-17s of the rear group." Hansell testified to the need for fighter protection. "When the fighters were along, the mission was going to be relatively easy. When they weren't along, it was tough."[64]

During the summer and fall of 1943, Winant and Hitchcock continued to plead for Mustangs. On July 9, Winant sent a cable to Hopkins: "Could you let me know when we can expect to get Mustangs with a Merlin engine here: ... I have pressed for the need of this plane for so long and so often that I hesitate to make further inquiries through Army channels."[65] Hopkins asked Lovett to respond to Winant.

On October 16, Winant sent Hopkins a more cheerful note about a milestone in the Mustang's career: "A small number of Mustangs have already arrived here. Last week I saw it fly with its new Rolls-Royce Packard engine. It is a better plane than I had dared to hope, and with its extra tankage it can go to Berlin and back."[66]

The efforts of Hitchcock, Winant, Hopkins, and Lovett to promote the Mustang were crucial in getting the legendary fighter to the U.K. in time to have a decisive impact on the battle for air supremacy.

Brigadier General Elwood P. Quesada came to England from the Mediterranean theater to command Ninth Air Force fighters. On January 20, 1944, he wrote to a friend about Mustangs: "The 354 Fighter Group arrived on November 4 ... received its first P-51Bs on November 14th ... participated in its first operational mission over France on 5 December [and on] December 13 escorted the heavies to Kiel.... Only a few planes had the 85 gallon tank but others are on the way."[67]

Major James H. Howard was one of the first AAF pilots to fly a P-51 from the U.K. He flew with the 354th Fighter Group, the pioneer AAF Mustang group in the U.K. Howard had flown with the famous Flying Tigers in China. With a Mustang he won the Congressional Medal of Honor. His depth of experience makes his comments on the P-51 exceptionally authoritative:

> All of the advanced rumors of the P-51's excellence proved true. It had a top speed of 425 miles an hour at twenty-one thousand feet, powered by a fifteen-hundred-horsepower Rolls-Royce Merlin in-line engine manufactured by Packard. There were four .50-caliber guns in the wings. It was a fighter pilot's dream. It had the latest "demand-type" oxygen system for altitudes up to forty thousand feet. It also had a superior static-free VHF radio with four push-button channels.[68]

Howard also remembered the P-51's defects: engine-mount bolts worked loose, guns jammed frequently, propeller shafts threw oil, oxygen tanks were too small, radiators leaked and sparkplugs often failed.[69]

An AAF report in April 1944 noted that "present preference of fighter pilots is, first, P-47 which is practically free from bugs, has 8 guns and engine reliability; second, P-51 which is not as well 'debugged' and the 4 guns of which are not considered as dependable

Eisenhower and Brereton greet Major James Howard, Congressional Medal of Honor winner. Coningham, Leigh-Mallory, and Spaatz are behind Eisenhower. (U.S. Air Force photograph.)

(probably corrected in the 6-gun D version); third, P-38 owing to difficulties with the new Allison [engine], poor cockpit heating and ease of recognition by the enemy which leads Germans to center attack on P-38s."[70]

AAF aircraft service personnel in the U.K. now had abundant experience removing bugs from aircraft; Mustangs would be debugged rapidly. The AAF Proving Ground Command tested P-51s and reported that the "rate of climb is outstanding.... acceleration in a dive is excellent, and its high speed zoom is superior. Above 20,000 feet, the overall fighting qualities of this aircraft are superior to those of all other types used in the trials."[71]

As AAF fighter numbers increased in the U.K., enough droptanks of various sizes became available, and relay systems allowed fighters to optimize fuel efficiency while providing escort for bombers throughout their missions. P-47s usually protected bombers during the first stage of penetration and the last stage of withdrawal. P-38s and P-51s took over escort duties at rendezvous points and went with the bombers to and from targets. P-51s could climb to escort altitudes on droptanks, proceed to a rendezvous point on gas from the extra internal tank, then escort bombers deep into Germany in proper fighting trim, retaining enough gasoline to get home. The prewar assumption that a long-range fighter could not survive in combat against enemy interceptors was valid as an exercise in Euclidean thinking but did not apply in the skies over Germany, where Mustangs were more than a match for GAF fighters.

AAF pilots and gunners also employed their new gunsights with great effectiveness. Hitchcock and Lovett had worked to make the sights available. Eaker explained the importance of accurate gunnery: "ammunition capacity cannot be increased and as missions grow longer it becomes increasingly necessary to have what ammunition is carried used more effectively and thus conserved so it will last."[72] Kepner believed that the Mark II gyro gunsight was the greatest advance in fighter effectiveness produced in the war. He recalled that "experienced pilots who are good shots have consistently bettered their shooting 400 to 500 percent.... Notoriously poor shots have, in some instances, increased their shooting effectiveness by 600 to 700 percent."[73]

In December 1943, before he left the U.K. for the Mediterranean theater, Eaker prepared a summary of Eighth Air Force's achievements during the period of his command. He still retained his faith in close escort and defended the gas-wasting maneuvers that it required. If fighter speed dropped too much, he explained, "pilots had to increase the angle of attack to maintain altitude; the nose rises, causing the pilot's search area to be limited ... the controls become sloppy, and the airplane becomes easy prey for any hostile aircraft in the vicinity." Eaker's argument depended on the assumption that close escort was necessary despite its drawbacks. It was a premise that Spaatz and Doolittle would reject. Eaker warned that fighters with a primary mission to escort bombers should not also carry out fighter-bomber missions. To do so would put too great a strain on maintenance facilities. This policy, too, would soon change.[74]

In a letter to Giles, Kepner summarized Eighth Air Force fighter problems in 1943. He recalled that the number of P-38s under his command had been few. The Lightnings had been used "right up to the hilt, so much so that the casualties have been higher than would normally be expected." Maintenance had been difficult in the winter months with short periods of daylight. Fighters had had trouble finding their airdromes in the "damnable haze and fog." Kepner had had to send P-38s out "beyond the P-47's when they were alone and frequently outnumbered three to one." He communicated a complaint moderately to Giles: "as you know all P-51s were turned over to IX Air Force.... Needless to say ... I would like to have them.... They are distinctly the best fighter that we can get over here...." Kepner informed Giles that P-47s were performing well now that their "bugs" had been eliminated. With new paddle blade propellers and water injection apparatus for engines, their performance had improved. The supply of droptanks was sufficient.[75] Kepner's gentle complaint about P-51s going to Ninth Air Force would be heeded. It was one of the first issues that Spaatz tackled after he took command of USSTAF.

Chapter 4

The Allied Expeditionary Air Forces

During the early planning stages of Overlord, it was clear that command of the air over the lodgment area was a prerequisite for a successful invasion. Time after time during World War II, both Allied and Axis armies had suffered heavy losses when they attempted amphibious landings on hostile shores without protective air cover.

When Allied leaders decided to launch an invasion of northwest Europe, the CCS appointed Air Chief Marshal Leigh-Mallory to plan air support for it. He had commanded fighters and had experience in close ground-support operations. The planning job led to his appointment to command Overlord's air organization, the Allied Expeditionary Air Forces.[1]

General Arnold felt antagonistic to AEAF from the outset. An American air force, Ninth Air Force, would be assigned to AEAF, but Arnold insisted that Leigh-Mallory would give only general operational direction to the Ninth's commander.[2] Arnold regarded AEAF as an unnecessary organization, one that would weaken communication between the supreme commander and his air forces. Arnold foresaw delay, confusion and acrimony resulting from AEAF's activities. Another drawback was AEAF's need for personnel. The AAF itself suffered from a severe shortage of qualified staff officers. Arnold procrastinated in making appointments to AEAF, and this policy motivated the RAF to fill most of the important positions.

Major General William O. Butler, an AAF career officer, became deputy commander of AEAF in November 1943. He soon felt a coolness emanating from AAF headquarters. In a letter to Giles, he explained the situation: "I asked for about 5 or 6 officers before I left.... So far none of these have arrived and there is no notice on their departure.... The Air Force here has furnished a few nondescripts and promises some more of doubtful ability soon.

"The RAF has set up a staff calling for 150 RAF officers with plenty of rank. Our share of this huge setup I have managed to hold to about 80 officers, but I am being pressed by Leigh-Mallory to begin to produce the bodies."[3]

Giles could offer little encouragement. The small pool of AAF officers qualified for staff jobs could not satisfy the worldwide demands on it.

Lack of AAF support weakened Butler's position in AEAF, and Leigh-Mallory's treatment of him lowered his status even more. An AAF officer reported to Arnold on a visit to AEAF: "It is true that the Air Marshal commanding the Combined Air Forces [AEAF] has an American officer as Deputy, but considering the personalities of this Commander and his Senior Air Staff officer, the Deputy will be completely ignored unless he is completely subordinate."[4] This proved to be an accurate estimate of the situation.

Leigh-Mallory's personality intensified the latent hostility existing between RAF and AAF airmen. Virtually every American who had contact with him described Leigh-Mallory as rude, overbearing and tactless. He also antagonized British personnel; he and Tedder clashed repeatedly. Tedder later wrote that Leigh-Mallory, "though earnest, zealous and brave, did not inspire confidence as Commander of the Allied Expeditionary Air Forces.... I did my best ... to explain gently ... that a less brusque manner would pay dividends."[5] Anyone in Leigh-Mallory's position would have encountered opposition, but his personality made conflicts much more difficult to resolve amicably. One of Leigh-Mallory's closest associates admitted that he was "so typically English, sometimes tactless, almost pompous in appearance and naive in character without any finesse, that it was difficult for the Americans to assess his ability...."[6]

Spaatz, however, promptly assessed Leigh-Mallory's ability and did not like the result. He concluded that the AEAF commander was incompetent to direct strategic air operations. The two strong-minded leaders were bound to clash; a major disagreement broke out over the objective of greatest concern to Spaatz at the time—winning air supremacy over the GAF. Spaatz recorded with amazement that Leigh-Mallory "apparently accepts possibility of not establishing air supremacy until landing starts."[7] An AEAF air plan contained the following statement: "Despite the present numerical superiority of the Allied Air Force, it may well be that air supremacy cannot be assured until the joining of the decisive air battle which will mark the opening of the Overlord assault."[8] This remarkably complacent attitude was challenged by General Frederick Anderson, now USSTAF's director of operations: "If such were the case, the assault [invasion] itself would be dangerously premature."[9]

Leigh-Mallory's policy on air supremacy may have been imprudent in Spaatz's judgment, but it was not inconsistent with Eisenhower's rocklike determination to control the strategic air forces. He insisted that they must come under SHAEF's direction to support Overlord several months before D-Day and remain so committed until invasion forces were established securely on the continent—possibly even longer if they were needed. Eisenhower believed that Overlord was the critical effort to which all forces must make a maximum contribution.

Spaatz wanted to employ the strategic air forces (with Ninth Air Force support) on Pointblank objectives until shortly before D-Day, a proposal that did not fit in with Eisenhower's plans. To bolster his case, Spaatz argued that a concentration on Pointblank would give USSTAF opportunities to achieve air supremacy, a condition vital to Overlord. Leigh-Mallory rejected this argument. He considered it unlikely that the GAF could be overwhelmed before the invasion. All it had to do—as the British had done in 1940—was to conserve an anti-invasion air force. Moreover, this eventuality did not disturb him unduly: Allied air forces were strong enough to protect invasion forces. Air supremacy could be won in air fighting over the beachhead. The RAF had conserved its fighters for just such a battle. Spaatz recognized the danger of GAF conservation of an anti-invasion force, but he planned to force it to fight. The issue was clearly defined—it was only a matter of time before it erupted into a confrontation between the Allied air commanders.

Spaatz informed Arnold of his concern about AEAF: "Leigh-Mallory has built up a huge headquarters which basically in my opinion, is much greater than necessary to control the Tactical Air Force. Whether or not he expects to have all Strategic Air Forces under his control also, I do not know."[10] Spaatz did not intend to let that happen.

Some of Spaatz's contemporaries believed he opposed immediate transfer of USSTAF to SHAEF because of his obsession to defeat Germany by strategic bombing. This simplistic thesis has been repeated by many writers and has become one of Overlord's myths. Nevertheless, it is untrue. An abundance of documentary evidence shows clearly that Spaatz was a loyal member of the Overlord team, not someone with a hidden agenda. He did have an obsession, but it was not to win the war with air power; he believed that USSTAF had to win air supremacy over the GAF before D-Day. Strategic bombing was the weapon USSTAF would employ to overwhelm the GAF. Without air superiority, the invasion would be too hazardous — in Eisenhower's mind, "foolhardy."

It is difficult to understand why so many historians misconstrued this policy, for Spaatz expressed it frequently in his writings and comments at the time. Strategic air operations, as Spaatz perceived them, had two major objectives — short term, to win air supremacy and long term, to weaken Germany by bombing its critical industries. Obviously, the two were not mutually exclusive. Air operations against German industries would force the GAF to fight and suffer attrition.

Early in January, Spaatz and Leigh-Mallory collided over an issue involving Ninth Air Force. Both men had authority over the Ninth. Leigh-Mallory had not created the problem, but he stood in the way of its solution. It involved the allocation of P-51s to Ninth Air Force. An unfortunate decision sent Mustangs — now recognized as the outstanding long-range escort fighter — to Ninth Air Force, where their principal responsibility would be to provide support for ground forces. As Spaatz prepared to take over USSTAF, Lovett called this strange allocation to his attention: "There has seemed to me to be considerable confusion as to who is going to do which to whom and with what...." Lovett reminded Spaatz that he had prodded the AAF for months to produce long-range fighters for bomber escort. He feared that "under the new set up which you will face ... we are going to wake up some day and find that our P-51B's ... are all controlled by some RAF officer."[11]

Lovett had once again intervened crucially in the career of the P-51, an intervention that exerted an important influence on the outcome of the war. Spaatz moved promptly to correct the situation. General Kepner, Eighth Air Force fighter command, remembered the meeting at which the problem was resolved: "General Brereton [Ninth Air Force commander] wanted the Mustangs — why, I don't know.... We argued all day long on this subject." Spaatz proposed to switch Kepner's P-47s for Brereton's P-51s. Leigh-Mallory pointed out the P-47's weaknesses — poor acceleration and slow climbing speed. Kepner maintained that they climbed well enough for ground support missions. Finally, Spaatz told Leigh-Mallory that he needed the Mustangs for bomber escort and, if necessary, would take the issue to the CCS. Leigh-Mallory then turned to Brereton and said, "Lewis, I don't think I can back you any longer.... Spaatz has demonstrated that this Thunderbolt probably is the plane for ground support and he should have the Mustang."[12]

Spaatz recorded the outcome in his diary: "Leigh-Mallory's attitude in this surprising to me ... he agreed to P-51s going to 8AF."[13]

During the next few months, most Eighth Air Force fighter groups gave their P-47s to Ninth Air Force, and received P-51s. In Ninth Air Force the P-47, an airplane designed as a high-altitude fighter, became the finest ground-attack aircraft of the war.

The forward-looking settlement of the P-51 allocation issue improved Spaatz's opinion of Leigh-Mallory only slightly. Tedder cited this distrust in a letter to Portal: "Spaatz has made it abundantly clear that he will not accept orders, or even co-ordination, from Leigh-Mallory...."[14] Spaatz's diary records his discussions with Eisenhower about the issue: "(15 February 1944) Discuss LM with Eisenhower and told him my feelings in the matter are that I have no confidence in Leigh-Mallory's ability to handle the job, and that I view with alarm any setup which places the Strategic Air Force under his control." A few days later Eisenhower "tried subtly to sell Leigh-Mallory" to Spaatz, who replied that his views "had not and would not change." Eisenhower continued to press Spaatz on the issue but with little success. On February 19, 1944, Eisenhower asked Spaatz to suggest how the present setup could be made to work under Leigh-Mallory. Spaatz expressed his firm conviction: "I do not believe it would work under LM."[15]

As Ninth Air Force burgeoned in the early months of 1944, Leigh-Mallory grew increasingly impatient about its failure to fully support AEAF's campaigns. Although Ninth Air Force was a part of AEAF, Eisenhower approved Spaatz's decision to employ its fighters to escort Eighth Air Force bombers on Pointblank missions. These escort duties interfered with AEAF's efforts to equip and train the Ninth's fighter groups for ground attack missions. Transfers of aircraft between air forces and aircraft modifications also caused delays in training. Leigh-Mallory and Brereton registered complaints repeatedly about the situation.

The controversy heated up when AEAF issued a directive regarding Ninth Air Force:

> 1. The Supreme Allied Commander has decided that the time has now come for the operations of U.S. IXth Air Force to be directed towards the preparation for Operation "Overlord." Henceforth IXth Air Force will therefore operate exclusively under Allied Expeditionary Air Force, and will be released from its commitment to assist U.S. VIIIth Air Force "Pointblank" operations under arrangements made by that Force.[16]

Spaatz promptly sent a curt note to Leigh-Mallory: "All three types of U.S. fighters are at the disposal of Eighth Air Force to assist them in Pointblank operations ... it will be my responsibility to determine how much diversion from Pointblank will be allowed for training."[17] When the dispute came to Eisenhower's attention, he decided that "long-range, deep penetrations by VIII AF will have priority for present."[18] It was another humiliating setback for Leigh-Mallory.

Ninth Air Force fighter groups continued to give first priority to Pointblank operations in the months before D-Day, but they squeezed in training exercises and re-equipment for ground attack. Ninth's bombers participated in AEAF's campaigns preparing for the invasion; Ninth Troop Carrier Command and other Ninth Air Force units prepared for their Overlord missions. Spaatz directed Brereton and Kepner to order fighter pilots to carry out ground attacks when they turned back from bomber escort missions. This was excellent training for tasks they would undertake during the invasion. Spaatz explained to Arnold that "future operational planning includes fighter sweeps over enemy territory at low level during withdrawal from escort duties."[19] Fighter sweeps, severely criticized by Arnold six months earlier, now became a means of training AAF pilots in ground attack. They also weakened the GAF by destroying aircraft on the ground.

By May 1944, Ninth Air Force had thirteen P-47 groups, three P-38 groups, and two P-51 groups. In addition to escort and ground attack missions, it executed photographic reconnaissance operations crucial to Overlord. Ninth Bomber Command had twelve medium bomber groups (B-26s) and six light bomber groups (A-20s). Ninth Troop Carrier Command trained to deliver airborne forces to France on D-Day using transport aircraft and gliders.

General Eisenhower rarely asked the British to replace an officer assigned to his command; faced with a counterproductive situation at AEAF, he acted consistently. Instead of asking the British to relieve Leigh-Mallory, the cause of much ill feeling, he relieved the unfortunate American deputy commander of AEAF. He advised Marshall that "Major General Butler of the Army Air Forces is now serving as Deputy to my principal Air Commander. I am not aware of this officer's past record and accomplishments in the Army Air Forces but he is not suitable for his present assignment."[20] Eisenhower described Butler as "diffident and uncertain." Major General Hoyt S. Vandenberg replaced Butler. No one ever described Vandenberg as diffident or uncertain. (After the war he became head of the U.S. Air Force.) Vandenberg did not allow himself to be ignored or intimidated by the AEAF staff or its commander, but his professionalism was sorely tested by the situation. He sought guidance from Spaatz and Eisenhower and was told that his first priority at AEAF was "safeguarding American interests."[21]

In the months before D-Day, Ninth Air Force medium bombers also became a subject of controversy between USSTAF and AEAF. Spaatz believed that the mediums were not contributing as much as they should to Pointblank. Since they were a component of AEAF, Leigh-Mallory would normally have to approve any changes in their operations.

Ninth Air Force's medium bomber, the B-26 Martin Marauder, was another AAF warplane that suffered agonizing growing pains. A single-winged, two-engined aircraft, it carried a crew of six and had originally been slated to carry out attacks at low altitudes. The AAF hoped that its speed of 285 miles per hour and its defensive armament would enable it to cope with enemy fighters. The B-26's sleek design, narrow wings and powerful engines gave it relatively high speed but also exceptionally fast landings, requiring long runways and skilled pilots. Early models had vicious stall propensities; young pilots, many fresh from flying schools, distrusted the B-26. Word spread throughout the Army Air Corps that the Marauder was a "widow maker." General Arnold asked Spaatz to head a board to investigate the B-26's "troubles." The board recommended several design changes, including wider wings.[22]

Arnold recruited Doolittle to help improve the B-26's reputation. He asked Doolittle to "take a B-26, fly it under any and all conditions and then go down to the B-26 outfit, take command, and show those boys that flying this ship was no different from flying any other."[23] Doolittle showed pilots how to fly B-26s safely. "The B-26 Marauder was an unforgiving airplane," he remembered, "and it was killing pilots because it never gave them a chance to make mistakes.... I checked it over, flew it and liked it. There wasn't anything about its flying characteristics that good piloting skill couldn't overcome. I recommended that it continue to be built and it was."[24]

In 1943 the AAF sent some B-26 groups to Eighth Air Force to participate in the strategic-bombing offensive. One of the first units to arrive was the 322nd Bomb Group. General Eaker urged its commander to "go after those enemy fighters where they live. Don't wait for body armor. The B-17 crews are operating without it."[25]

On May 14, 1943, the 322nd Bomb Group sent eleven B-26s to attack a power plant at Ijmuidan, Holland. The force flew at low altitude across the North Sea, skimming wave tops to evade detection by German radar operators. No aircraft were lost; bombing results were poor. Three days later the 322nd attacked power stations at Ijmuidan and Harlem. Only one bomber survived the mission.[26] This disaster exemplified every air commander's worst nightmare. Eaker ordered a review of medium bomber tactical doctrine. Investigators concluded that the B-26 had to be given fighter escort and enough altitude to provide a reasonable chance to survive anti-aircraft fire. Eaker informed Arnold that in future he would give the B-26s more protection: "We have put bombsights into the lead aircraft

4. The Allied Expeditionary Air Forces 57

B-26 medium bombers attacking a target in France. (U.S. Air Force Photo Collection [Neg. No. 72989 AC], courtesy of National Air and Space Museum, Smithsonian Institution.)

and we will, within a few days, start our mediums battering the German airdromes and other targets ... with fighter cover.... This will train the medium units so that they will be ready to support the ground troops in an invasion."[27]

When Spaatz examined the record of medium bombers, he was not impressed. He agreed with a high-ranking AAF officer who had written that "the loss rate [of mediums] is very low, less than 1% due to shallow penetration, fighter escort and targets of less importance.... In my opinion the medium bomber force is not carrying its weight in support of Pointblank, either by causing any appreciable attrition of the GAF, disruption of its facilities or destruction of vital industrial objectives."[28]

General Fred Anderson, then commander of Eighth Bomber Command, reported that his heavy bombers did not receive much help from Ninth Bomber Command: "The medium bombers do not serve to divert enemy fighters from heavy bomber formations and we have long since ceased to count upon them for that function."[29] GAF fighters generally ignored escorted mediums, which usually attacked targets of slight importance to Germany. Anderson advised Spaatz that the mediums "should extend their operating range to the maximum.... This should be done at least a couple of times beyond Fighter escort...."[30]

Complaints that Ninth Bomber Command did not support the strategic-bombing offensive seemed somewhat irrelevant to Leigh-Mallory and Brereton. Their primary goals were to employ Ninth Bomber Command against targets which would help Overlord and to get it ready to support ground armies in the coming invasion.

Spaatz, of course, had other priorities. He asked Portal for help in getting more cooperation from AEAF: "I do believe ... that there will sometimes be excellent possibilities of catching the enemy fighters as they are returning to airdromes within range of mediums.... [This would be] the most effective kind of support they can give to our bomber operations."[31] Portal replied: "Leigh-Mallory is bound by his directive ... to lend maximum support to the strategic air offensive." He promised to call this point "urgently" to Leigh-Mallory's attention.[32]

General Brereton was not enthusiastic about sending mediums out without fighter escort. He advised Spaatz that "the mediums can go in with fighter support, leave their fighter support at its maximum range and proceed 15 minutes further and be picked up by fighter support on withdrawal without incurring unduly large losses. [But] ... this could be done once or twice only ... not regularly without incurring prohibitive losses."[33]

In the period prior to D-Day, Brereton's Ninth Air Force hustled to try to satisfy many different obligations. His medium bombers attacked airfields, rail centers, radar sites, bridges and secret weapon installations. They steadily improved their techniques and operated more effectively; they came to be one of the principal AAF weapons to employ against relatively small but critical targets.

Ninth Air Force reconnaissance groups performed an extremely valuable service in the pre–D-Day period: they carried out a prodigious photo-reconnaissance campaign to collect information about enemy defenses on the continent.

Ninth Air Force engineer units constructed airfields and other installations in the U.K.; it was excellent training for jobs they would have to do after D-Day on the continent. Ninth Troop Carrier Command flew transports and gliders in training exercises preparing to take airborne soldiers to Normandy on the eve of D-Day. Each week, Brereton withdrew some fighter and bomber groups from operations for training.

One of Ninth Air Force's major obligations, however, could not be met. It had to reject some requests from U.S. Army divisions training in the U.K. to participate in air-ground exercises. It was a serious neglect, and it had unfortunate consequences. Air-ground cooperation was a new field, one in which a multitude of techniques and policies had yet to be developed.

Perhaps the operations that motivated Ninth Bomber Command most forcefully to improve its bombing accuracy were those directed against V-weapon installations. Intended for launching rockets and flying bombs against England, these sites were relatively small and difficult to attack effectively; they were protected with massive concrete shelters and formidable anti-aircraft defenses.

Spaatz was distinctly unenthusiastic about Operation Crossbow, the campaign to disrupt Hitler's plans to assault England with V-weapons–flying-bombs (V1s) and rockets (V2s). Spaatz believed the danger was not as great as the British believed it to be. He worried about the diversion of air effort from critical campaigns.

Spaatz's major concern was to bring the GAF to battle, and he consistently opposed operations which did not help accomplish this objective. As always, weather was the most frustrating deterrent to precision bombing. In February 1944, Spaatz and USSTAF waited for a period of clear weather over Germany so that the crucial battles for air supremacy could be fought.

Chapter 5

USSTAF's Campaign to Weaken the German Air Force

Spaatz took command of USSTAF in January 1944 with clear instructions from Arnold: "It is a conceded fact that Overlord ... will not be possible unless the German Air Force is destroyed. Therefore, my personal message to you — is to, '*Destroy the Enemy Air Force wherever you find them, in the air, on the ground, and in the factories.*'"[1] Rarely has a field commander received a more explicit directive from headquarters.

To insure central leadership to accomplish AAF goals, Arnold gave Spaatz authority over all AAF units in Europe. In spite of tangled lines of command resembling a bird's nest, Spaatz exercised authority over Brereton and Eaker and worked smoothly with Eisenhower, Portal and Tedder. With Arnold's support he had little difficulty establishing his authority and exerting leadership.

As USSTAF's commander, Spaatz coordinated strategic operations of Eighth and Fifteenth Air Forces. These were designed to weaken Germany so that her defeat became a certainty. To direct air forces operating in different theaters under different supreme commanders required tact, firmness and a high level of competence. Arnold depended on Spaatz to coordinate the AAF efforts in Europe.

Until strategic air forces in the U.K. came under Eisenhower's control, Spaatz received direction from Air Chief Marshal Portal with regard to strategic operations. He worked closely with Eaker, who now commanded Allied air forces in the Mediterranean theater. He and Eaker had collaborated on many projects in peace and war; they would continue to do so without much friction.

Ninth Air Force, commanded by General Brereton, was a component of AEAF, but Spaatz exercised control over its administration — personnel, equipment, supplies. Indeed, Spaatz established general authority over Ninth Air Force in all important matters affecting it. He later commented that "Brereton was never in any doubt about who commanded Ninth Air Force." The Ninth mushroomed, in the six months prior to D-Day, to become a huge tactical air force with a primary mission to provide close support for invasion armies. Before the invasion it carried out various missions given to it by both AEAF and USSTAF.

In the first quarter of 1944, the CCS continued to direct USSTAF through Portal. At some still unspecified time, Portal and Eisenhower would negotiate the terms of its transfer to SHAEF. Yet, even before the formal transfer of authority, Tedder directed planning for employment of Allied air forces in support of Overlord. He dealt with Spaatz, Leigh-Mallory and Harris as if they were on a "coordinate plane." AEAF did detailed planning of air operations in support of the invasion, including those which would involve Eighth Air Force and RAF Bomber Command.

Operating in such a tangle of lines of command, it was inevitable that Spaatz would encounter short circuits. One of these incidents occurred in January. Portal continued to give directives to Fifteenth Air Force. Spaatz sent him a protest that did not mince words:

> I have already issued target directives to the United States Strategic Air Forces in the Mediterranean through MAAF [Mediterranean Allied Air Forces]. If target priorities are also issued by you that are not sent through my headquarters, confusion and lack of definite direction of the American operating forces will result.... My directive charges me with the responsibility of the strategic direction of the American strategic forces, and all directives to them must definitely come through my headquarters.[2]

Spaatz had to be forthright about the extent of his authority. Not only did USSTAF direct operations of the Eighth and Fifteenth Air Forces, it also ran a vast service organization that satisfied the supply and personnel needs of these air forces and Ninth Air Force too.[3]

Eighth Air Force had grown steadily since the day in August 1942 when it had sent twelve B-17s to attack the railroad yard near Rouen. It would soon be able to send a thousand heavy bombers escorted by as many fighters to carry out a single mission. Spaatz reminded Doolittle of the main objective and the critical time factor: "We are committed to the destruction of the GAF. One requirement is the destruction of the German fighter and ball bearing factories.... Sometime before Overlord [the invasion] we will probably be committed to its direct support and there is a possibility that our freedom of action may be restricted."[4]

Spaatz traveled constantly throughout the European theater visiting air stations, conferring with airmen, inspecting facilities, listening to suggestions and complaints. He identified a number of practices that would have to be changed to make AAF units more effective. One such change lengthened tours of duty for air crews. Their relief from combat duties came after they had completed a specific number of missions, but research showed that they were then at peak proficiency. In 1942, when Eighth Air Force had consisted of only a few groups, replacements had been slow in coming, and morale had suffered. Eaker had told his staff: "Of this I am certain and you can count upon it, that as long as I retain command ... a combat crew must be told what their combat expectancy is, and further they must be told that when they have completed that period, they will never again be required to man a combat crew station in an airplane on operations against the enemy."[5]

Spaatz believed that such a policy wasted resources. Air-combat conditions had changed dramatically since 1942. At one time early in Eighth Air Force's career, with a loss rate of 10 percent per mission, airmen (wrongly) calculated their chance of surviving ten missions to be zero. A research report stated clearly that competence of crews and the probability of surviving a mission increased steadily with experience:

> 67 percent of initial combat-crew members complete 5 missions.
> 70 percent of those completing 5 missions complete 10 missions.
> 75 percent of those completing 10 missions complete 15 missions.
> 77 percent of those completing 15 missions complete 20 missions.
> 91 percent of those completing 20 missions complete 25 missions.[6]

These figures give airmen a 25 percent probability of surviving twenty-five missions. Arnold dealt with the sensitive issue and sent an unpopular but unequivocal memo to his air force commanders: "If you have made any policies or understandings that combat personnel will be returned to the U.S.[after a specific number of missions], those policies will be rescinded at once. Our combat personnel must understand that we plan to use combat crews in accord with war demands."[7] Now, bomber crews would remain on operations until their commander decided that their relief was in keeping with the needs of the AAF, and U.S. forces generally. Spaatz reported to Arnold that airmen no longer believe they will be "through with the war" after a certain number of missions.[8] This change risked damaging morale, but it brought AAF rotation policies in line with those of ground and naval forces.

Weather continued to stifle Eighth Air Force operations. Spaatz urged commanders to take greater risks in poor weather, to get their bombers and fighters into the air even in the face of a threatened storm if better conditions were forecast for the time of their return: "Send out a portion of the forces so it can be formed more rapidly and return before weather closes in on home bases.... Another portion of the force can be sent out same day ... and continue on to Italy."[9]

Doolittle and Spaatz exchanged angry words about weather. Doolittle had little faith in weather predictions. He organized a scout force that used fighter aircraft to fly to targets in advance of bombers and report to them on weather conditions.[10] Radar systems guided bombers to targets and helped them bomb "through the overcast," a phrase Arnold recommended in preference to "blind bombing." Aircraft with special navigation equipment acted as "pathfinders" for bomber formations so that they could fly in weather that would previously have kept them grounded.

At times, Spaatz became impatient with Doolittle. On February 9, 1944, he recorded the following complaint in his diary: "Today is to go on record as completely wasted. Good weather at bases, good weather over target, and Doolittle sent *no* bombers."[11] Doolittle's air force operated under severe stresses. Next day, an Eighth Air Force assault on the industrial area of Brunswick met fierce opposition; more than 20 percent of the bomber force was lost. But battles like this were necessary to weaken the GAF and achieve air supremacy.

Doolittle did not really need much prodding to employ Eighth Air Force aggressively. His experience in North Africa and Italy had taught him that constant effort would be needed to overwhelm the GAF. At one of his first meetings with Eighth Air Force commanders, he announced that he wanted the largest possible number of aircraft participating in each mission. Non-operational periods due to weather would suffice for recuperation.[12]

When Doolittle took command of Eighth Air Force, it had been operating from the U.K. for eighteen months. Enemy fighters had forced its bombers to fly in large formations so that Allied fighters could give protection and fire from bombers' weapons could be massed. But such a system had many drawbacks, principally the time, effort and gasoline consumed to assemble aircraft in precise formations. The boxes of heavy bombers could be located swiftly by enemy fighters, and these boxes were vulnerable to flak. It was extremely difficult for bombers, endangered by fighters and flak, to place bombs on targets from high altitudes. Most groups had only a few bombardiers who could be relied on to bomb accurately. Moreover, such formations were only one of many disadvantageous countermeasures that enemy fighters and flak imposed on the AAF and Allied forces. Reduction of the fighter threat would permit Allied air, sea and ground forces to operate with greater freedom and effectiveness.[13]

Doolittle, with a doctorate in aeronautical engineering and years of experience doing research on aviation problems, often delved into technical matters. One of his reports angered Spaatz. It concerned the B-24 heavy bomber that had been "improved" so much that it was far over its designed weight and difficult to fly in formation; it had a tendency to go out of control. Doolittle explained the situation in a memo to Arnold: "Fully loaded B-24s become difficult to fly properly in formation at 28,000 feet. ... the lower elements in formations of the size flown here will be below 20,000 feet, where the flak is lethal." Doolittle wanted the B-24s lightened. Morale of crews flying the Liberators was dropping. He informed Arnold that "B-17 crews state, and only half jestingly, that they would rather have a B-24 group with them than a fighter group as the enemy fighters generally single out the B-24 units if everything else is equal.... We are endeavoring to build up a spirit of healthy competition between the B-17 and B-24 units but are experiencing great difficulty due to the consummate confidence of the B-17 units in their equipment and the lack of confidence on the part of the B-24 units in theirs."[14]

Spaatz sent an unusually strong protest to Arnold about Doolittle's complaints: "I must say that I can not sponsor any extensive modification or redesign program in the B-24 airplane which would prejudice the now scheduled deliveries to this theater. I consider that I do not have an unlimited time to do this job, and I must, in the best way possible, do it with the tools you furnish me. The German Air Force must be liquidated if Overlord is to be successful, and I can not liquidate it with airplanes resting in modification centers...."[15] Arnold calmed both commanders without interfering substantially with the bombing offensive. He started a modest weight-reduction project for B-24s.

Critics charged that Eighth Fighter Command under General Hunter had lacked aggressiveness. Its defensive-minded escort tactics did not result in a rate of destruction of GAF fighters that would lead to air supremacy. In a report to staff members at AAF headquarters, a former Eighth Fighter Command intelligence officer described its escort policies: "A fighter pilot could fly fifty missions, never get a chance to shoot his guns and still be one of the best, doing a good job."[16]

Under the leadership of Spaatz, Doolittle and Kepner, a fighter pilot who flew fifty missions without firing his guns would definitely not be commended for "doing a good job." They urged fighter pilots to seek combat with enemy fighters and to attack ground targets. The time was right for Eighth Fighter Command to adopt more aggressive tactics. Many of its pilots now had about one hundred hours of operational experience, and many leaders had developed. Moreover, most of its groups now flew P-51s, not P-47s. But P-47 pilots, too, were more offensive-minded. Kepner later recalled the transformation:

> We once thought ... that they [P-47 pilots] did not dare to come down to low altitude, because the Thunderbolt was a big heavy plane; they had found that it could out-dive anybody in the world — dive after somebody, or being attacked, dive and get away. They were perfectly satisfied ... that if they had that height they could always take care of themselves. Then along in January [1944] we commenced to come down lower and lower. In the beginning the boys didn't want to get below 27,000 feet ... by February they had convinced themselves that they could fight the Germans any place in the sky with a Thunderbolt.[17]

Spaatz reported to Arnold on February 11 that "the most significant factor [in combat] is ability of our fighters to take on GAF fighters on deep penetrations. From 1st January to 11 February inclusive, AAF fighters based in U.K. have destroyed in the air 354 German Air Force fighters for a loss of 112."[18] Much of this achievement must be credited to P-47s and P-38s; they made extensive use of droptanks. P-51s did not begin to have a major impact on the air war until February and March.

B-24 Liberators attacking a target at Tours. (U.S. Air Force Photo Collection [Neg. No. 52170 AC], courtesy of National Air and Space Museum, Smithsonian Institution.)

American fighters in the U.K. had reached a high level of effectiveness at a most opportune time. To increase their impact on the GAF, Doolittle ordered changes in bomber escort policy — he later judged these orders to be his most important decisions of the war. During a visit to Eighth Fighter Command, he noticed a sign which read "The first duty of Eighth Air Force fighters is to bring the bombers back alive." Doolittle told Kepner to replace it with one that declared "The first duty of Eighth Air Force fighters is to destroy German fighters."[19] Thereafter, AAF fighters would not be tied to bomber formations. GAF pilots could no longer escape by diving for the deck. German fighter losses soared. Kepner welcomed the new policies. By late February 1944, Spaatz believed that air superiority, perhaps even supremacy, could be achieved if northwest Europe had fifteen or twenty days of clear weather.

Many bomber crews resented the new escort policy. At an Eighth Air Force bomb group commanders' meeting, one of the officers challenged it: "It seems to me that it was decided sometime ago that the policy would be adopted of having the fighters chase enemy aircraft even if they had to leave the formation. If we are going to a target having terrific opposition, it would be better if the fighters stayed with the formation."[20] But conditions now favored change; the fighter force was large enough to provide protection for bombers, not by weaving close to them, but by searching for enemy fighters and attacking them. Equipment problems had been sharply reduced: radios worked, engines operated reliably, droptanks were available, fighter ranges extended and guns did not jam so often. Pilots could initiate combat from advantageous positions, and their gunnery was more accurate. They attacked ground targets on the way home if they had managed to conserve enough gasoline and ammunition.

Reichsmarshal Goering ordered GAF fighter pilots to avoid combat with fighters and concentrate on bombers. This policy gave AAF pilots time to build up competence and confidence. A German fighter pilot commented on the situation, possibly with some exaggeration: "The flight of an American fighter over GERMANY was the safest flying in existence. Not a soul attacked him.... To start with, the Americans were rather apprehensive and attacked very unwillingly. But once they noticed that nothing happened to them they grew increasingly cheekier and more dare-devilish."[21]

The commander of GAF fighters, General Adolf Galland, opposed the defensive fighter policy; he recognized it as a prescription for defeat. Faced with superior AAF numbers, the GAF should not take away from its pilots the option to initiate combat with fighters. He informed Goering that "the ratio in which we fight today is about 1:7. The standard of the Americans is extraordinarily high. The day fighters have lost more than 1000 aircraft during the last four months, among them our best officers, and these gaps cannot be filled."[22] The spectacle of hundreds of AAF bombers flying over Germany in daylight "as if on parade" was a severe humiliation for Goering and a condemnation of his leadership of the GAF. In desperation he made matters worse by exhorting his pilots to ignore fighters and concentrate on bombers.

Unfavorable weather in January and February curtailed USSTAF's attacks on Germany's aircraft industry. Finally, on February 19, 1944, forecasters predicted a period of fair weather over Europe. Next day, USSTAF dispatched more than 1,000 heavy bombers and 850 fighters to attack aircraft factories. A week of consecutive missions and furious air fighting ensued. AAF losses were high during "Big Week," as it came to be known: 226 heavy bombers and 28 fighters were lost. But Eighth, Ninth and Fifteenth Air Force fighters destroyed 533 aircraft in February.[23]

In March, USSTAF attacked a target that the GAF had to defend regardless of losses. On March 4, Eighth Air Force bombers, escorted by P-38s, P-47s and P-51s in relays, went all the way to Berlin. Two days later 660 bombers attacked ball-bearing, electrical equipment and aircraft-engine plants in and around the German capital. Eighth Fighter Command operated an intricate escort shuttle service to permit each type of fighter to make the most effective use of its fuel. P-38s with two 150-gallon droptanks could fly to targets 600 miles from their bases; P-51s with 75-gallon droptanks could exceed that distance; and P-47s with droptanks of various sizes extended their tactical radius to 450 miles.[24]

As expected, the GAF response to the Berlin attacks was fierce. On March 8, Eighth Air Force hit Berlin again: 462 heavy bombers struck ball-bearing plants in clear weather. Four groups of P-51s, numbering 174 aircraft, protected the bombers over the target area.

A total of 1,015 AAF fighters flew escort sorties. Eighth Air Force lost 37 bombers and 17 fighters. AAF fighters shot down 87 aircraft. Fighter claims were checked by photographic or eyewitness evidence and tended to be less exaggerated than those of the bombers' gunners.[25]

In a postwar interrogation, General Galland confirmed that the GAF had transferred fighters from other theaters to defend against Pointblank operations: "We threw nearly all of them in in the West," he stated. "This fighter arm had been built up during the preceding months with our last breath." Galland gave an authoritative review of GAF and Allied air tactics:

> When at first you appeared ... without fighter protection, we only had to reckon with bombers ... which had very effective defensive fire. We first had to learn the methods of concentrated attack.... Then you hesitatingly started employing fighter-protection.... [They] hovered about 1000 to 2000 m. above your formations.... As a result we took no notice of your fighters and continued adjusting our tactics, training and armament to deal only with bombers. That was the first step in the wrong direction.... a fatal error, quite apart from our inferiority in numbers and quality.... Your fighter-protection became the last word in offensive spirit ... they carried out low-level attacks on their homeward flight and shot down landing aircraft.[26]

Anti-aircraft fire brought down many AAF aircraft. The 88mm artillery weapon was formidable against both air and ground targets. Nevertheless, Germany's decision to rely heavily on anti-aircraft fire to repel Allied bombers was a costly mistake. Weapons that could have helped German armies instead guarded cities of the German homeland; at any given time only a small part of the vast flak force had targets to fire at. It numbered some 900,000 men and women with 14,250 heavy guns, 34,750 light and medium guns, 1,500 barrage balloons and 6,750 searchlights. To keep such a force diverted from battlefields was a major achievement of Allied air forces.[27]

In February 1944, Field Marshal Ehrhard Milch confirmed the error involving the anti-aircraft force. Speaking to a conference of German officials responsible for aircraft production, he called for an extraordinary effort to maintain the fighter output. "There is only one counter-measure [to Allied bombing] and that is day and night fighter operations. Let us not delude ourselves about the effectiveness of flak."[28]

Soon after this conference, Milch could see, in the skies over Germany, that the AAF had solved the problem of long-range fighter escort. In less than a year of operations, Eighth Fighter Command had adapted equipment and tactics to achieve this goal. During the period, August to October 1943, four new P-47 groups became operational, while 108-gallon tanks extended the P-47's tactical radius to 320 miles. A group of P-38s arrived in October which provided escort after P-47s had to turn back. The P-38s were too few for their task and suffered heavy casualties both from enemy fire and from mechanical malfunctions. In December, more P-38s and P-51s arrived. With droptanks, Mustangs had a tactical radius of 650 miles. AAF escort fighters made daylight precision bombing a feasible operation; in the process they won air supremacy in time for the Normandy invasion. An AAF operational summary noted: "Much of the destruction and damage to the German Fighter Force at this time was due to a change in tactics initiated by the Eighth Fighter Command.... The new policy did not mean any relaxing of bomber protection but if the enemy was sighted, he was to be pursued and destroyed. This meant leaving the bombers at times to search for the Hun, but it helped them indirectly and in the long run would more quickly bring about the destruction of the German Fighter Force."[29]

The great air battles of February and March 1944 convinced Spaatz that air supremacy could be won. He had, moreover, a valuable source of intelligence to help him make judgments about the air war: an allied program of interception and decryption of German radio communications provided information, codenamed Ultra, about GAF losses and the condition of its units. Spaatz received this priceless information almost as soon as enemy headquarters. Unlike most intelligence data, it was timely and highly reliable.

The German code system used a complex electrical machine called Enigma to encipher and decipher messages. Germans believed the system to be unbreakable, but Polish mathematicians had broken it in the Thirties. Poland later gave this precious secret to French and British intelligence services; they then established the Ultra system that made a major contribution to Allied victory. For many years Ultra was a closely guarded secret, and the Polish mathematicians never received the recognition they deserved.[30] British writers who gradually divulged bits and pieces of the Ultra story failed to acknowledge the great debt owed to the Poles.

After the February battles, Spaatz decided that it was time to exploit GAF weaknesses; he sent a message to his air force commanders urging them to increase the intensity of their operations:

> Our effort, requiring the enemy to oppose us on our terms, must be pushed relentlessly every day it is humanly possible to operate over Germany.... Greater risks are justified, and infinitely greater demands on personnel are mandatory. Further, for the immediate future, it is even desirable to invite air opposition when we have fighter escort, rather than to attempt to evade.[31]

Air supremacy won primarily by the AAF in fierce air fighting in the first quarter of 1944, had far-reaching consequences. It substantially improved the prospects for Overlord; it gave USSTAF greater freedom to pinpoint its destructive power against critical points in the German war machine; it permitted Allied fighter groups to equip aircraft and train personnel for ground attack.

RAF Fighter Command participated only marginally in the Allied effort to win air supremacy. The renowned British fighter pilot, J. E. Johnson, summarized the situation: "The greatest daylight air battles of late 1943 and early 1944 were fought out over Germany between the fighter arm of the Luftwaffe and the bombers and fighters of Eighth Air Force.... But the Spitfire, which had achieved immortality in the earlier battle, played no part in this great conflict...."[32]

Spaatz urged his air force commanders to "seek out the enemy's sore points." He explained that Allied air supremacy, "toward which all our efforts have been leading ... is now well within our reach." He predicted that the GAF would practice conservation of aircraft and pilots. It would be faced with a choice between severe attrition in battle and giving the Allies unlimited bombing freedom all over Europe. Spaatz warned his commanders not to cling to defensive tactics that were no longer necessary. It "will become possible to send out the bomber force in small units. ... support becomes area cover, and this will remove many [bomber] assembly difficulties, thereby decreasing the number of days that bases are non-operational due to weather. Assembly time saved can be added to the depth of penetration while increase in number of separate forces makes it possible to cover wide areas in search for openings under borderline target visibility conditions."[33]

As the GAF fighter threat diminished, Allied fighters began to pay greater attention to ground targets. Kepner praised the P-47 in ground attack: "When we are shooting up airplanes on airfields, shooting up gasoline tanks and munition dumps, tanks, etc. there

Colonel Donald J. Blakeslee, commander of the 4th Fighter Group standing before his P-51 Mustang. (U.S. Air Force Photo.)

are eight guns shooting on a Thunderbolt.... One day we ... shot down — in the air and on the ground, probably better than half of them on the ground — on the order of 150 aircraft ... we got 229 locomotives...."[34]

The P-47's eight machine guns could destroy box cars, locomotives, oil storage tanks, trucks, lightly armored vehicles, artillery equipment and horse drawn wagons. An Eighth

Fighter Command history described the effects of P-47 attacks on a railroad yard: "We ... started systematically, cutting every box-car to shreds.... We sprayed practically every car in that freight yard with armour-piercing incendiary [bullets]. ... fires were everywhere.... About every 30 seconds another large explosion would go off throwing incendiaries and cases of exploding shells all over the countryside."[35]

The 4th Fighter Group was Eighth Fighter Command's leader in aerial victories. Many of its pilots had transferred from RAF Eagle Squadrons. In AAF service they had flown P-47s first, then had switched to P-51s. The commander, Colonel Donald Blakeslee, described ground-attack missions in a Mustang:

> I consider surprise as one of the chief factors in a successful strafe.... I ask for all the photographs available. I want to know what the terrain around the airdrome is ... I use terrain — hills, gulleys and trees — for cover, and such airdrome installations as hangers, etc., to screen my approach. I never come right in on an airdrome if I can help it.... But once I hit the drome, I really get down on the deck ... I mean so low the grass is brushing the bottom of the scoop.[36]

AAF fighter attacks on airfields were often costly. Ground fire brought down many experienced fighter pilots; the Mustang was more vulnerable in this sense than the Thunderbolt. But the results of ground attack were impressive. On April 5, 1944, Blakeslee's group attacked airfields deep in Germany and claimed fifty German airplanes destroyed and forty-nine damaged. Blakeslee described his rather crude approach to dive bombing: "I have no particular method of bomb aiming. I go down in a steep glide from 3000 feet and when I am so low I think I am going to hit the deck, let the bombs go, then pull up and turn off to one side, never ahead."[37]

During the first quarter of 1944, Allied air forces mortally weakened the GAF and thereby assured air supremacy over the lodgment area during the invasion. It was primarily an achievement of the AAF strategic-bombing forces: heavy bombers attacked targets the GAF had to defend, thereby exposing GAF fighters to bombers' guns and to escort fighters superior in the number and quality of both pilots and equipment. AAF fighter pilots had achieved a high level of offensive spirit.

With D-Day less than three months away, all Allied air commanders turned their attention to plans and preparations for the Normandy invasion. AEAF drafted an air plan that would, if adopted, require the full participation of all available air forces in the months before the landings.

Chapter 6

The Plan to Bomb French and Belgian Rail Centers

In battles fought over Germany in the first quarter of 1944, Allied air forces won air supremacy — a victory that later prevented the GAF from effectively interfering with invasion forces. The landings in Normandy would still be most hazardous, and many crucial tasks remained for Allied air forces to accomplish in support of Overlord before D-Day. Principally, air power had to disrupt transportation facilities that anti-invasion forces relied on for access to the beachhead. Overlord's planners warned that "the situation will be critical for the first seven to fourteen days."

General Eisenhower directed Tedder to develop an air plan that would make maximum use of all available air strength to support Overlord both before and after D-Day. As anticipated, the role of the strategic air forces in Overlord became the most controversial matter and Tedder's most difficult problem. He arranged to have Solly Zuckerman assigned to AEAF to help plan air operations. Zuckerman had worked closely with Tedder in planning and evaluating air campaigns in the Mediterranean theater. He had helped plan the bombing of the island of Pantelleria, which convinced the Italian garrison to surrender without an assault by ground forces.

While on the faculty staff of Oxford University, Zuckerman had used animals to investigate the effects of explosions. This had led to research on bomb damage and casualties. Prewar books and journals treated the subject of bombing in a sensational style that misled many people into believing that urban populations would be exterminated and their cities pulverized. Fears of unstoppable air assaults provided support for the appeasement policies of the Thirties. Zuckerman's research brought him to the attention of the RAF; he received assignments to study the effects of air attacks.

Tedder admired Zuckerman's abilities and had great confidence in his judgment. He appreciated Zuckerman's clear and detailed reports and the rhetorical skills with which he defended his proposals.[1] Zuckerman used scientific jargon like a bludgeon to intimidate opponents. Few military officers could stand up to him in a debate on technical and scientific issues.

After a brief review of the AEAF air plan, Zuckerman convinced the staff that it was inadequate. "We agreed," he later explained, "that I should develop an alternate plan." His experience in Sicily convinced him that the destruction of railroad centers, especially repair facilities, contributed significantly to Allied victories. He remembered that attacks on only six centers had practically paralyzed the Sicilian and southern Italian rail systems.[2]

Zuckerman's selection of rail centers as targets meshed smoothly with Eisenhower's obsession to bring the strategic air forces under SHAEF's control in the months before D-Day. Tedder explained SHAEF's principal guideline: "We would waste much of our power if the U.S. Strategic Air Forces were to operate against one system of objectives, Bomber Command against another, and AEAF against yet another."[3]

To bring the strategic air force under SHAEF's authority, Tedder and Zuckerman had to select a target system for them which Harris and Spaatz could not dismiss as inappropriate. Tedder approved Zuckerman's choice of rail centers in Belgium and France as primary objectives.

Harris and Spaatz could hardly deny that disruption of the railways serving anti-invasion forces would contribute significantly to the success of Overlord. Rail centers were targets large enough for Harris's night bombers to hit. According to a top-level AEAF planner, "Railway areas that cover from 50 to 500 acres ... [are] ideal targets either for precision-bombing by day ... or, in a large number of cases, bombing at night...."[4] Moreover, they were dispersed widely so that on any given day USSTAF could probably find some not hidden by cloud cover.

The railroad network in northern Europe had been under consideration for air attacks for years. The targets in the Zuckerman plan are often referred to as "marshaling yards," but this was only a convenient term to indicate locomotive depots, junctions and rail centers with their servicing, signaling and switching equipment. Attacks on rail centers would also destroy locomotives, boxcars and roundhouses. Zuckerman expected that massive bombing of the kind he proposed would paralyze the rail system.[5]

By February 1944, the AEAF staff, under Zuckerman's direction, had developed a plan for the employment of Allied air forces, including the strategic air forces, in support of Overlord. In the three-month period before D-Day, they would concentrate on rail centers. The railroad system available to German forces could be disrupted most effectively, according to the AEAF plan, by attacking the motive power of the system. Planners named seventy-eight railway centers in northwest France and Belgium as targets; others in southern France and Germany would be bombed later. Zuckerman asserted that rail centers were the only suitable objective for the 45,000 tons of bombs that the strategic bomber forces would have available to assist Overlord.[6]

On February 12, 1944, high-ranking officers received top-secret copies of the AEAF air plan to study prior to a meeting to be held a few days later. The section devoted to railway targets, which became known as the "Transportation Plan," proposed to "paralyze railways from Western Germany to the assault area to such an extent that major reinforcement by rail would be virtually impossible. When this was achieved the Allied air forces would concentrate their power on other targets which could affect the tactical situation during the opening phases of the land assault."[7]

In a general way the rail-center plan conformed with AAF doctrine, which assigned second priority to "isolating the battlefield." (Winning air superiority was first priority.) The AAF, however, did not approve the means proposed in the plan to accomplish its objectives. It preferred to block enemy military movements toward a battlefield by destroying key transportation installations in and near a battle area. Proponents of this approach, usually called "interdiction," believed it to be efficient and effective because it blocked bridges, tunnels, viaducts, roads and railways leading directly to the battlefield.

The Transportation Plan, however, selected targets scattered throughout France and Belgium. Interdiction blocked transportation lines directly; the Transportation Plan proposed to paralyze a large part of the rail network in the west. This difference in outlook caused sharp disagreements. AAF planners believed that results promised by the rail-center plan were nebulous compared to those derived from knocking down a rail bridge on a main line to the lodgment area. Execution of the AEAF plan would cause far more civilian casualties and property damage than interdiction.

AAF antipathy to AEAF's railway plan was countered by the latter's conviction that interdiction alone could not bring about the required degree of interference with German movement to the lodgment area. Interdiction, according to Leigh-Mallory, should be seen as supplementary to the transportation plan, not a substitute for it. Zuckerman's research in Sicily convinced him that targets like bridges and viaducts were difficult and costly targets, while track cuts were easily repaired. If started too soon, interdiction would endanger the secrecy of the intended beachhead because its targets were close to the lodgment area. Interdiction, to be fully effective, required good weather in the period immediately prior to and following the landings. Leigh-Mallory did not believe that the success of the landings in Normandy should depend on good weather.

Eisenhower and Tedder favored the Transportation Plan. They believed that the strategic air forces should attack targets selected by SHAEF. Full reliance on interdiction did not appeal to them because it was not a suitable program for heavy bombers and because it could not be carried out in the months before D-Day. They argued that destruction of the railway system could only be accomplished by massive bombing of the important rail centers, which required the heavy bombers. The Transportation Plan would bring the strategic air forces under SHAEF's direction in the months before D-Day, and the targeted rail centers were so widely dispersed that their destruction would not direct particular attention to Normandy.

"Elimination of a number of adjacent railway centers, would paralyze movement in the whole region they serve," the plan stated: "If all the targets are effectively dealt with the result will be a railway desert...."[8] Severe cuts in railway service would force German units to move by roads, a slower means of transportation, with increased expenditures of fuel, excessive wear of equipment, especially of armored vehicles, and long periods of vulnerability to tactical air attacks.

Leigh-Mallory used a favorite British ploy to gain swift approval of the plan. AEAF's staff prepared a detailed statement of it and sought approval before its opponents had time to study it carefully. General Eaker had described this gambit many months earlier: "We always find ourselves overmatched in these conferences [with the British] and consequently the plans, as might be expected, are other people's plans and not ours."[9]

AEAF hopes for swift approval of the Transportation Plan were dashed when USSTAF denounced it. Spaatz offered an alternate plan which his staff had prepared, the "Plan for Completion of the Combined Bombing Offensive." It proposed that USSTAF concentrate on Pointblank objectives and also attack Germany's oil industry. Fourteen synthetic fuel plants and thirteen oil refineries were identified as targets. This program would be appropriate for strategic air forces and the resulting fuel shortages would handicap the German war effort generally.[10]

The Transportation Plan sparked a brushfire of opposition that spread to the highest levels of Allied governments. Many officials and military leaders condemned a plan that would bring death and destruction to towns in friendly nations. Many experts expressed doubts that bombing rail centers would achieve the objectives of the transportation plan. Questions arose during bitter debates that remained unanswered for fifty years. Principally, these questions were threefold:

1. Could AEAF's plan possibly achieve its objectives?

2. Would its cost be commensurate with the results?

3. Could its objectives be achieved by other means, principally interdiction?

In the weeks following the distribution of the AEAF plan to commanders whose cooperation would be needed to implement it, Tedder and Zuckerman found themselves fully engaged in defending it. The extent and intensity of the opposition surprised them. Zuckerman later wrote of this debate: "Rational discussion of what was being proposed was at an end. All the opposing parties joined to defeat the apparent threat which the AEAF plan implied to the independence of the strategic air forces."[11] Characteristically, even long after the war, when he wrote those words, Zuckerman assigned ulterior motives to his opponents.

Chapter 7

Opposition to the Transportation Plan

A surprisingly large number of agencies and individuals condemned the AEAF railways plan, including Prime Minister Churchill, most of his War Cabinet, the Joint Intelligence Committee, the Chief of the Imperial General Staff, the Ministry of Economic Warfare, the Enemy Objectives Unit (EOU) of the Economic Warfare Division, Air Marshal Harris, General Spaatz General Doolittle, most other AAF commanders and many staff officers. Formidable opposition also came from General Montgomery's 21st Army Group headquarters.

The plan was top-secret and its circulation restricted, but this did not silence its opponents. They castigated AEAF for the death and destruction the plan proposed to bring to inhabitants of French and Belgian towns near the bombed rail centers. Military critics concentrated on what they perceived as the plan's major flaw: the campaign to implement it could not achieve its objectives. Furthermore, it would be a gift to the German propaganda services; it would sour relations with France and Belgium and alienate friends of the Allies in those countries.

In a note to Eisenhower, Churchill described bombing rail centers as "cruel and remorseless"; it might "well do more evil than good." The British War Cabinet concluded that a "bad effect … will be produced upon the French civilian population by these slaughters, all taking place so long before 'Overlord' D-Day."[1] Churchill feared that RAF Bomber Command would bear the brunt of criticism because of its inaccurate night bombing. Civilian leaders based their opposition on the civilian casualties the campaign was expected to cause — 80,000 deaths according to one estimate. Military experts emphasized the plan's basic military defects. They did not believe it could achieve its primary objective — to cause substantial delay in German military movements by rail after D-Day. The execution of the plan would waste an enormous quantity of Allied resources. During the early discussions of the plan, opposition to it was so widespread that rejection seemed certain.

Doolittle's Eighth Air Force would be responsible for a major share of the plan's execution. He objected to it on "practical" grounds. He classified rail centers as pinpoint targets and, in many cases, very difficult ones. "To attack them efficiently and effectively," he explained, "they must be attacked visually. This means that the same limitations apply to them as targets as to the German aircraft factories — mainly weather. We cannot go out at will and destroy communications targets. Not only are the critical points too numerous but the damage done is easily repaired and therefore is of only temporary value."[2]

Doolittle had little confidence in the ability of Eighth Air Force to bomb accurately "through the overcast" using radar instruments. "Our experience to date with this type of bombing technique indicates that it is closely allied with area bombing and does not lend itself to the precision bombing of pinpoint targets.... On those occasions when we have hit a precision target [using radar] it has been largely luck. Ordinarily bombs are scattered over at least ten times as much area as with visual bombing."[3]

As Tedder anticipated, Air Marshal Harris opposed the Transportation Plan. It would divert RAF Bomber Command from more important objectives — German cities. Harris never pulled his punches when defending Bomber Command from people he labeled "panacea mongers," including staff officers at RAF headquarters who wanted "to have the fun of running the Bomber Offensive ... while I take the responsibility...."[4] Harris was "seldom open to persuasion," as an RAF history put it, but in Tedder and Eisenhower he met his equals in stubbornness.

Zuckerman refused to accept the claim that RAF bombers could not hit targets as small as rail centers. He conferred with squadron commanders and learned that RAF Bomber Command had greater potential for accurate bombing than Harris had admitted. Harris grudgingly ordered trial bombing attacks carried out on a few rail centers using Pathfinder crews and elaborate target-marking techniques. The results amazed him, so he later claimed: they showed that RAF night bombers could attack rail centers with acceptable accuracy. Harris muffled his opposition to AEAF's plan, at least for a time.[5]

AEAF had not involved USSTAF in the planning of its air plan for Overlord, but Spaatz sent representatives to meetings to consider the finished product. An officer on his staff reported on such an experience. "Every means were utilized by [Leigh-Mallory] ... to obtain endorsement of his plan rather than a true presentation of technical advice...."[6] Many USSTAF officers resented Leigh-Mallory's obvious maneuvers to squelch debate. One of USSTAF's chief planners described a meeting he attended at AEAF headquarters. Railway experts were there apparently to give rubber stamp approval to the AEAF plan. Instead of testifying to the main point at issue, "namely whether the plan proposed would be successful in ... preventing the movement of strategic reinforcements within a limited period of time," they were "driven into a discussion of the best type of railway objectives to attack, assuming that the attack of railway transportation has been adopted as a primary object of policy...."[7]

Although Leigh-Mallory tried to avoid discussion of the plan's weaknesses, the railway experts managed to make the point that an air campaign aimed at destroying rail nodal points, such as heavy girder railway bridges and key road bridges, would be more effective than attacks on rail centers.

General Fred Anderson, USSTAF's director of operations and an AAF bombing expert, criticized the AEAF plan. Characteristically, he went straight to the crux of the matter: the vast rail system available to the enemy could not be paralyzed by bombing. It was too efficient; it offered too many possibilities for rerouting trains. Anderson favored interdiction — blocking selected railway lines in and on the periphery of the lodgment area. "And any block which is established must be maintained in order to be effective," he advised. Anderson rejected the AEAF contention that interdiction would not be effective without prior destruction of rail centers. "The decision of the A.E.A.F. to seek destruction of German railway potential rather than establish blocks, seems to have been based in part upon a belief that bridge destruction and other blockings are impractical ... [but] a study made in the Mediterranean ... [shows] that such destruction is practical."[8]

Bridge-bombing became a most controversial issue in discussions about targets whose destruction would be likely to help Overlord.

Surprisingly, the British Air Ministry condemned the Transportation Plan. It favored interdiction and recommended that "all available effort ... be put into a short-term offensive to be put into effect on or about D-Day aimed at preventing the enemy from bringing his reinforcements into the lodgment area, this to be effected by cutting specific points (including bridges) on the lines serving that area."[9]

Perhaps the most comprehensive critique of the plan came from the Enemy Objectives Unit of the Economic Warfare Division, a unit staffed in large part by personnel of the Office of Strategic Services (OSS), an American intelligence agency. EOU operated from the U.S. Embassy in London with Ambassador Winant's support. Winant had an intense interest in Allied air operations: his son was an Eighth Air Force bomber pilot. EOU analyzed German resources to pinpoint vital installations that could be destroyed by bombing. In agreement with other critics, EOU concluded that the rail network serving France was too large, well-equipped and efficient to be paralyzed by bombing. Of course, bombing rail centers on a scale proposed by the plan would reduce traffic sharply, but the Germans would cut civilian traffic before they allowed military movements to be affected. They would go to any lengths to insure that lines were open for military trains. Thus, in addition to the deaths and destruction inflicted on towns adjacent to bombed rail centers, civilians throughout northern Europe would suffer from shortages of fuel, food and other essentials.

The EOU report estimated that only 4 percent of the total number of locomotives would be destroyed by bombing rail centers. Trains could be marshaled far to the east; they would need only a few lines to supply divisions along the front in Normandy. German forces would round up civilians to repair bomb damage. They would bring German railway workers to the west in the spring to make sure that essential railroad lines remained open during the invasion. AEAF claimed that two-thirds of the French rail system was used for military traffic; EOU gauged it to be only one-fifth. Rail traffic would have to be cut by 80 percent before German military forces began to feel a pinch.[10]

EOU agreed with USSTAF that interdiction was a far superior alternative to a bombing offensive against rail centers. Interdiction would block German military transportation by destroying key facilities near the lodgment area — bridges, viaducts, tunnels, tracks and a few marshaling yards. Fighter-bombers would attack trains and traffic on roads, rivers and canals. Allied air forces had such superior numbers that they could afford to strike supply dumps, staff cars and even horse-drawn vehicles. A large number of experts believed that an interdiction campaign could disrupt German troop movements sufficiently even without the preliminary assault on rail centers, but Tedder and Leigh-Mallory disagreed and Eisenhower backed them.

Targets for interdiction were selected in "rings" on the periphery of a battle area. In this way a battlefield could be "isolated," as AAF guidelines recommended. Efforts to maintain a ring of interdiction could be eased or stepped up according to the progress of the battle. Executed properly, interdiction minimized both pointless destruction and damage which was likely to hurt the Allies more than their enemy.

Interdiction would only begin shortly before D-Day to delay as long as possible giving the enemy clues about the location of the landing beaches. This timing would make it difficult for Germans to repair damage to railways and to organize alternative transportation before the invasion. Bad weather would hamper interdiction but not as much as it had curtailed heavy bomber operations. Tactical air forces, which would execute a major share of an interdiction campaign, could often operate in weather conditions that kept heavy bombers grounded. Fighters and medium bombers of the tactical air forces generally bombed with greater accuracy than the heavy bombers.

Zuckerman, Tedder and Leigh-Mallory stoutly defended the Transportation Plan. They claimed that interdiction should be thought of as supplementary to the transportation campaign, not as an alternative to it. They pointed out that the AEAF plan provided for a modest interdiction offensive to begin shortly before D-Day. But, they insisted, its effectiveness would depend on the prior assault on rail centers.

In a paper he distributed in defense of AEAF's plan, Tedder challenged the assumptions of interdiction advocates: "Attack on railway and road bridges has very occasionally in a tactical area in ITALY, been successful in causing temporary delay," he wrote, "but, for both technical and tactical reasons, it has in general been both ineffective and highly uneconomical. Attack on railway tracks has also been considered. ...this method was tried to a considerable extent in ITALY (where conditions were specially favorable) but proved highly unproductive."[11]

Each side in the dispute labeled the other's proposal "ineffective and highly uneconomical." Zuckerman and Tedder also challenged the competence of their critics. They cited their experience in the Mediterranean and Africa to silence opponents. Zuckerman referred to the plan's critics as "theorists,"— unscientific amateurs who relied on a priori conjectures. He enjoyed the arguments and long afterward remembered that he had been "exhilarated, not cast down, by the opposition...."[12] He and Tedder made a formidable team in debates. Zuckerman provided data to support their positions; Tedder promoted the plan in a smooth, confident manner. His high rank tended to overawe military personnel. Occasionally, he asked Zuckerman to skip a conference to "keep the heat down."

However, no one could overawe Spaatz in discussions of air-power issues, even if he did not shine in conferences. He had commanded American air forces in combat operations in the North African and Mediterranean campaigns and was definitely not a "theorist." USSTAF requested reports about interdiction and rail-center bombings from AAF units in Italy. General Eaker sent a statement that refuted Zuckerman's claims: "All our experience in attacks on communications in this theater has shown that even the most successful bombardment of a marshaling yard does not cut traffic for more than a few hours."[13] Eaker's deputy, Air Chief Marshal John C. Slessor, was even more emphatic: "The fact is that, especially if you don't care a damn about the [civilian population] ... the proportion of the transportation potential ... which is required to meet the minimum needs of the Army and Air force is so small that you have, so to speak, a tremendous cushion against interference with military supply...."[14] Slessor disagreed with AEAF policy on bridge bombing: "One of the remarkable developments in the past three months to my mind has been the emergence of the bridge as a worthwhile bombing objective. At the present time, of the twenty-five clean cuts in the Italian railways, sixteen are bridges." Slessor attributed the effectiveness of bridge-bombing to the "astonishing accuracy of the medium bomber in the low attack. ...it is something new since Tedder's day out here."[15]

Target planners at EOU received reports from their OSS colleagues in Italy. One report noted that bridge attacks were not excessively difficult and costly. Of thirty railroad bridges bombed, eighteen were blocked. The average weight of bombs dropped per blockage was 196 tons.[16] OSS agents sharply criticized Zuckerman's report on bridge bombings. In fact, they questioned the integrity of his research and the honesty of his reporting. Zuckerman had not taken the length and sturdiness of bridges into account, nor their anti-aircraft defenses. "Only two specific railroad bridge bombings are discussed in support of ... [Zuckerman's] proposition that such attacks are ineffective.... These examples support a proposition contrary to that for which they are cited." Zuckerman's claim that bridge bombing was too costly was also disputed. OSS data indicated "that if 100 tons or more are dropped, the chances of securing a blockage are very high indeed and that only 2.5 attacks will be required for 50% destruction of the target. Compared to ... 1280 tons per square mile showered on the Messina yards, this does not seem uneconomical."[17]

OSS investigations in Italy also provided evidence to justify use of a tactic disparaged by Tedder and many others — track cutting. The OSS report explained: "A succession of craters at say 170 yard intervals over a stretch of say 30 to 40 miles would completely overburden the repair facilities." Scattered along the line as they would be, the craters would have to be repaired successively by gangs working in from the ends of the bombed section.[18]

In debates about the Transportation Plan one of its important weaknesses did not receive much attention — bombing rail centers would have little if any impact on transportation near the beachhead. During the first few days, invasion troops would be threatened more by German forces moving on roads than by those using railways. Interdiction, on the other hand, would disrupt railway, road, canal and river transportation in and near the lodgment area. Moreover, it could be adjusted to concentrate on those sectors needing attention at any given time.

In their efforts to bring the strategic air forces under SHAEF's control, Tedder and Eisenhower worked closely with Portal; he would have to approve any change in their status. Discussions dragged on, but by March, Portal and Eisenhower were close to agreement. The formal transfer of authority would take place when they jointly approved the AEAF air program. Portal demanded a number of concessions from Eisenhower. He wanted Overlord's air operations directed by Tedder, a change Eisenhower had already made. He wanted assurances that SHAEF would return British air forces to RAF control if the security of the U.K. were threatened. Eisenhower agreed to this condition.

As part of his review of the Transportation Plan, Portal collected opinions on it from key associates. Harris informed him that he wanted "full discretion as to what German target I shall attack on any given night."[19] The chief of the Imperial General Staff advised: "The destruction of the GAF must remain our primary object, and must have overriding priority. The railway plan should not be approved if it will involve any such diversion." The British Ministry of Economic Warfare identified serious drawbacks in the AEAF plan. The three-month campaign against rail centers would give the Germans time to make repairs, improvise solutions to problems and set up organizations to deal with them.[20]

Tedder worked hard to retain Portal's backing. He told him that his critics were not well-informed about railroads, and they had not consulted railway experts: "Nor was Prof. Zuckerman of the Home Security Department (who alone has had unique opportunity of directing the systematic analysis of actual bomb damage ...) [been] consulted." Tedder labeled the plan's opponents "illogical" because they recommended a short-term attack on communications while condemning a long-term attack. Portal felt some uncertainty about Tedder's reasoning: "Is this illogical?" he wrote in the margin of Tedder's letter."[21]

With so many officials and agencies opposed to the Transportation Plan, Portal scheduled a meeting of the chief interested parties to discuss the issues. He and Eisenhower would be there to listen to the pros and cons. Tedder would defend AEAF's plan and Spaatz would speak in favor of an oil plan.

Throughout the war, Allied air planners paid close attention to Germany's oil situation. Until 1944 Germany had vast oil resources at its disposal, and Allied air forces could not attack them effectively. Now, as German forces in retreat abandoned oil-rich territories, they faced a fuel shortage that would worsen as the Allies opened a front in Normandy and Fifteenth Air Force started to attack oil-production facilities in eastern Europe.

During the Thirties Germany built hydrogenation plants to convert its plentiful coal into liquid fuels. Spaatz proposed to attack these installations. The Oil Plan called for the destruction of some twenty-seven plants, including fourteen synthetic fuel plants, which produced 80 percent of Germany's synthetic oil and gasoline, and thirteen oil refineries, which comprised 60 percent of its crude-oil refining capacity. USSTAF would also continue to strike at the GAF by attacking aircraft and ball-bearing factories.[22] Spaatz sent one of his chief planners, Brigadier General Charles Cabell, to AAF headquarters to drum up support for the Oil Plan. Arnold told Cabell that "Spaatz has his hose turned on the wrong garden." It was Eisenhower he had to convince.

On the day before the meeting to discuss future employment of strategic air forces, Spaatz distributed a paper describing the Oil Plan. Tedder also distributed a paper to help promote AEAF's Transportation Plan.[23] "What is now required," he wrote, "is an adjustment of Pointblank, which, while maintaining the G.A.F. as the primary objective and continuing the deep penetrations into Germany, will directly prepare the way for the assault and subsequent land campaign." He expressed his conviction that attacks on bridges and tunnels were "ineffective and highly uneconomical." Attacks on them in Italy had been "highly unproductive."

With Portal's support, Tedder restricted the agenda of the meeting to consider only one question: should the strategic air forces attack oil or transportation in the months before D-Day? It was a clever maneuver; Tedder believed he could show that the Oil Plan was inadequate. By concentrating on employment of strategic air forces, Tedder neatly skirted the issue of interdiction, a campaign primarily executed by tactical air forces and one that its proponents claimed would make the bombing of rail centers unnecessary. In the paper he distributed the day before the conference, Tedder claimed that "the choice lies between the Oil Plan and the Transportation Plan. It is difficult to see any evidence to suggest that the Oil Plan can, in the short time available, seriously affect the enemy ability to meet the Overlord assault, or fight the immediately following campaign...." Tedder's paper alluded to his common denominator premise: "The Oil Plan is not a plan in which Bomber Command can take any really effective part, and it is one in which A.E.A.F would be unable to take any part at all."

USSTAF hurriedly prepared and distributed a paper to respond to Tedder's claims.[24] It rejected the common-denominator argument: "We [cannot] subscribe to the theory that transportation is an essential target on the grounds that all three [air forces] tactical and strategic are capable of attacking it. Three wrongs do not make a right, and if the plan is wrong this theory would simply commit all our air power to the wrong course of action. We believe, rather, that any sound plan should make the most of the maximum capabilities of the forces to be employed, not the minimum." USSTAF's paper expressed confidence that the German synthetic-oil plants and refineries could be put out of operation for many months by air attacks and that the oil offensive would achieve an objective of major importance — defeat of the GAF. The Luftwaffe would "defend oil to their last fighter plane." It would not risk serious attrition to defend French and Belgian rail centers. An oil offensive would weaken German forces on all fronts simultaneously and "expedite the success of Overlord in the period subsequent to D-Day." The USSTAF paper failed to challenge Tedder's assertion that RAF Bomber Command could not take "any really effective part" in an oil offensive." The months of wrangling about employment of air forces nearly exhausted Eisenhower's patience. He regarded the situation as a challenge to his authority. The air commanders were interfering with his efforts to make Overlord as strong as possible. In his diary he recorded his determination to bring air matters to a head: "The actual air preparatory plan is to be the subject of a formal meeting on this coming Saturday, March 25.... If a satisfactory answer is not reached I am going to take drastic action and inform the Combined Chiefs of Staff that unless the matter is settled at once I will request relief from this command."[25]

One week before this conference, Spaatz felt confident about the outcome. He informed Arnold that "there is an excellent chance that Tedder will repudiate AEAF Plan of his own accord ... [and] avoid hard feelings."[26] It was one of Spaatz's few errors of judgment. There was not even a remote possibility that Tedder would repudiate the plan. The key person still open-minded on the issue was Portal. In his position as director of the strategic-bombing offensive he might be expected to support Spaatz, but it would be a drastic move for him to come out in opposition to both Eisenhower and Tedder. Portal agreed with Eisenhower that a policy had to be established and supported by the entire Overlord team. Portal's biographer described him as having a keen respect for order; his school, Winchester College, strived to develop this attitude in its students. A graduate of this school "despises a shambles.... He expects to know exactly to whom and for what he is at any time responsible, and expects every contingency to be covered in advance."[27]

Eisenhower and Portal met with senior air commanders and other interested parties on March 25, 1944, at Norfolk House, St. James Square, London. In attendance were Tedder, Leigh-Mallory, Harris, Spaatz, Fred Anderson, three major generals from the British War Office, two other RAF air marshals and representatives of the Joint Intelligence Committee and the Ministry of Economic Warfare.[28]

Portal asked Tedder to explain the AEAF plan. Tedder assured the group that the GAF would remain a first-priority objective. He recommended that rail centers be given second priority. Allied bombers would pulverize approximately seventy-six rail centers, most of them in France and Belgium. Destruction of these facilities would cripple the rail network the enemy relied on to move anti-invasion forces to Normandy after D-Day. He conceded that the offensive would not block all traffic, but it would funnel German rail shipments into a few lines which could be monitored by the tactical air forces. Tedder's calm, pipe-smoking manner exuded confidence. He tried to avoid ruffling feathers.

When Tedder concluded his opening remarks, some of the group expressed doubts about the Transportation Plan. Lower-ranking officers were not comfortable disagreeing with Tedder. A British general recalled that attacks on railway targets in Africa and Italy had interrupted traffic for only a brief time. An intelligence officer pointed out that any cuts in rail traffic would be borne by the civilian economy before they affected military transportation.

Eisenhower soon showed how he felt about what he believed to be issues of secondary importance. He did not intend to let critics of SHAEF's proposals dominate the meeting. Very early in the discussions he introduced his major concern forcefully: the first five or six weeks of the invasion would be the most critical period for Allied forces. Every possible assistance must be given to them to insure that they got ashore and stayed there.

Whatever the air forces could do to help them achieve this objective they must do. Acting more like an advocate than a judge, Eisenhower said that the AEAF plan gave the strategic air forces a chance to make a crucial contribution to the success of Overlord in the months before D-Day. His words left no doubt about the intensity of his conviction: "It was only necessary to show that there would be some reduction [in railway traffic], however small, to justify adopting the plan provided that there was no alternative available."

Spaatz spoke for the Oil Plan but without the eloquence and finesse of Tedder. On a fitness report, Eisenhower had noted that Spaatz was not impressive in writing or speaking. The air commander must have been shaken to hear that the supreme commander did not consider the Oil Plan a viable alternative to Tedder's proposal. He predicted unequivocally that an oil offensive would create a fuel crisis for the Germans. A few synthetic-fuel plants produced a large part of the enemy's gasoline, and they were vulnerable to attack by bombers. An oil offensive would have a decisive impact on the German forces within six months. It would handicap them on all fronts including their homefront. He was convinced that the transportation offensive would not have a serious effect on German forces in any measurable length of time.

A representative of the Ministry of Economic Warfare offered an opinion crucial to the debate: he estimated that an oil offensive would not have a significant effect in the west for four or five months. This statement, which Spaatz did not challenge, was devastating to his proposal, and it came from an agency known to favor an oil offensive.

Portal immediately pointed out the importance of this estimate: "it showed conclusively that the Oil Plan would not help Overlord in the first few critical weeks." He admitted that an oil offensive had "great attractions" and should be reconsidered after the first critical phase of Overlord. Eisenhower agreed, promising to review the Oil Plan after Allied forces were securely established on the continent. Against all odds, the Transportation Plan had survived.

Portal's commitment to consider an oil offensive represented a change of heart for him. Earlier in the war he had written: "The advantage of bombing for devastation is of course that the vast majority of the bombs have a direct effect on something — at best an important factory, at worst the morale of the German people — whereas the very high percentage of bombs which I expect to miss a small target will often do no good whatever. Picture an isolated synthetic fuel plant. Bombs missing this small target and falling harmlessly in the surrounding fields and waterways."[29]

At the close of the March 25 meeting, with the major issue settled, at least for a time, Portal asked for comments about problems likely to arise in the offensive against railways. Harris said he disliked both plans, but the AEAF plan less than the oil plan. He doubted that Bomber Command would be able to "dispose of all the rail centers assigned to it." Eisenhower asked Spaatz if USSTAF could carry out its part of the transportation offensive. Spaatz replied that he would have to devote one-half of USSTAF's effort to Pointblank targets. It was essential, he explained, that the other half should be directed at some target system that would produce substantial enemy fighter reaction and attrition. The transportation campaign would not do this, he warned. Clearly, the strategic air force commanders felt little enthusiasm for the Transportation Plan.

Portal did not want the plan raised again as an issue. With some asperity, he challenged Spaatz's assertion that the GAF would not defend rail centers. It would respond to the attacks, he predicted, as soon as it realized that the entire railway system was at risk. Spaatz could only shake his head in amazement at a claim he knew to be preposterous.

Tedder and Eisenhower could not have been pleased by the lack of enthusiasm of the strategic air commanders, but at least these commanders had not claimed that they could not execute the campaign. Portal asked the group for an estimate of how much the bombing of rail centers would handicap future Allied operations. Eisenhower predicted that the Germans would blow up railway installations during retreat. The Allies should not spare any rail facilities in hopes that they might be able to use them later. Portal directed Harris and Spaatz to work with AEAF on detailed planning for attacks on rail centers.

Before the meeting adjourned, Portal mentioned an issue that eventually provoked the most powerful opposition, primarily from civilian authorities, to the transportation offensive. He reminded the group that bombing rail centers in France and Belgium would cause many civilian casualties and extensive destruction of property in towns adjacent to the rail yards. Allied political leaders would have to approve the Transportation Plan.

There was little discussion of interdiction, although many experts had recommended it as a superior alternative to an assault on rail centers. When Eisenhower declared that he saw no alternative to the Transportation Plan, he was presumably taking interdiction into account, as well as an oil offensive. The tactical air forces who would have most of the responsibility for execution of an interdiction offensive, were represented at the meeting only by Leigh-Mallory, who spoke little. His primary concern was to defuse opposition to the Transportation Plan.

Spaatz had been overconfident and had failed to have the case for interdiction presented. The chief proponents of the transportation campaign believed that interdiction was mostly irrelevant at a meeting concerned with strategic bomber employment. Moreover, Tedder would not have been eager to see another air campaign put forward as an alternative to the AEAF plan, and he may have used his influence to see that interdiction was not on the agenda for the meeting.

The meeting on March 25, 1944, has often been described as a debate on the question "Oil or Transportation," with Eisenhower sitting as judge. Actually, the supreme commander was more of an advocate than a judge. He came to the meeting committed to the AEAF plan. He regarded opposition to it to as bordering on disloyalty. Recognizing the danger of damaging his relationship with Eisenhower and Tedder, Spatz decided to bide his time and mute his protests.

In the weeks following the March 25 meeting, Spaatz made up some lost ground. On March 30, 1944, he complained to Portal that the minutes of the meeting did not include a paper he had distributed. He wanted the record to show that although he could not guarantee that an oil campaign would have an "appreciable effect on the initial success of Overlord ... it would be decisive in six months." Bombing rail centers, he warned Portal, "could not have a decisive effect within any measurable length of time."[30] Portal may now have understood what Tedder meant when he had referred to Spaatz as a "stubborn Dutchman."

Spaatz also continued to badger Eisenhower about an oil offensive. On March 31 he sent the supreme commander a sharp denial of assertions made by Tedder. An oil campaign could cause disaster for Germany, whereas the transportation offensive would cause only harassment. Spaatz rebuked Eisenhower for sloppy reasoning: "In weighing these two [plans], it appears that too great a price may be paid merely for a certainty of very little."[31] This criticism referred to Eisenhower's point that any operation that made a contribution to Overlord, "however small," should be executed provided there were no better alternatives.

A little more than two weeks after he received this complaint from Spaatz, Eisenhower gave USSTAF permission to conduct trial attacks on oil plants to see how the GAF reacted. It was the start of an oil offensive.

In April, RAF Bomber Command began an intensive campaign against rail centers. Protests about the killing of civilians poured into London and Washington. Spaatz felt compelled to make his feelings known to Eisenhower. He did not send the following statement officially, but he showed it to the supreme commander:

> Many thousands of French people will be killed and many towns will be laid waste in these operations.... I view with alarm a military operation which involves such widespread destruction and death in countries not enemies, particularly since the results to be achieved from these bombing operations have not been conclusively shown to be a decisive factor. I believe the possibilities of cutting rail and road lines of communication at sensitive points outside of centers of populations, attacking large concentrations of German troops, supply and ammunition dumps, and tank depots should be given careful consideration, together with the constant endeavor to emasculate the German Air Force.[32]

It was a forceful, unequivocal statement, but it was tardy. It should have been made at the meeting on March 25. Spaatz's weakness as a debater and a bureaucratic manipulator, a result in part, of his distaste for staff jobs and desk work, handicapped him in the confrontation with Tedder.

A directive from SHAEF, dated April 15, 1944, notified Allied air forces that USSTAF and RAF Bomber Command were now under the supreme commander's authority. Tedder would direct air operations in support of Overlord. An air advisory committee would function at SHAEF to assist him. Spaatz appointed Brigadier General Charles Cabell, to the committee. Cabell reported that "twelve Englishmen and one American were invited to the first meeting" and he concluded that the committee would be little more than a rubber stamp for Tedder.[33]

While arguments went on about the best ways that air power could assist Overlord, American air forces executed campaigns already underway and prepared to carry out whatever missions they eventually received to support invasion forces. Eighth Air Force executed Pointblank missions in coordination with Fifteenth Air Force; Ninth Air Force struggled to satisfy demands on it from AEAF and USSTAF while making ready to provide the best possible close air support to Eisenhower's armies after D-Day.

Chapter 8

Air Preparations to Support Invasion Forces

Ninth Air Force grew rapidly in the first half of 1944. Diagram 2 illustrates its command structure on June 1, 1944. Some of its groups arrived in the U.K. before aviation engineers had completed construction of their airstrips in the English countryside. General Brereton described a visit to the 405th Fighter Group: "The men are living in tents under simulated field conditions. The field, like many others occupied by our fighters much resembles what we may expect in France. It is a sod field with only temporary wire mesh landing strips put down by our engineers…. There is no housing or shelter. Officers and men live in tents hidden in the trees…."[1]

Aircraft-modification centers operated night and day to equip aircraft for a variety of missions. Ninth Air Force received P-47s from Eighth Air Force groups that were switching to P-51s. Many of the P-47s were combat-worn and had to be reconditioned and given bomb racks, paddle blade propellers and water injection systems to improve engine performance. New electrical bomb releases were more reliable than manual types. Improvements such as these helped to make the P-47 the AAF's best fighter-bomber. Some P-47s carried rockets—a major advance in ground attack weaponry. The speed of the fighter-bomber helped propel the rocket, and its lack of recoil enabled fighters to fire a projectile with a powerful explosive force. A P-47 with rockets was a formidable anti-tank weapon.

Ninth Air Force reconnaissance units performed highly valuable missions in the pre-invasion period. They photographed the enemy's coastal artillery positions, airfields, V-weapon installations, transportation facilities and beach obstacles, as well as targets for strategic bombers, both before and after attacks. Intelligence agencies studied these photographs and distributed prints to units that needed them. The 67th Tactical Reconnaissance Group carried out extensive, low-altitude oblique photographic-mapping operations over enemy-controlled territory. Ground forces used these photographs to prepare campaign maps. Missions to Normandy were paired with others outside the lodgment area to avoid tipping off the locations of beaches where Allied troops would land on D-Day.

AEAF's plan for the Normandy Invasion provided for a campaign of direct air support for ground forces after D-Day—during what it called the "tactical phase." Influenced by Zuckerman, both Tedder and Leigh-Mallory opposed extensive bridge bombing. AAF units in the U.K. disagreed with this policy and planned to carry out extensive bridge interdiction. Spaatz ordered his subordinates, including heavy bomber group commanders, to have their forces ready to cut bridges on the Seine and Loire rivers.

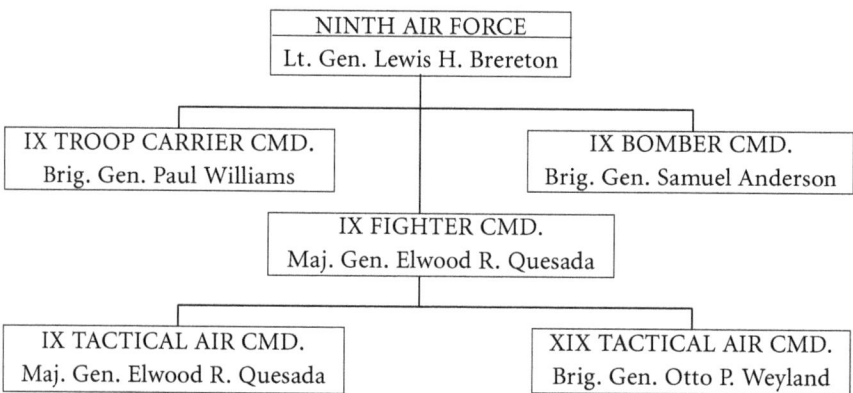

Arnold sent Spaatz a summary of his thinking about AAF operations in the European theater:

> I want to be very sure that the overall United Kingdom Air Forces are doing everything possible to: (1) reduce the GAF, and (2) accomplish the respective Overlord responsibilities. Perhaps it might be well to inform every combat pilot in the United Kingdom as to what we are trying to accomplish, namely: (1) a reduction of the German Air Force in order to gain air superiority, (2) isolation of the Overlord area, and (3) 100% day and night support for the ground forces. Will you keep these tactical requirements foremost in your mind and give General Brereton all required support to build up the Ninth Air Force.[2]

In this important message no hint appears that Arnold expected the AAF to defeat Germany by air power alone. Arnold also communicated directly with Brereton. In February he wrote that "the increasing effectiveness of light flak indicates to me that the major part of the low altitude attack burden must fall on your fighters. I think they may be fast enough and elusive enough to make results justify costs. I will be extremely interested in hearing of the techniques you evolve to get the best low altitude results at the least cost."[3] Arnold's reading of the ground-attack situation agreed with recommendations of the former deputy U.S. commander in the U.K., Major General Idwal Edwards, a career AAF officer who had inspected AAF units in the U.K. Edwards had concluded that fighters and medium bombers should make a greater contribution to the destruction of the GAF. He recommended that they attack enemy airdromes and that fighters employ dive bombing and minimum-level tactics.[4]

But the development of equipment and guidelines for dive bombing, and for ground attack generally, lagged in the prewar era, in part because of Army Air Corps' apathy to ground support. An Army Air Corps Pursuit Board, headed by Spaatz, had warned that dive bombers were too vulnerable to fighters. As noted in a previous chapter, this board condemned efforts to build one airplane to "fight hostile pursuit, cooperate with ground troops, take photographs, drop bombs, engage in long cross-country flights and perform many other functions aside from their primary mission of knocking down bombardment aircraft."[5]

This summary of fighter missions, dismissed then as a "fallacy," actually describes what fighters were called upon to do in World War II. The Pursuit Board reasoned that "to make provision in the design and equipment of pursuit aircraft to better fit it for secondary missions is generally unsound, in that such provisions almost invariably penalize the pursuit in its ability to perform its primary function." It was a case of theory failing to anticipate wartime demands that could not be ignored. De Seversky, whose Republic Aviation designed the P-47, criticized the Army Air Corps for its failure to foresee that fighters would have to execute different kinds of missions in wartime. His *Victory through Air Power*— published during the war — reminded the AAF that manufacturers in peacetime had been forbidden to install bomb racks on fighters.[6]

During the explosive growth of the AAF in 1942, air-ground cooperative training received little attention. As late as September 1942, the commander of U.S. armored forces complained that there was no air-ground support training.[7] Not until August 1943 did the AAF expand fighter-pilot training to include dive bombing and ground attack.[8]

Combat experience in the North African and Italian campaigns showed that fighters would be required to perform many different missions, including reconnaissance, air fighting and direct support of ground troops by bombing and strafing enemy positions.

The P-47's size and strength enabled it to employ a variety of equipment. It could carry bombs with ease and endure the strains of dive bombing. It could carry a 1,000-pound bomb or droptank under each wing and its "belly." This exceptional capability made it a formidable weapon in ground attack. Moreover, its eight .50-caliber machine guns could destroy ground targets as efficiently as they did enemy aircraft. The P-47's size made it a likely target for ground fire, but its speed and sturdiness of construction helped compensate for this liability. Its air-cooled engine offered some protection for its pilots from light flak, and it was far less vulnerable to ground fire than liquid-cooled engines which overheated and died after their cooling systems were hit.

Pilots of the 353rd Fighter Group were among the first to use P-47s in ground-attack operations from the U.K. In September 1943, Major Glenn E. Duncan, the group's executive officer, sent a memo to his wing commander about the GAF's practice of avoiding combat with AAF fighters. He explained that the GAF "knows the performance of the P-47 and that it does not operate at low altitudes." German fighter pilots often ignored Thunderbolts; they posed no threat to their airfields. Duncan suggested that if the P-47 were used as a fighter-bomber it would "give the Hun something to worry about [and] ... his attrition rate would grow."[9]

Eighth Air Force headquarters welcomed Duncan's memo, and, in traditional Army fashion, he got the job of developing dive-bombing techniques and equipment for P-47s. No bombsights were available. The AAF had not assigned a high priority to ground-attack methods and equipment. An Army Air Corps commander in the Thirties had expressed his frustration with current bombing methods: "It is impossible for any airplane crew regardless of type of airplane, to bomb from these altitudes with any degree of accuracy without sights."[10]

The situation had not improved substantially by the time Duncan and some fellow pilots took off and headed for an island off the coast of Wales to learn how to dive bomb. Duncan later recalled the situation: "Everybody said it couldn't be done. They argued that the P-47 was designed for high altitude fighting: that we lacked a bomb-sight; that we had no air brakes ... and that flak would be too tough for us anyway." None of these warnings discouraged Duncan. He worked out evasive tactics to help reduce the danger of flak. "As for lacking a bomb-sight," he recalled, "one important point seems to have been overlooked. We do have one ... two good eyes."[11]

Duncan's team used shackles and release mechanisms developed for droptanks. They painted lines on their cockpit canopies to help them estimate angles of dive. Duncan advised pilots learning to dive bomb to "load up a 100-pound practice bomb ... approach the target straight and level. Fly close enough to the target so that it will pass out of sight

Kepner, Spaatz, Colonel Glenn Duncan, Doolittle and Woodbury. (U.S. Air Force photograph.)

under the wing at about the position of the guns. After the target has passed from view ... for ten seconds, pull the bomb release. Fear of the bomb striking the propeller is unfounded."[12]

Duncan's methods were crude, but none better were accessible. He was an aggressive fighter pilot who wanted to exploit the P-47's capabilities. During his tour of duty in the U.K. he destroyed 19.5 enemy aircraft in the air and 6 on the ground. He was later shot down during a ground-attack mission and made a prisoner of war.[13]

The 353rd Fighter Group carried out its first dive-bombing mission on November 25, 1943. Sixteen P-47s carrying 500-pound bombs attacked an airfield near St. Omer. The Thunderbolts encountered heavy flak, and most of the bombs missed their targets. The group lost its commander on this mission when an anti-aircraft shell hit a fuel tank. He and Duncan were two of many fighter pilots shot down on ground-attack operations.[14]

To fill gaps in fighter-bomber knowledge, AAF commanders in the U.K. asked for help from their counterparts in Italy. Major Gilbert Wymond, Jr. sent a report in which he described his experience in ground attack: "From all we heard about how inadequate the P-47 was below 20,000 feet, we entered the venture fully expecting negative results. After one month's operations this organization gives 100% approval of the aircraft for close support ... it will prove to be the most successful dive bomber we have today...."[15]

Wymond described how his group flew Thunderbolts bearing two 1,000-pound bombs and a 500-pound bomb from a dirt field: "On close support we can take 2500 pounds of bombs for each ship within a radius of 125 miles, return, and be serviced and bombed up again in one hour and fifteen minutes." Wymond called the P-47's strafing ability "devastating."[16]

During the first quarter of 1944, despite many commitments, Ninth Air Force trained its pilots in ground-attack methods and equipped its aircraft for such operations. It was a remarkable achievement, done "in the field" while actively engaged in several campaigns.

The 365th Fighter Group of Ninth Air Force received orders to develop effective techniques to bomb V-Weapon installations — sites from which Germans would launch flying bombs and rockets. The Group's history shows that it proceeded "from the basic premise that the greatest bombing accuracy could be obtained by releasing bombs as close to the target as possible." Pilots practiced ground-level bomb runs at high speed. Bombs with delayed-action fuses were released at pointblank range "after being literally flown into the target."[17]

The AAF's tendency in the prewar era to neglect air support for ground operations was not easily eliminated. After a year of war, the AAF's ground-attack capabilities still did not satisfy General Arnold. He let his staff know how he felt about the failure:

> This is something I have been pounding on now for over a year — apparently with little success. I have emphasized time and time again the urgent necessity for having perfect team play between Air Support units and Ground troops. I have brought out, and I thought in no unmistakable terms, the fact that this cannot be accomplished without thorough training in communications, in technique, and in procedure.[18]

Commanders of ground forces complained throughout the war about inadequate air support. They wanted to be able to order air attacks, not request them. It was difficult to convince them that air power could only be employed effectively if directed by a central agency manned by airmen. The RAF had such a system, and Tedder used his influence to convert Eisenhower's staff to the policy. In the abstract it is obvious that a squadron of fighters, capable of attacking targets in an area of more than 100,000 square miles, should not be controlled by a division commander and made to restrict its operations to a small section of the front. Obvious it was — abstractly — but not convincing to a ground officer in need of air support who is told that the air forces are busy elsewhere or that his target is not important enough or appropriate for an air attack.

Ground units sometimes got air action closer than they wanted; they were bombed and strafed by "friendly" aircraft. This happened regularly and was one of many problems that fostered air-ground discord. Actually, air-ground hostility had its roots in the prewar Army organization which treated airmen with disdain and discrimination. The fault was not all on one side. General Quesada, who became an outstanding tactical air commander in World War II, recalled that "Air Forces didn't really understand what they could contribute to a ground campaign.... I don't like to admit this but it is true. There was an attitude that went all through the Air Force, that I adopted, my juniors adopted and my seniors adopted, that this was not our mission. It was not our mission to participate that close in battle."[19]

Like Spaatz, but at a higher level, Arnold wore several hats. He was chief of the AAF, but subordinate to Marshall. He was a member of the U.S. Joint Chiefs of Staff and thus a member of the CCS, but in these positions he generally remained in Marshall's shadow. Also like Spaatz, the ambiguity of his position did not trouble him since he retained

Marshall's trust. As Arnold's messages to Spaatz and Brereton spelled out, Overlord demanded the establishment of a powerful tactical air force. He reminded his subordinates that the U.S. Army's ground forces believed that they had not received effective air support in North Africa and Italy.

The North African campaign served as a laboratory for development of AAF ground-attack doctrine and of air combat and command principles generally. New guidelines appeared in Army Field Manual, FM 100-20, approved by the War Department in July 1943. It called for central direction of air units in a theater by an air commander working closely with the theater commander. "Land power and air power are co-equal and interdependent forces," it stated, "neither is an auxiliary of the other." This did not give the AAF autonomy, but it was a large step in that direction. It established policies that airmen had promoted for decades. As a first-priority objective, an air force must win air superiority, for without it land forces "must take such extensive security measures against hostile air attack that their mobility and ability to defeat the enemy land forces are greatly reduced."[20]

Interdiction of enemy supply and reinforcement operations received second priority, and close air support of ground forces, third priority. FM 100-20 warned that it was a misuse and waste of air power to parcel it out among ground units directed by commanders concerned primarily with local objectives.

The tendency of ground forces to expect too much of air forces was a major problem. FM 100-20 explained the difficulties faced by pilots: "Enemy ground positions are most difficult to locate. In addition, there is always a considerable chance of striking friendly forces."[21] There were times during Overlord when Spaatz and Doolittle wished that every ground commander, including Eisenhower, had memorized this admonition.

Despite a wide range of commitments to Pointblank and Crossbow [the campaign against V-weapons], Ninth Air Force prepared to carry out its primary mission — support of Overlord's invasion armies. Spaatz, Kepner and Brereton encouraged fighter groups to combine ground-attack missions with bomber escort by attacking airfields and other targets after leaving the bomber formations. Ninth Air Force had so many obligations that it could not attend to some critical areas. One of them was air-ground exercises with the First U.S. Army waiting in the U.K. to invade the continent. Its commander, Lieutenant General Omar Bradley, retained a bitterness about this omission for a long time. Years later, he wrote of his grievance:

> If our pre-invasion confidence in air support were to be measured by the indifference shown us in England by Ninth Tactical Air Force, we would have sailed on the invasion with misgivings. Part of our uneasiness stemmed from the brush-off we experienced at the hands of Brereton himself, for in attempting to pin him down on air-ground training, I was told his air force was then too heavily committed in the air battle for France.[22]

This blunt criticism indicates the depth of what Eisenhower called the "incipient air-ground hostility" and verifies the need for the official policies expounded in FM 100-20. In his preoccupation with his own problems, Bradley did not appreciate the vital importance of the campaign for air superiority and other air campaigns which had to take precedence over air-ground training exercises in the pre-invasion period.

As the tempo of Ninth Air Force operations accelerated, mechanical problems proliferated. Heavy use of fighters on tasks for which they had not been designed led to equipment breakdowns. Aircraft modification sometimes brought about structural weaknesses. Wings buckled and empennages ruptured on the extensively modified P-51s.

Brereton notified Spaatz in February that P-51B aircraft had to be grounded "until inspection is made for loose fuselage nuts and bolts in empennage assembly."[23]

While mechanics, ordnance experts and sundry aviation specialists wrestled with technical problems, Ninth Air Force ORS's analyzed operational tactics. A dire need existed for standardized fighter-bomber guidelines. It was a complex task to compile and analyze data related to aircraft, targets, bombs and enemy defenses — to name only some of the variables involved. Many questions remained unanswered about attacking railroad tracks and equipment, motor vehicles, bridges, missile sites, gun emplacements, beach obstacles and V-weapon installations.

Brereton decided to form a tactical research section to help find some answers. He appointed Lieutenant Colonel Tommy Hitchcock to command the unit. It would conduct trials using a few P-38s, P-47s and P-51s. Hitchcock had achieved his goal of flying fighters on operations; he had transferred to Ninth Air Force when his fighter group became a training unit. The job with Ninth Air Force would at least get him near the battle and exploit his technical abilities. He directed trials to develop fighter-bombing tables. In April 1944, during a dive-bombing exercise near Middle Wallop, England, Hitchcock's Mustang broke apart, and he died in the crash.[24]

Ninth Air Force suffered from deficiencies beyond lack of equipment and tactical guidelines. Most of its fighter groups were inexperienced: pilots lacked proficiency in instrument flying, night flying and bad-weather operations. One report noted that they "can't pinpoint [targets] ... don't know how to jink [evade flak] ... can't read a map."[25] But in pre-invasion operations, they improved their skills on tasks such as these.

In the months before D-Day, the probable strength of the GAF's response to the invasion remained a topic of intense interest to Allied commanders. Many crucial decisions depended on this estimate. A report distributed in late May described the GAF as having substantial strength available to attack invasion troops.[26] (See Table 2.)

A force as strong as this posed a serious threat to Overlord. Concern over such danger gave support to USSTAF's decision to give first priority both to the campaign to reduce GAF fighter strength and to the RAF's decision to keep its fighters ready to fight a decisive air battle over the beachhead.

The British controlled the best Allied intelligence sources. AAF commanders suspected that they doctored or withheld from circulation data that challenged policies they favored. A report claiming that the GAF had strong forces in reserve would lend support to the RAF's contention that the GAF could not be overwhelmed before D-Day and that air supremacy would have to be won during the invasion. This supported the RAF's refusal to modify its fighters for long-range bomber escort and fighter-bomber missions. If the British intelligence reports were accurate, they weakened Spaatz's contention that air supremacy could and should be achieved before D-Day.

Ninth Troop Carrier Command, commanded by Brigadier General Paul Williams, concentrated on training and buildup in the pre-invasion period. Its transport aircraft and gliders would carry airborne soldiers to Normandy on and after D-Day. Ninth Air Force engineers constructed air-base runways, roads and buildings. It was valuable training for jobs they would do during the invasion.

Ninth Air Force also planned to carry out extensive rail-cutting operations to help isolate the battle area. In anticipation of this commitment, Ninth Tactical Air Command's [IX TAC] ORS prepared a paper, "Paralyzation of a Railroad System by Fighter-Bombers."[27] It claimed that the rail system in an area along the French coast from Cherbourg to the Somme river, sixty miles in depth, could be paralyzed with a minimum of

Table 2: Estimated GAF Strength in May 1944

Aircraft Type	Quantity
Long-range Bombers	440
Fighter-bombers	70
Single-engine Fighters	650
Twin-engine Fighters	600
Long-range Reconnaissance Aircraft	95
Tactical Reconnaissance Aircraft	45
Coastal (Anti-shipping) Aircraft	50

thirty-eight "strategically selected cuts." If this number rose to fifty-one, it would neutralize the system even if some cutting efforts were not successful. Evidently, the authors of this paper were not aware that the region they chose for a hypothetical example included the intended lodgment area. A startled General Quesada, who did have that knowledge, stamped "Top Secret" on the ORS paper. The report estimated that seven fighter-bomber groups could keep a rail system paralyzed in an area two hundred miles long and sixty miles wide. It declared that track-cutting was preferable to attacks on rail centers: "Even if a marshaling yard is completely obliterated [it] … can still be bypassed. Only a comparatively small result [is achieved] at great cost. …attacks can be carried out more effectively and efficiently by cutting the rail links between the junction points. It has been shown, furthermore, that a comparatively small number of cuts can be scattered through the system in such manner that traffic is blocked in any direction."[28] The ORS paper recommended that initial attacks should be made simultaneously in a magnitude sufficient to produce a crippling of the designated part of the rail network with the first blow. It denied assertions that track-cutting had only short-term value.

Brereton planned to direct Ninth Air Force from headquarters at Uxbridge, England, during the early period of the invasion. Quesada would direct IX TAC's close support operations from Bradley's headquarters on the beachhead.

A few days before D-Day Brereton wrote of Ninth's readiness: "As far as Ninth Air Force is concerned, the invasion started back in May when we went to work … maintaining air superiority and isolating the battlefield.… The Luftwaffe was attacked wherever it could be found in the air or on the ground. To prevent the enemy's movement, 2,791 sorties were flown in which 35 bridges were destroyed or damaged and numerous marshaling yards severely damaged."[29]

Brereton reported to Arnold on the eve of D-Day that his two tactical air commands, IX TAC and XIX TAC, were "completely organized and operational." Ninth Bomber Command was experienced and efficient: "Bombing by flight of sixes and fours had become standard." Ninth Troop Carrier Command appeared to be in "an effective state of readiness.…"[30] Brereton's pride in Ninth Air Force would be justified in the coming months. After many command failures and tragedies, he now commanded a great tactical air force that would give invasion forces close air support of unparalleled effectiveness.

Part II
Air Operations in Support of Overlord

Chapter 9

Attacks on Rail Centers, Oil Plants and V-Weapons Before D-Day

RAF Bomber Command carried out the first bombings of the transportation campaign. In March 1944, Lancaster bombers attacked rail centers in France and Belgium to determine whether bombing accuracy was adequate for such relatively small targets. Bombs fell on the rail center at Trappes late on the night of March 6/7. Next night, heavy bombers struck the marshaling yard at Le Mans. Bombing accuracy in these trial missions reassured Tedder that the Transportation Plan was feasible. RAF Bomber Command executed fourteen attacks on rail centers in the next few weeks.

German-controlled newspapers expressed outrage at the "Anglo-American terrorist bombings." On March 13, the RAF bombed Le Mans again; forty-eight civilians died in the carnage. Bombs dropped on Lille's rail center on April 9 killed 465 inhabitants and damaged more than five thousand houses.[1]

After the war, Air Chief Marshal Harris recalled his surprise about the transportation campaign: "I myself did not anticipate that we should be able to bomb the French railways with anything like the precision that was achieved."[2] However, despite postwar recollections like this, RAF Bomber Command's accuracy in the transportation campaign should not be overrated. Admittedly, it was generally better than it had been in 1941, when a study of bomb-damage photographs determined that "of those aircraft recorded as attacking their target, only one in three got within five miles of it."[3] Yet, in 1944, many bombs intended for rail centers still fell on adjacent towns. RAF night-bombing accuracy depended on a large number of variable conditions. Radar equipment (which malfunctioned occasionally) guided Pathfinder aircraft to a target area where they dropped flares to mark aiming points. Bomber Command's most accurate radar navigation system guided aircraft at most for 270 miles at 28,000 feet.[4] Bomber crews struggled to cope with darkness, wind, defective flares and radar equipment, enemy searchlights, errors of navigation, anti-aircraft fire, GAF fighters, deception by the enemy, clouds and the dust and smoke created by exploding bombs.

According to an official history of the RAF's strategic air offensive against Germany, 45 percent of the bombs dropped on the first fifteen transportation targets were not "effectively aimed," which presumably means that they hit the ground far from their targets. How far may be inferred from a report that the average bombing error for those bombs that were "effectively aimed" was 680 yards. RAF investigators reported that 25 percent of the bombs dropped during missions against rail centers were "gross errors, and had fallen far away from their targets."[5]

Bomber Command worked hard to improve bombing accuracy. An offset, target-marking technique involved dropping flares some 300 or 400 yards from an aiming point so that dust and smoke stirred up by the first attackers would not hide marker flares from those attacking later. Aircraft with "master" bomb crews remained in target areas to give directions to the main forces. They could, for instance, warn others about misplaced flare markers.

Many things could go wrong during a bombing mission, as demonstrated during the attack on Aulnoye on the night of April 10-11. All but one pair of target markers fell to the southwest of their respective aiming points; flare markers hovered about 500 yards from one aiming point and 1,100 yards from another. Similar errors occurred on the same night during attacks on Laon, Tergnier and Ghent. At Laon, only a corner of the railway yard was hit. At Ghent, 428 civilians died and 300 were injured; and bombs destroyed 584 buildings including schools, convents and an orphanage.[6]

When SHAEF assumed direction of RAF Bomber Command and Eighth Air Force, the CCS issued a directive to Eisenhower that assigned first priority to attrition of the GAF and attacks on the aircraft industry. It assigned second priority to the railroad network that Germans would use to strengthen their positions in Normandy. With just six weeks remaining before D-Day, most of Eisenhower's air-power demands had been satisfied, but one major problem remained unsolved. British civilian leaders protested against the killing of French and Belgian civilians that was an inescapable part of the transportation campaign. Portal notified Churchill that "very heavy casualties among civilians living near the main railway centers will be unavoidable.... I hope you will agree ... the plan must go ahead after due warning has been given."[7]

The prime minister did not agree. He informed Eisenhower that "the British War Cabinet took rather a grave and on the whole adverse view of the proposal to bomb so many French railway centres, in view of the fact that scores of thousands of French civilians, men, women and children, would lose their lives or be injured. Considering that they are all our friends, this might be held an act of very great severity, bringing much hatred on the Allied Air Forces."[8]

Eisenhower responded with a firm defense of Overlord's air offensives. He reminded Churchill that "one of the fundamental factors leading to the decision for undertaking Overlord was the conviction that our overpowering air forces would make feasible an operation which might otherwise be considered extremely hazardous, if not foolhardy." AEAF had consulted transportation experts, Eisenhower explained, and "it was decided that the only preparatory field in which our air force could be profitably employed, other than in its normal task of destroying the hostile air force, was against the enemy's transportation system." Eisenhower also reminded Churchill that civilians were endangered by almost all air actions, but his air forces would drop leaflets on French towns to warn inhabitants of the dangers. He disputed Churchill's estimate of "scores of thousands" of deaths. There would be fewer fatalities than critics had predicted. The supreme commander reiterated a position from which he never budged: "I think it would be sheer folly to abstain from doing anything that can increase in any measure our chances for success in Overlord."[9]

Churchill remained unconvinced. He warned that the transportation campaign would create a "volume of dull hatred" in France that would disturb relations with that country for decades. The RAF would be looked upon with "odium and accused of killing our friends by blind bombing attacks." He feared that "odious comparisons" would be made "between the daylight precision bombing of the AAF and the scattering of bombs at night [by the RAF]...."[10]

Churchill's fears could not have been eased by USSTAF's obvious lack of enthusiasm for the Transportation Plan. Late in April, Portal reported to the British War Cabinet: "The U.S. forces had hardly started their program...."[11] Bomber Command dropped about 2,500 tons of bombs on rail centers in March; by June 1944, a total of 28,000 tons had been dropped on rail centers by the RAF.[12]

Throughout the debates on the rail-center offensive, Tedder claimed that its critics exaggerated the probable casualties. He estimated that not more than 10,500 French and Belgian civilians would be killed. This estimate did not mollify the British War Cabinet. It asked Tedder to keep close watch on casualty totals and to postpone attacks on heavily populated centers until it became clear that they were necessary. Tedder reported to the War Cabinet nightly. He called attention to the bombing of the rail center at Tergnier which "resulted in seven days' delay in the movement of an S.S. division.... An attack on March 13/14 on Le Mans proved so effective that ten days later normal operation was still suspended...."[13] Opponents of the air offensive challenged such claims. They pointed out that the enemy would not feel a sense of urgency to restore interrupted rail transportation until D-Day. Then the Germans would act with their customary energy, efficiency and ruthlessness. If some bombed rail centers remained out of service in the pre-D-Day period it could mean that the enemy had decided that he did not need them.

Some bombed rail centers returned to service promptly. An intelligence agency reported on these targets: "Repairs are being carried out rather more quickly than we might have been led to expect from a sorely taxed railway system. ...Repairs are being carried out simultaneously at six major centers which would seem to indicate that the Germans have made plans for such an eventuality."[14] To be prepared to keep lines open for high-priority military trains, German rail officials in the west had sent for 50,000 railway workers from Germany.

On April 25, the British Directorate of Intelligence reported that "in the past week no fresh evidence has been received of delay to German troop movements ... indeed it is known that troop movements have been taking place ... notably between Amiens and Valenciennes."[15]

With some critics charging that attacks on rail centers were killing too many civilians and others claiming that they were not accomplishing their objectives, Tedder kept busy defending the campaign. He needed reliable evidence, above all, to show that it was effective. Ultra, the decryption of German radio communications, apparently did not furnish much information about French and Belgian railroad operations. Reports from newspapers in German-occupied countries had to be heavily discounted. Reports from Resistance groups came to London, but many of their members condemned a bombing offensive they perceived as useless and destructive.[16] Tedder's most difficult judgments concerned explanations for German reactions to the bombings. A lack of effort to repair rail centers could mean that they did not feel an urgent need for them or, as Tedder hoped, that the bomb damage had already overburdened their repair facilities. Similarly, if traffic slowed in one area, did it mean that the offensive was achieving its goals or merely that the Germans were routing trains on open lines?

Protests about the bombings continued to arrive in London from neutral and occupied countries. A group of French bishops issued an appeal for an end to the slaughter of civilians: "We are convinced ... that it should be possible to distinguish with more care, between military objectives and the humble dwellings of women and children, with which they are surrounded." The church leaders pleaded with the Allies to spare "monuments in our towns the treasures of art and memorials, our churches...."[17]

German-controlled newspapers portrayed the attacks as wanton terrorism. They published stories of delayed-action bombs which exploded after workers had started to rescue people trapped in rubble. Stories of damage to schools, orphanages and hospitals circulated throughout the world. Marshal Pétain, the French leader, visited Rouen — a city of historic importance to the French — to express sympathy for 1,800 deaths which occurred during the week of April 15–22.

Along with Churchill, some of the U.K.'s most prominent political leaders opposed the transportation campaign. At a meeting of the War Cabinet on April 27, Anthony Eden and Clement Atlee (future prime ministers) condemned it.[18]

The widespread devastation from bombing did not silence critics; they did not equate demolition with effectiveness. Lord Cherwell, Churchill's trusted scientific advisor, explained: "We have never denied that dislocation would be caused. The whole question is whether it will be sufficient to hamper appreciably military movement, which remains to be seen. I still believe that attacks on bridges will be far more effective for this purpose...."[19] Lord Cherwell exerted a profound influence on Churchill, who favored an Allied air offensive against French bridges.

Eisenhower continued to defend the air offensive but did agree to postpone attacks on targets in heavily populated cities.[20] Tedder reported that fewer bombs fell in populated areas than predicted. General Cabell, USSTAF's representative to SHAEF's bombing advisory committee, warned Spaatz not to accept Tedder's claims at face value. He had attended a meeting that dealt with casualty totals: "The figures can and will be juggled within wide limits to prove whatever point is to be made at the moment."[21]

Tedder not only juggled figures to defend the transportation campaign, he also shifted ground smoothly to counter criticism. In a letter he drafted for Eisenhower, he disposed of claims that bombing a rail center would block traffic for only a short time: "It has never been suggested that these Operations by themselves will stop essential military movement. The object of the whole Operation is to so weaken and disorganize the Railway system as a whole that, at the critical time of the assault, German rail movements can be effectively delayed, and the rapid concentration of their forces against the lodgment area prevented."[22] It was a clever restatement of the campaign's rationale to counter intelligence reports, now widespread, that German military movements continued regularly despite the rail-center bombings. Tedder predicted a collapse of the rail system as a cumulative result of the transportation campaign, but achievement of this objective appeared highly problematical, and doubters worried whether the main goal — to block troop movements to Normandy — would be attained.

To blunt the increasing clamor for interdiction, Tedder made the following observation in the same letter: "Some of these [interdiction operations] fit into the Tactical phase [after D-Day], and were already scheduled to be included in the final stage of Air operations. They do not, themselves, however, in any way constitute a plan by which our Air power can, in the final stages, effectively delay and disrupt enemy concentrations."[23]

Protests about the killing of civilians and the destruction of beautiful and historic town centers continued to flood into SHAEF. Looking ahead to the invasion, Eisenhower reminded his commanders to exercise restraint during future battles on the continent so that "cultural treasures are not destroyed needlessly."[24]

9. Attacks on Rail Centers, Oil Plants and V-Weapons Before D-Day 97

Devastation in the city of St. Lô, France. (U.S. Air Force Photo Collection [Neg. No. 61321 AC] courtesy of National Air and Space Museum, Smithsonian Institution.)

In May, as the bombing offensive moved into its final phase, intelligence agencies continued to report alarming evidence that it was not accomplishing its major objective. SHAEF's own intelligence section issued a report so negative that its director felt obliged to attach a disclaimer to it. Readers were forewarned that the report did not intend to belittle the effects of the transportation campaign. The paper's principal conclusion came as no surprise to the campaign's critics: there were so many railway lines available to the enemy that "there is no need to enter into argument as to the extent to which line capacity through the heavily attacked area may have been reduced." Furthermore, the enemy did not suffer from a shortage of locomotives. "The number of conveniently located locomotive servicing centres in France and the Low Countries, which remain, after taking account of the effects of rail centre attacks, are greatly in excess of those which will be needed to handle the small number of locomotives needed for military supply traffic." According to SHAEF's intelligence analysts, "the programme of rail centre attacks has clearly not impaired the enemy's ability to move the necessary daily supply and maintenance tonnage by rail into the bridgehead area." German forces had three times the number of railway lines they needed, four times the quantity of rolling stock, eight times as many locomotives and more than enough servicing facilities.[25]

This remarkable report, coming from the headquarters of the organization that produced the Transportation Plan, created an uproar whose echoes still reverberate. A U.S. Army official history denigrates this document: "Seldom have intelligence estimates been so wrong. They ... took no account of either cumulative or critical damage." This was only one of many official statements that attempted to scuttle reports that the transportation campaign had failed. The British Ministry of Economic Warfare also found fault with the offensive against rail centers: "The Germans appear to have adopted a policy of re-distributing to other sheds locomotives formerly stationed at the heavily attacked centres, of transferring the marshaling work from the larger centres to a number of smaller yards.... the worst of the effects have so far fallen on the French...."[26]

Meanwhile, USSTAF had procrastinated in starting its part of the transportation offensive and continued to concentrate on the GAF. Eisenhower understood Spaatz's goal and explained it to Marshall: "We are seizing every opportunity to force the Luftwaffe to fight. When our penetrations go very deep we have to pay a good price but Spaatz' crowd is taking a big toll of the enemy and once we get a really good operation against about three or four important targets east of Berlin we won't have to go that far for a long time."[27]

Tedder and Portal felt uneasy about USSTAF's delay in executing its share of the rail-center attacks. A SHAEF report on May 2, compared the efforts of three air forces (see Table 3). These data can easily be misinterpreted. True, Eighth Air Force had attacked fewer targets than Bomber Command, but its bombing was more accurate; 38 percent of its targets were judged to be in Category A—demolished and out of service. Bomber Command, with a far greater expenditure of bombs, had 42 percent of its targets in Category A, while Ninth Air Force had 24 percent.[28]

Spaatz and Doolittle were confident that Eighth Air Force could complete its share of rail-center missions before D-Day; the closer to D-Day they were bombed, the greater the probability that they would be out of service during the critical period. As always in daylight, precision bombing, weather strongly influenced operations.

Doolittle's B-17s and B-24s struck marshaling yards at Blainville and Châlons-sur-Marne on April 17. On April 22, Eighth Air Force's tempo accelerated; 631 heavy bombers struck the rail center at Friedrichshafen. Attacks on rail centers in France, Belgium and Luxembourg followed. Bombing was excellent, but, as Spaatz had forecast, the GAF did not send fighters to defend these targets. Flak, however, took its customary toll of aircraft.

On May 1, Eighth Air Force sent 328 heavies and sixteen groups of fighters to attack marshaling yards at Troyes, Reims, Brussels, Liège, Sarreguemines and Metz. In clear weather a relatively small number of Eighth Air Force bombers could put a rail center in "Category A"; a number of important centers could be hit on the same day. Ninth Air Force medium bombers demonstrated impressive accuracy as they bombed from about 12,000 feet. On May 2, ten separate forces, each made up of about twenty-eight aircraft, hit rail targets in France and Belgium. With D-Day only weeks away, USSTAF launched a major effort to disrupt the rail centers allotted to it. Late in May, Fifteenth Air Force joined the offensive by attacking rail centers in southern France including those in Nice, Lyon, Grenoble, Avignon, Marseille and Nîmes.[29]

RAF Bomber Command completed its share of attacks on rail centers in May. The brief reports below, taken from a postwar Bomber Command history, testify to the fury of the assault:

> 30 April/1 May
> 143 aircraft attacked Somain. OBOE [radar] marking was inaccurate. Most of the air crews did not hear or ignored warnings of the master bomber not to bomb. Some bombs fell on railway-men's housing or open country.
>
> 1/2 May
> Malines in Belgium was bombed and extensive damage caused to civilian homes—171 killed.
> 120 aircraft bombed Chambly which contained a major railway supply and repair depot which was knocked out of service for 10 days. Only 5 people were killed as the result of bombs falling on a nearby village.
>
> 19/20 May
> 113 RAF heavy bombers bombed a rail yard in the center of Tours.

Table 3: Effort Expended on the Transportation Campaign

	Percent of Allotted Targets Attacked	Bombs Dropped (Tons)
Bomber Command	93%	26,320
Eighth Air Force	36%	1,433
Ninth Air Force	78%	6,703

> 28/29 May
> The bombing of a rail center at Angers was described as a "good, concentrated attack." Town officials claimed [in postwar interviews] that many bombs fell on residential area — 800 buildings destroyed, 254 people killed.[30]

In June, RAF Bomber Command bombed towns in and near the Normandy invasion beachhead primarily to create rubble that would delay German road movements. The same postwar history of Bomber Command summarizes some of these missions:

> 6/7 June
> 3,488 tons dropped on targets including Acheres, Argentan, Caen, Coutances, St. Lô, Lisieux and Vire.
> A new weapon — a 12,000-pound bomb — was used against a railway tunnel at Saumur. Damage blocked the rail line for a considerable time.

On May 25, shortly before Tedder called a halt to the transportation campaign, SHAEF issued a summary of its results. Since February 9, seventy-three rail centers had been bombed, and 48,795 tons of bombs expended on them. Locomotive servicing in forty-two centers was either impossible or severely restricted. The offensive destroyed 4,000 locomotives. In the period April 10–May 15, 4,615 French and Belgian civilians perished in rail-center bombings.[31]

French newspapers gave extensive coverage to the Anglo-American bombing of their towns. Rouen occupies a special place in the hearts of the French people. Joan of Arc was burned at the stake there; French and German newspapers often reminded readers of her fate during the martyrdom of the city in World War II. Its importance as a transportation gateway, and it nearness to England, meant that it would be bombed often. Marshal Pétain visited Rouen on May 13 to call worldwide attention to the destruction and deaths wrought by Allied air forces.

On May 22, *Le Républicain* of Orléans, another city associated with St. Joan, had a tragedy close to home to write about: "In the same week that our city suffered 46 deaths in bombardment ... a new aerial aggression ravaged our districts and suburbs, causing a hundred deaths and many injuries." The headline charged "L'Aviation américaine bombarde violement." The story observed for its readers that "so, as in the past, France is atrociously ravaged by a ferocious adversary, always the same one after ten centuries...." The RAF had attacked Orléans on the night of May 19/20; 118 Lancasters and four Mosquitoes carried out a mission that was reported as "particularly accurate."[32]

While political and military leaders of the U.K. and U.S. argued about the transportation campaign, the people most painfully affected by it had little influence on Allied decisions. The U.S. refused to grant diplomatic recognition to any person or group to represent France. It was a sore point in Anglo-American relations: the British backed General Charles de Gaulle as the leader of the French people; President Roosevelt, however,

The marshaling yard at Rouen, France, after an Allied bombing. (U.S. Air Force Photo Collection [Neg. No. 52893 AC], courtesy of National Air and Space Museum, Smithsonian Institution.)

did not trust de Gaulle, who was reputed to despise democratic institutions and clearly had a burning ambition to become head of the French government when France was liberated. De Gaulle opposed American policies ceaselessly, and frequently came into conflict with the U.S. in his efforts to bolster his position and undermine the Pétain regime. Churchill pleaded with Roosevelt to temper his hostility to the French leader but with little success.[33]

Roosevelt's antagonism virtually forced de Gaulle to assume an uncooperative stance with regard to Overlord, and there was little Eisenhower could do to correct the situation. This situation was especially disturbing since de Gaulle had won the allegiance of the French Resistance groups. Churchill reminded Roosevelt that "General Eisenhower attaches great importance to the action to be taken by the French resistance groups.... Undoubtedly we must take care that our joint troops do not suffer heavier losses owning to the fact that no agreement has been made for the employment of French resistance groups."[34]

Eisenhower recorded his disgust about French relations: "All our information leads us to believe that the only authority these Resistance Groups desire to recognize is that of De Gaulle and his committee.... the whole thing falls into a rather sorry mess. De Gaulle is, of course, now controlling the only French military forces that can take part in this operation.... He, however, takes the attitude that military and political matters go hand in hand and will not cooperate militarily unless political recognition of some kind is accorded him."[35]

Roosevelt's frigid attitude regarding de Gaulle thawed slowly. Not until October 1944, did the President recognize the Committee for French National Liberation as the provisional government of France. By that time, de Gaulle's functionaries were governing the liberated parts of France.

Allied decisions to treat de Gaulle's claims as illegitimate meant that French power was not fully mobilized on the side of the Allies. French Resistance forces contributed to victory, but with only token support from the Allies. De Gaulle later recalled that SHAEF did not know "precisely the striking power of these [Resistance] groups which furnished neither statements nor lists to anyone." As a professional soldier he understood that the "Allied command was behindhand in measuring the effectiveness of this form of warfare, quite new, for its general staffs prepared only for battles conducted according to the rules."[36]

Overlord's planners expected assistance from Resistance groups but did not count on it. It was known at SHAEF that Resistance groups sometimes betrayed each other to the Germans. German counter-intelligence agents were able to infiltrate many Resistance groups. Efforts to aid the Resistance sometimes resulted in helping the Germans.

Allied agents of the British Strategic Operations Executive (SOE) and the American OSS infiltrated France to assist Resistance groups; they helped plan sabotage of key services such as railroads and public utilities. But SHAEF's policy was to treat any benefits derived from such efforts as "windfalls." Many Resistance members gave allegiance to international communism and looked to the Soviet Union for guidance. Resistance groups did receive some supplies by air drop, although Allied air forces felt little enthusiasm for these operations.[37] As feared, many of these arms fell into German hands.

Assaults on French rail centers dampened the enthusiasm of many Resistance fighters. They perceived the attacks to be pointless and costly. Likewise, French railway workers believed that labor strikes and sabotage could have achieved most of the objectives of the transportation campaign. In postwar years the chief proponents of the transportation campaign have cited the words of de Gaulle's representative at SHAEF, General Joseph Pierre Koenig. Referring to French civilian casualties, he supposedly said, "This is war, and it must be expected that people will be killed. We would take twice the anticipated loss to be rid of the Germans."[38] This remark, if ever uttered, was certainly taken out of context and did not represent the feelings of the French about the bombing of their towns by the Allies.

Soon after the first reports reached London of rail-center bombing casualties, Churchill told his War Cabinet that there was "a limit to the slaughter ... [beyond] which we could not go."[39] He asked Roosevelt to decide the issue as a matter of high political significance. Roosevelt responded promptly: "However regrettable the attendant loss of civilian lives is, I am not prepared to impose from this distance any restriction on military action by the responsible commanders that in their opinion might militate against the success of 'Overlord' or cause additional loss of life to our Allied forces of invasion." According to Churchill, "this was decisive."[40]

While the transportation campaign went forward, the oil offensive remained on hold, causing frustration at USSTAF where Spaatz and his associates believed that attacks on German oil resources could make a decisive contribution to victory. Allied air forces had the strength to devastate the twenty-three synthetic fuel plants and thirty-one refineries that accounted for over 90 percent of Germany's oil and fuel production. The EOU reported that "oil offers the most promising system of attack after fighter aircraft and ball bearings, to bring the German armies to the point where their defeat in the field will be assured." This report recommended an operational schedule for USSTAF:

> Period 1
> Until D-30: complete Pointblank, police Pointblank to prevent German recuperation, and begin an offensive against oil.
>
> Period 2
> From D-30 to the establishment of a firm Allied beachhead in Normandy: direct support for Overlord.
>
> Period 3
> After the beachhead is secured: police Pointblank, provide tactical support for ground forces if absolutely required; complete attack on oil.[41]

At the March 25, 1944, meeting, Portal and Eisenhower promised to reconsider an oil offensive after the beachhead was firmly established. Spaatz urged Eisenhower to give authorization to begin one sooner. He wanted to exploit the good weather of late spring for oil attacks before the needs of the invasion assumed overriding priority. The ever-present fear of a resurgent GAF—a fear Spaatz used like a cattle prod—motivated Eisenhower to permit trial attacks on oil before D-Day. On April 19 the supreme commander gave Spaatz permission to bomb oil plants on the next two days of clear weather. Eighth Air Force was ready, but suitable weather did not occur until May 12. On that day, 935 heavy bombers attacked synthetic-oil installations at Zwickau, Merseburg-Leuna, Brüx, Lützkendorf, Böhlen and other cities. It was the start—long delayed—of the most successful Allied strategic bombing offensive.[42]

The GAF reaction to the attacks on oil vindicated Spaatz's judgment. Luftwaffe fighters attacked AAF bomber formations savagely; forty-six heavy bombers went down. Allied fighters destroyed seventy-five GAF fighters and lost ten of their own. Fifteenth Air Force joined the oil offensive with attacks on major installations around Ploesti, Romania, and crude-oil refineries in Austria, Hungary and Yugoslavia.

The German official chiefly responsible for industrial production, Albert Speer, later remembered May 12 vividly: "Until then we had managed to produce approximately as many weapons as the armed forces needed," he wrote; "But ... [attacks on oil plants] in central and eastern Germany ... meant the end of German armament production."[43] Speer rounded up hundreds of thousands of workers from other critical activities to repair damaged oil plants and restore them to production. By September, 7,500,000 foreign workers labored in Germany. Speer directed an extraordinary program which managed to maintain at least a minimum of oil production for many months. The effort weakened German forces on all fronts. Time after time, when an oil plant returned to production, Doolittle scheduled it for another attack.

Ultra confirmed that Germans regarded attacks on oil as a mortal danger. Anti-aircraft gun batteries and fighter squadrons moved from the Russian front and Italy to protect oil installations. Many units in the German forces suffered fuel shortages. An order went out from GAF headquarters forbidding flights whose sole purpose was to escape destruction on the ground.[44]

Allied air planners now understood that it was counter-productive to launch untimely attacks with inadequate resources. Portal explained to Churchill: "It would be wrong to attack these [oil] targets piecemeal with small forces over a long period. The enemy would then doubtless start organizing very efficient smoke screens and would greatly increase his Flak defences."[45]

On June 5, Ultra provided more evidence of the German oil crisis. The high command of the GAF informed its units that "most essential requirements for training and carrying out production plans can scarcely be covered by quantities of aircraft fuel available.... It has been necessary to break into ... [the] strategic reserve."[46]

Soon after D-Day, Portal and Eisenhower fulfilled their promise to review oil as a strategic target. On June 8, 1944, Spaatz issued a historic directive making oil a primary objective.[47] With some difficulty, Portal convinced Harris to participate in the oil offensive. On June 12 and 13, Bomber Command launched attacks on synthetic-fuel plants in the Ruhr.

As Overlord's crucial moment neared, the Allies faced a major threat that appeared to be reaching the level of a crisis. The Germans had V-weapons — pilotless flying bombs and rocket missiles — apparently ready to launch against England. The program to cope with the threat — codenamed Crossbow — consumed a large share of Allied air effort. British intelligence agencies had watched the V-weapon program closely for years. An intensive, photographic reconnaissance campaign showed ski-shaped launch ramps sprouting up in many parts of France and the Low Countries. British leaders took the V-weapon threat very seriously, but Spaatz had reservations about putting so much effort into an essentially defensive operation, especially since air attacks did not appear to do much damage to launch sites. In a moment of exasperation, he suggested to Tedder that "if England were so worried for its own safety, the RAF night bombers should be sent on this target."[48] Tedder reminded Spaatz that Bomber Command did not have enough accuracy to hit such small, well-concealed targets.

Eighth Air Force first attacked flying-bomb launch sites—"ski sites"—in August 1943. Massive amounts of concrete and steel protected them. According to the British, who directed the intelligence effort against V-weapons, they could be destroyed only by accurate, heavy bombing by daylight precision bombers. On December 24, 1943, Eighth Air Force sent 722 heavy bombers escorted by fighters to attack twenty-three ski sites. Ninth Air Force also took part in Crossbow.

Intelligence agencies had located some 120 V-weapon targets, most of them launch sites for flying-bombs [V-1s], but some installations would be used to launch giant rockets [V-2s].

Arnold, like Spaatz, had doubts about using heavy bombers against V-weapon installations. In January 1944, he ordered the AAF Proving Ground Command to carry out a rush program to determine the best way to destroy them. "I want the job done in days, not weeks," he told the test commander; "It will take a hell of a lot of concrete ... give it first priority...."[49]

Construction crews rapidly erected structures simulating V-weapon sites at an AAF base in Florida; airmen employed many different kinds of weapons against them. The trials showed that minimum-altitude attacks by fighter-bombers were most likely to damage the installations significantly. British leaders evidently considered this finding to be self-serving, for they ignored it and continued to call on USSTAF's heavy bombers and Ninth Air Force mediums to carry out Crossbow missions.

Spaatz, however, acted on the trial results and ordered AAF fighter groups to attack ski sites. On May 3, 1944, the 365th Fighter Group attacked four flying-bomb sites without loss and with good results. Each aircraft carried two 1,000-pound bombs with eight-to-eleven-second delay fuses. Three squadrons flew the mission under the leadership of Colonel Lance Call. On the approach to their targets, the flights gradually lost altitude

Table 4: Sortie Totals for U.S. Aircraft

	No. of Sorties	Fighters Damaged per 1,000 Sorties	Fighters Lost per 1,000 Sorties
Bomber Escort	31,638	23	10
Sweeps	1,999	35	13
Ground Strafing	1,723	80	36
Fighter-Bombing	1,722	49	9

and then began a steep dive to the ground pulling out several miles before the target. The bomb run was made as close to the ground as feasible. A report by one of the pilots describes his experiences:

> I was down to 8000 feet, so I pushed over violently in a near vertical dive 3 miles South of target, turned on course to Northeast and dove in on target at full throttle. I aimed my plane at the "Q" building, trimmed the ship and checked to observe my wingman in position.... We struck the target simultaneously at 340 MPH at zero level. I released two 1000-pound bombs at pointblank range.... I had no idea of the height of the trees since no oblique photos were available.[50]

During this attack, German defense forces directed heavy fire at the P-47s. Near the target the Thunderbolts were rocked by exploding land mines the Germans had installed in trees.

Allied attacks on V-weapons were futile for the most part. With characteristic skill and energy, Germans modified the installations to cope with air attacks. They made them smaller and designed them so they could be moved and set up in other places quickly. They upgraded security precautions and flak defenses. Camouflage, smoke screens and dummy sites confused attackers. A substantial part of the bomb tonnage expended on V-weapons in the spring of 1944 fell on sites the Germans had abandoned.

Ninth Bomber Command attacked V-weapon sites and a variety of other targets in the pre-D-Day period. Formations of eighteen medium bombers proved to be efficient against large airdromes; flights of six bombers were used to attack bridges and V-weapon facilities. Toward the latter part of April, Ninth Bomber Command concentrated on rail centers. A common bomb load for B-26s attacking rail centers was eight 500-pound bombs or sixteen 250-pound bombs; on some missions they carried 1,000-pound and 2,000-pound bombs.

German radar stations along the continental coastline posed a serious danger to invasion forces. Air efforts to knock them out had been underway for months. In March, RAF rocket-firing Typhoons struck a radar station near Ostend on the Belgian coast and demonstrated conclusively that these installations could be eliminated by air attack. The RAF launched more attacks at widely scattered targets to confuse Germans about the location of the beaches chosen for invasion. By D-Day only a few radar stations still operated. The RAF suffered heavy losses, but it was a most effective and significant effort. Not only did German forces not receive timely warning of the invasion but the attacks blinded their radar-directed coastal guns.[51]

Combat conditions facing Allied air crews changed drastically in 1944. As the GAF weakened, Allied bombers and fighters suffered less from air attack but relatively more from ground fire. The vastly increased effort put into ground attack by Allied air forces meant that German gunners had more targets and, consequently, claimed more victims.

9. Attacks on Rail Centers, Oil Plants and V-Weapons Before D-Day

First Lieutenant John T. Godfrey standing before the victory board of the 4th Fighter Group. (U.S. Air Force Photo.)

P-47 Thunderbolts suffered less damage and loss per sortie than other AAF fighters in the period of August 24, 1943, to May 31, 1944, although damage and loss rates from ground fire increased generally by 300 percent. Table 4 gives sortie totals for the last third of that nine-month period. Of those AAF fighters hit by flak, about three of every four P-47s returned, compared to about three of every five P-38s and P-51s. The higher loss rate for the P-51 was offset by the toll it took on enemy fighters, mostly on bomber-escort missions.[52] P-38s and P-51s operated a greater distance from their bases, on average, than P-47s, which also lowered their probability of surviving.

Questions arose about the practice of sending skilled fighter pilots to attack ground targets. Their air-fighting skills did not help them much in ground attack. Frequently, they had to fly through storms of flak where luck meant more than skill. Captain John Godfrey was one of the highest-scoring aces in the European theater. He was shot down during a strafing attack on an airfield. "Each time I'd tell myself this was the last [pass], but eagerness overcame caution," he wrote in his autobiography, "until on the fifth pass the firing at me was so heavy I could literally smell the hot lead about me."[53]

Arnold asked his air force commanders to comment about the use of fighter aces in ground attack. Doolittle did not favor giving special treatment to high-scoring aces, who, he believed, already received too much attention.

Allied air forces expended an enormous effort on rail centers and V-weapons installations in the six months before D-Day, much of it wasted. Opponents of the bombing of rail centers made a strong case against these operations, but SHAEF decided that they were among the few targets suitable for RAF Bomber Command. The campaign went on and brought great suffering to the French and Belgian peoples.

Germans did not usually set up V-weapons launch sites in the heart of urban areas, so the Allied effort to destroy them caused fewer civilian casualties and less property damage than the transportation campaign. But Crossbow was enormously costly, and its results were meager relative to its expenditures.

Allied air forces made only a modest beginning on an oil offensive in the months before D-Day, but even this small effort produced reactions from the Germans that showed it was potentially crippling. Its results convinced Eisenhower and Portal to authorize an oil campaign as soon as the air effort could be spared from Overlord.

In the months before D-Day, the AAF executed its part of the transportation campaign reluctantly and made only a beginning of an oil offensive; however, it put a full, enthusiastic effort into an interdiction program, especially into a campaign against bridges. The outcome completely vindicated the claims of its proponents.

Chapter 10

Attacks on Bridges and Airfields Before D-Day

In pre–D-Day operations Ninth Air Force attacked V-weapons launch sites, rail centers, bridges and airfields. General Brereton was not satisfied with Ninth Bomber Command's performance: "I am disappointed with the bombing results of the B-26s and A-20s [light bombers] and have decided on a change in bombing technique. Instead of having a large element drop on signal from the lead plane, bombing will be done by smaller flights within the squadrons. The squadrons will have two or three flight leaders for sections of six planes each."[1] Smaller bomb patterns resulted from this change. With GAF fighter numbers sharply reduced, AAF medium bombers could operate with greater flexibility and less fighter escort. Flak, however, remained a serious menace: medium bombers bombed from about 10,000 feet on most missions; as Ninth Bomber Command's commander, Brigadier General Samuel E. Anderson explained, "Their light stuff [flak] was effective to about 7,500 feet, and their heavy stuff didn't become effective until about 13,000 and on up, and we fly in between."[2]

B-26 Marauders could carry two tons of bombs of various sizes and combinations including 1,000-pound and 2,000-pound bombs. Ninth Air Force used various kinds of bombs: general-purpose high explosive, fragmentation, armor-piercing and incendiary. The B-26, a problem aircraft in its early career, became a highly versatile weapon of great effectiveness. But, as a Ninth Air Force instructional manual explained, it could not be all things to all men:

> It is never worthwhile to operate fewer than six medium bombers, and on certain occasions not less than eighteen. Given the aiming error and pattern size of a single aircraft the possibility of hitting a target is remote. This means that medium bombardment is not appropriate for relatively small and unimportant targets because, to guarantee a reasonable probability of destruction, eighteen aircraft will normally have to be assigned, resulting at best in wasting a major part of the bombload.[3]

Ninth Bomber Command's bombing accuracy improved steadily. The percentages of bombs placed within five hundred feet of aiming points in the first seven months of 1944 were as follows.

January–March	10.4%
April	15.0%
May	25.0%

IX TAC reconnaissance photograph of a bridge at Vernon, May 1944. (U.S. Air Force photograph.)

June   29.0%
July   32.0%

Ironically, some of this improvement came from wasteful operations against V-weapon sites — missions that sharpened crews' skills without doing much damage to targets. A report describes Ninth's anti–V-weapon efforts: "All day, every day the processions of mediums visited the Pas de Calais area, and with every break in the weather, bombs were showered on these targets.... From March on, it was necessary to parcel out the mediums on other priority targets, but even as late as 17 May 1944, 10% of their effort was still being committed against V-launching sites."[5]

The goal of the Allied interdiction offensive, begun a few weeks before D-Day, was to delay German movements of troops, equipment and supplies to the lodgment area; many targets were key parts of the transportation system, including bridges — despite AEAF's belief that bridge attacks were difficult and costly. A report signed by Leigh-Mallory, dated April 30, stated that "it has been suggested that 5 bridges over the River Seine should be destroyed by bombing, but in view of the heavy expenditure of effort that would be involved (6,000 short tons) and the fact that the lines could be cut at other points ... for a smaller expenditure of effort, this commitment can be included ... [only] if the effort can be spared from other essential commitments."[6]

The AEAF staff believed that bridges were difficult to bomb, and even those bombs that hit bridges often did little damage. Tedder agreed with Leigh-Mallory about bridges. He believed that Germans would prepare alternate means to cross rivers — pontoon bridges, barges and ferries.[7] Many bridges, like rail centers, were located in the most congested, historic sections of the communities they served; bombs that were aimed at bridges often fell on nearby towns, causing tragic loss of lives and property. Opponents of bridge bombing warned of the costs. A British railway expert estimated that bridge destruction would cost 1,200 tons of bombs per bridge.

However, other Overlord units joined the AAF in support of bridge interdiction. General Montgomery's 21st Army Group headquarters requested destruction of key bridges over the Seine before D-Day. One of Montgomery's subordinates suggested "this would be of more decisive value than pin-pricking on rail communications."[8] Lord Cherwell urged Churchill to voice support for bridge bombing. The commander of the RAF 2nd Tactical Air Force, Air Vice Marshal Sir Arthur Coningham, suggested that his fighter-bombers carry out a few trial bridge attacks.

Leigh-Mallory acceded to the clamor and grudgingly authorized a few experimental attacks on railway bridges "provided that such attacks were technically practicable, and for this purpose it appeared that 8th Air Force would be the best force to employ."[9]

This designation disturbed Spaatz; at the next meeting of the target committee at SHAEF, he expressed his conviction that fighter-bombers and medium bombers would be better bridge busters than heavy bombers.

Another group was working quietly but effectively to promote a bridge offensive. Four young AAF generals, each assigned to a different headquarters, billeted together. Brigadier General Frederick H. Smith, Jr., AEAF operations director, recalled that in "evening conclaves at 49 Harefield Road" in London they kept each other informed about various proposals. The plotters agreed that "the first bridge system that seemed amenable to cutting communications as well as not disclosing objectives, would be bridges along the Seine River from Rouen to Paris (see Map 1). There were some thirty-two bridges which crossed the Seine and were connecting links between the German Army in the Pas de Calais area and the German armed forces in the Normandy and Brittany areas."[10] Smith encouraged Ninth Air Force to prepare to bomb bridges.

Allied deception schemes aimed to convince Germans that the invasion was coming in the Pas de Calais. Attacks on bridges over the Seine between Paris and Rouen were compatible with this program and would hinder powerful German forces stationed north of the river when they attempted to move quickly to the beachhead. One of these bridges crossed the Seine near Vernon.

On May 6, AEAF ordered Ninth Air Force to carry out a trial bridge-bombing mission. The RAF's 2nd Tactical Air Force had already executed some effective bridge attacks. The 365th Fighter Group was one of the Ninth Air Force units chosen to bomb Seine bridges on May 7, 1944. It would attack three railroad bridges—a steel bridge at Vernon and two concrete bridges at Mantes-Gassicourt—"further attacks to await study of results obtained," in the words of the AEAF directive.

Twelve P-47s, each armed with two 1,000-pound, general-purpose bombs, fuses set at eight–eleven second delay, approached Vernon at 1157 hours. A fighter-bomber dove from 10,000 feet, leveled out and drove its bombs at high speed and pointblank range into an abutment supporting the north end of the bridge. The group commander, Colonel Lance Call, bombed next, then circled the area to direct subsequent attacks. The Thunderbolts flew through showers of light flak during their bomb runs. Colonel Call recorded the attack:

> The remaining bombers ... were brought down through the overcast individually. The bombing results were excellent and as the smoke cleared away from the sixth attack, the north end of the bridge collapsed into the water.... Two planes were already committed to the attack however, so they were ordered to hit the center bridge support, which they did with such effectiveness, that the entire north span

Map 1: River Seine Bridge Targets

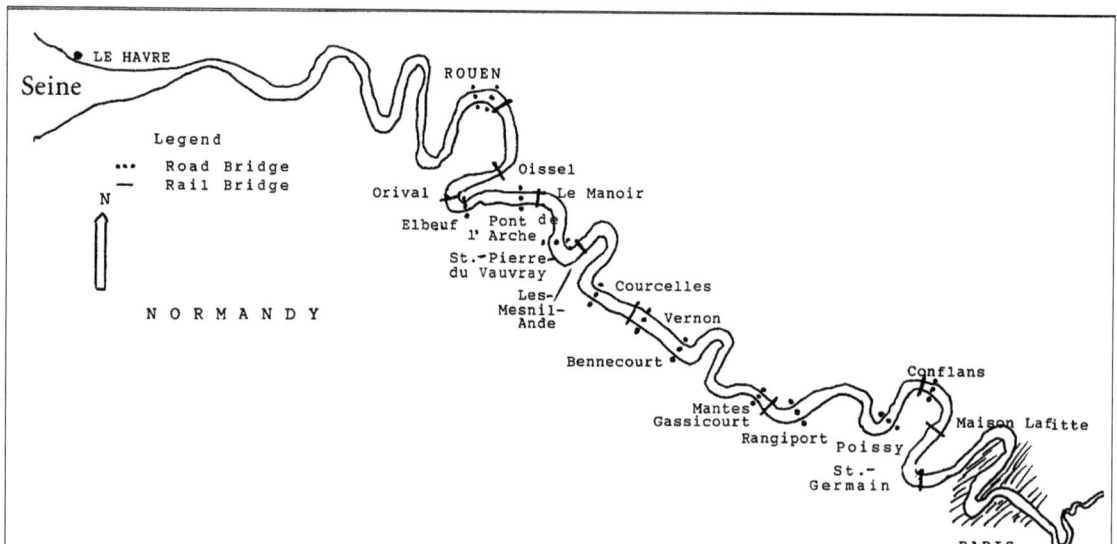

collapsed and crashed into the water, thus paralyzing not only rail transportation but probably water transportation as well.[11]

The 365th Fighter Group lost two aircraft to flak during the bridge attack; the successful mission had been neither unduly difficult nor excessively costly. Staffs at Ninth Air Force and USSTAF reacted to news of the bridge destruction at Vernon with near euphoria; it was seen as a striking vindication of the AAF's faith in bridge bombing.

To divert German attention away from the Seine, AEAF ordered attacks on bridges near the Belgian frontier on May 8. Brereton recorded with glee: "Thunderbolt fighter-bombers destroyed a double-track 8-span railroad bridge crossing the Oise at Hirson, France, and remained over the target to see the wreckage float down the river."[12]

The success of the bridge bombing at Vernon helped AAF commanders get approval for a full-scale bridge offensive. The 365th Fighter Group achieved spectacular results at Vernon, but its efforts to knock down a rail bridge at Mantes-Gassicourt brought only frustration. Concrete abutments, although hit repeatedly, deflected bombs so that they merely glanced off the structure. Sixteen Thunderbolts of the 365th hit the railroad bridge at Mantes again on May 9, but it withstood the onslaught. Clearly, much more study was needed to discover how to destroy bridges by bombing. AEAF had not been entirely wrong about the difficulties of bridge bombing. On May 10, the 365th again hit the sturdy rail bridge at Mantes, releasing bombs at pointblank range; when the last P-47 completed its bomb run, the tough bridge remained uncut.[13]

An intercept of a German radio message indicated that the bridge attacks of May 7–10 had attracted unwanted enemy attention to Lower Normandy. On May 10, Leigh-Mallory ordered a postponement of the bridge offensive; the pause lasted until May 24 when bridges were struck again. The intermission gave Allied ORS's time to work on problems associated with bridge bombing. Methods used to attack the bridge at Vernon would not always be effective. The bridge there had been particularly vulnerable to low-altitude, fighter-bomber attack, but most bridges could not be destroyed in this way. Medium bombers, even heavy bombers, would have to participate in the bridge offensive; bombs, fusing, aircraft and tactics would have to be selected according to the essential characteristics of each bridge.

The bridge offensive went on as scientists searched for ways to make it more effective. Allied air forces executed a major effort against Seine bridges in the two weeks before D-Day, learning by experience. Medium bombers and fighter-bombers struck bridges at Le Manoir and Poissy on May 26, and at Mantes-Gassicourt, Rouen, Meulan, Bennecourt and Conflans on May 30.[14] Fighter-bombers employed three approaches to bridge-bombing: zero altitude; a steep glide from about 4,000 feet, releasing bombs at 2,000 feet; and dive bombing from 8,000 feet, releasing bombs between 4,000 and 6,000 feet. Fuse settings were chosen so that bombs would be effective against the part of the bridge designated as most vulnerable.[15] Unless bombs of an appropriate size and fusing struck vulnerable parts of a bridge's structure, they would often bounce off the concrete or steel components to explode harmlessly in air or water.

Ninth Bomber Command played a major role in the bridge offensive. General Sam Anderson visited medium-bomber groups in Italy to study effective bridge-busting techniques. As Leigh-Mallory had forecast, most bridges were difficult targets, although not as costly as his advisors had estimated. The relatively small size of bridges made them hard to hit; flak took its toll of aircraft; cloud cover, smoke screens, dust and smoke from exploding bombs and ground fire all made bombing difficult. All this while ORS scientists labored to identify tactics and techniques that would help bomb crews place bombs on targets. Intelligence officers and photo-reconnaissance groups collected data on bridges that were likely to become targets.

Ninth Air Force medium bombers attacked bridges at Oissel and Namur on May 8. The attack order directed Ninth Bomber Command to bomb these bridges "until the destruction of at least one span was accomplished."[16] The mediums made bomb runs at altitudes of 10,000 to 12,000 feet along paths perpendicular to the bridges. The center of each bridge was the aiming point. Twenty-four B-26s attacked the rail bridge at Oissel causing no visible damage. Thirty-six mediums attacked the bridge again next day and the south section sustained a direct hit which holed its center span. Thirty-two mediums went after the Oissel bridge on May 10, and a center span of the south section collapsed. On these missions each B-26 dropped four 1000-pound general purpose bombs.[17]

The 365th Fighter Group escorted medium bombers to Oissel on May 10. Orbiting pilots judged the bombing to be poor by their standards: "The bombs hit in a wide circle around the bridge target." Many of the fighter pilots considered the operation to be a "waste of bombs."[18] The B-26 crews had a lot to learn about bombing bridges, but they learned fast. And they could deliver 2,000-pound bombs, a size required to cut some bridges. The mediums soon became premier bridgebusters. At times, their accuracy was extraordinary. Two B-26 groups attacked the Poissy highway bridge on May 26, dropping 134 bombs and getting eight hits. They completely destroyed the bridge.

After P-47s failed to knock down the arched masonry bridges at Mantes-Gassicourt, B-26 groups attacked them six times. During one of these strikes, two bombs hit the north bridge but ricocheted off, and two bombs with fast-fusing succeeded only in blowing off small chunks of masonry. The bomb that finally cut a span had a delay fuse. During their retreat in 1940, French forces had destroyed two spans of the south bridge. The replacement spans were evidently not as strong as the rest of the bridge; they were finally cut by B-26s. A highway bridge at Mantes-Gassicourt collapsed during an attack on May 30 by Ninth Bomber Command.[19]

The railroad bridge at Maisons-Lafitte was a sturdy structure. In a two-day period,

May 27–28, Allied air forces aimed a total of 324 tons of bombs at it with ten hits. Those bombs with instantaneous nose-fusing only succeeded in "dusting off the surface." Bombs with delay-fusing, however, caused significant damage to this important rail bridge near Paris.

Many of the bombs dropped on Seine bridges, even some that hit vital parts, failed to do any damage; but the campaign achieved its objective. General Anderson summarized Ninth Bomber Command's contribution:

> On eleven days between 19 May and 30 May 1944 the eleven groups of IX Bomber Command flew a total of 174 missions.... These missions were flown against the most important and most heavily defended targets within your radius of action and caused you your heaviest losses to date. In contrast to these losses, and completely overshadowing them, are the following results: BRIDGES, of 13 attacked 12 were destroyed....[20]

A report by the British Air Ministry on June 3, also expressed great satisfaction with the Seine bridge campaign: "The results have been outstandingly successful, far more successful in fact than was considered possible a few months ago...."[21] Nine railway bridges across the Seine below Paris were cut or damaged so severely as to be out of service. In addition, Allied air forces had seriously damaged twelve road bridges below Paris.

The historic city of Rouen is a transportation center with major rail, road and water connections to the interior, especially to Paris. The direct route for German forces moving from the Pas de Calais to the Normandy beachhead crossed the Seine at Rouen. This made the city's bridges high priority targets for Allied bombers. B-26s bombed road bridges at Rouen on May 30. They demolished the approach span of the upstream bridge with four hits. The downstream bridge suffered less damage. It was struck repeatedly by both fighter-bombers and mediums in the months of June and July with an inconclusive outcome, probably as a result of incorrect bomb fuses.

The 366th Fighter Group attacked the important rail bridge at Rouen on May 7 and on each of the next three days with poor results. On May 27, the 373rd Fighter Group dropped forty-five fused-instantaneous 1,000-pound bombs that hit the center, both ends and the right abutment; the Rouen bridge buckled.[22]

ORS's analyzed the Seine bridge offensive and promptly sent their findings to operational groups. ORS guidelines gave recommendations that concerned bomb size, fuse, aircraft, direction of attack and the vulnerable parts of various types of bridges. They urged groups to use the largest bomb their aircraft could carry: "Bombs are cheaper than sorties." Pilots were warned that intelligence dossiers on bridges were full of errors: "A well-planned attack requires that the *construction details* and surrounding territory be known." To execute successful low-level attacks, pilots had to know the whereabouts of power lines, flak batteries, trees and other obstacles. Most bridges required 1,000-pound or 2,000-pound bombs: "The 500-lb. G.P. will give such poor results that it should never be employed. This excludes the P-51 from heavy-bridge low-level operations."[23] Bridges suitable for minimum-altitude attack were those "of such a character that the bombs will penetrate and stick into vulnerable parts.... the things to look for are soft abutments surrounded by earth, or wooden piers. In general, such targets are rare among the permanent bridges." Proper fusing was critical in bridge attacks. Fuses had to function so that the bombs exerted maximum destructive force on vulnerable parts of bridges. Different sections of bridges required different fusing, but the IX TAC ORS concluded that "it is best to fuze for the part of the bridge which has the greatest vulnerable area."[24]

Allied invasion plans called for interdiction to reach a peak of intensity on D-Day.

Attacks on Seine bridges would direct the attention of German intelligence staffs to the Pas de Calais and Lower Normandy, but an elaborate deception program encouraged them to favor the Pas de Calais. Destruction of transportation facilities at this time would make it difficult for the Germans to complete repairs on them before the invasion started. Moreover, Allied air strength was so great that reconnaissance aircraft could monitor the most important transportation targets continuously.

On May 21, Allied fighters fanned out over northwest Europe to attack trains. Pilots claimed seventy locomotives destroyed. These attacks caused many deaths and injuries to civilians; some railway workers abandoned their jobs. Allied air forces dropped leaflets warning people not to use trains, but German authorities made certain that each train carried some civilians to discourage air attacks and sabotage.

During the week before D-Day, Eighth Air Force attacked airfields, aircraft factories, synthetic-oil plants, V-weapon sites, rail centers and coastal defenses. Penetrations deep into Germany forced the GAF to remain committed to defense of the homeland. On May 28, heavy bombers attacked synthetic-oil plants and airfields at Cologne, Zeitz, Königsberg and Magdeburg. The cost to the Eighth was high as an estimated 450 enemy fighters attacked the bomber formations. On May 29, 881 Eighth Air Force heavy bombers attacked the synthetic-oil plant at Politz, aircraft factories at Tutow, Leipzig, Cottbus, Sorau, Krzesiny and Poznan, and airfields at Höhn and Schneidemühl. Enemy fighter and flak action were intense; the Eighth lost forty-nine heavy bombers on these two days.[25]

In the pre-D-Day period the 467th Bombardment Group participated in Eighth Air Force operations. On April 10, its B-24s bombed an airfield at Bourges. The group's history calls this attack a "milk run"— an easy mission; 1,000-pound bombs made a shambles of the field, hangars and factory buildings. "We went out each day and all the early missions were against German airfield factories. Air crews were given only the information they needed to know. It was not until D-Day that we found out what a Noball or Crossbow target was — a V-1 launching platform on the coast of France — but during three months we went after them every time the weather was bad over Germany. Mostly we potholed the countryside about these installations and got few bombs on the small ski-launching ramps."[26]

The bombing offensive against French and Belgian rail centers ended in June, except for a few attacked as part of the interdiction campaign. Early in June, SHAEF G-2 distributed a top-secret paper summarizing the results of the air offensives and making recommendations for future uses of air power to disrupt enemy supply and transportation activities. The paper expressed disillusionment with the transportation campaign. Attrition — wearing down the transportation system as a whole — would not be effective unless "virtual total destruction of the system is achieved and maintained." This was hardly possible even if the Allies could stomach its terrible costs. Rail center attacks "failed to so reduce the railway operating facilities as to impair the enemy's ability to move up reinforcements and maintain his forces in the West." The paper also expressed confidence in interdiction, provided "repeat attacks [are made] on points that can be repaired quickly ... [and] less frequent attacks at points where repair is slow." It recommended two lines of interdiction so that the enemy is "forced to revert to long road hauls with all its problems and what are for him, especially evil consequences." The paper described some of these consequences. About 180 trucks would be needed to match the load-moving capability of a single train. "Thus, it is clearly most uneconomical to have a great number of vehicles and men tied down to lifting large quantities of supplies over long distances." The Allies would soon have the truth of this assertion demonstrated to them painfully.

A German soldier and civilian study the Fieseler aircraft factory near Bettenhausen after a bombing by Eighth Air Force. (Courtesy of the National Archives and Records Services.)

Two highly damaging effects of a railway shortage would soon be felt by German armored forces: tanks would suffer extensive wear on road marches; the German fuel shortage would become critical.[27]

Although the oil offensive had barely started, SHAEF G-2 had evidence to show that the "recent series of attacks on synthetic plants in Germany and refineries in the Balkans had provoked immediate repercussions." German headquarters had issued orders for "even more restricted use of fuel of all types both for the Army and the Air Force…. It seems clear from a recent study of the enemy's oil situation, that he is facing an oil crisis which, with our assistance, can possibly be made a collapse." The oil and interdiction offensives, moreover, were seen to be distinctly complementary: "By denying the enemy the use of rail transport, we shall be increasing his vital need for fuel in the west, and by attacking oil production we shall be reducing the supply; the two are mutually supporting."[28]

The air campaigns designed to prepare the way for invasion forces paused in June, and Allied air forces turned their attention to missions of direct support for ground forces attempting to establish a beachhead in Normandy.

Chapter 11

Air Support for the Landings in Normandy

A dispute erupted at SHAEF a few days before D-Day about the plan to drop airborne forces in Normandy. Leigh-Mallory warned Eisenhower that the 101st and 82nd Airborne Divisions would be butchered if they carried out their scheduled landings south of Utah Beach. He estimated that the casualty rate could go as high as 70 percent. Eisenhower later described his feelings about the issue:

> It would be difficult to conceive of a more soul-racking problem. If my technical expert was correct, then the planned operation was worse than stubborn folly, because even at the enormous cost predicted we could not gain the principal object of the drop. Moreover, if he was right, it appeared that the attack on Utah Beach was hopeless, and this meant that the whole operation suddenly acquired a degree of risk, even fool-hardiness, that presaged a gigantic failure, possibly Allied defeat in Europe.[1]

Ultimately, Eisenhower decided to allow the airborne operation to go forward as planned. It was essential to capture the port of Cherbourg quickly; this required a landing at Utah Beach and a rapid drive inland over causeways secured by airborne troops. On the eve of D-Day, Eisenhower mingled with soldiers of an American airborne division as they boarded their aircraft.

Transport aircraft of Ninth Troop Carrier Command dropped paratroopers of the 101st Division near Utah Beach in the general area of Sainte-Mère-Église beginning at 0200 on June 6. Glider-borne forces of the 101st landed in the same area at the same time. At approximately 0130 hours, paratroopers of the 82nd Division jumped from 369 aircraft west of the Merderet River, which coursed generally parallel to Utah Beach and five miles inland. Another part of the 82nd, in fifty-two gliders, landed in the same area at 0400 hours. Additional gliders brought reinforcements and equipment on the evening of D-Day and morning of D+1.

To protect the airborne operations, Allied air forces attacked searchlights and anti-aircraft batteries and provided fighter cover over the Channel and enemy territory.

Ninth Troop Carrier Command had not reached a peak of proficiency by D-Day. Like other parts of Ninth Air Force, its buildup had been hectic, but unlike them it had not had opportunities to sharpen its techniques gradually in combat operations. D-Day conditions confronted Ninth Troop Carrier Command with severe challenges. More than nine hundred transports assembled in darkness smoothly but transport pilots encountered problems on flights to drop zones in Normandy that some of them were unable to handle competently. Anti-aircraft fire, continuous and heavy, endangered the low-flying

Map 2: Normandy Lodgment Area

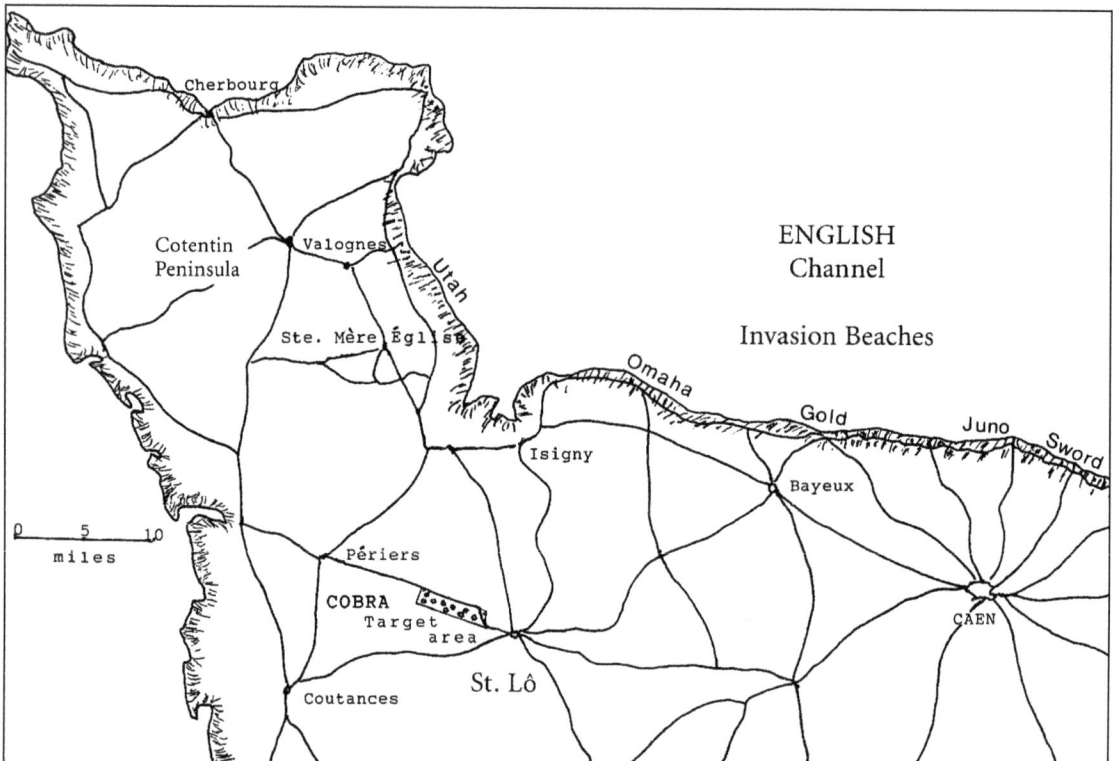

planes. Fog and clouds interfered with identification of landing areas. Some airborne troops came down far from their planned drop zones. A few pilots flew too fast, making parachute drops exceedingly hazardous. In violation of orders, some pilots broke formation to climb to higher altitudes. Despite difficult conditions, glider forces carried out their mission successfully: forty-eight of fifty-two gliders landed within two miles of their planned drop zones. They suffered moderate casualties although some of the landings were extremely rough. The assistant division commander of the 101st Division lost his life in a glider crash.[2]

By early afternoon of D-Day, U.S. airborne soldiers had captured vital causeways leading inland from Utah Beach through marshy terrain. The U.S. Seventh Corps, commanded by Major General J. Lawton Collins, landed on Utah Beach on D-Day, then drove southwest to cut off the Cotentin Peninsula. The U.S. Fifth Corps went ashore on Omaha Beach and moved toward St. Lô, with the British Second Army on its left flank.

An official U.S. Army history records that: "The airborne troops had done their job well and the 4th Division therefore had little difficulty getting ashore."[3] Casualties among airborne soldiers were high but not as high as Leigh-Mallory had feared they would be. Soon after D-Day he apologized to Eisenhower for expressing doubts about the operation and thereby adding to the supreme commander's worries.

Major General Maxwell Taylor commanded the 101st Division and jumped with it into Normandy on D-Day. He later wrote a report sharply critical of troop-carrier pilots. He noted that the confidence of airborne troops in Ninth Troop Carrier Command was low and would remain so until those pilots "who failed conspicuously [were replaced] …

and the proficiency of groups to navigate accurately through cloud and bad weather has improved."[4]

Brigadier General James M. Gavin, assistant commander of the 82nd Division, seconded Taylor's criticisms. Some of the troop-carrier pilots had "climbed as high as 2000 feet and stepped up their speeds to 150 miles an hour.... This resulted in severe opening shocks and loss of equipment on the part of the jumpers."[5]

In his report of the airborne operation, Major General Matthew Ridgeway concentrated on positive results achieved by his division: "Enemy reaction to the landing of the 82nd Airborne Division in the Normandy area was prompt and severe, but from the time the first member landed until 33 days later, when the Division was finally relieved, every mission was accomplished and no ground gained was ever relinquished."[6]

In the hours before dawn on D-Day, RAF Bomber Command attacked ten heavy coastal batteries in the assault area. Soon after dawn medium bombers blasted coastal artillery emplacements and beach obstacles. Eighth Air Force heavy bombers attempted to hit selected points in the beach defense system beginning at H-hour minus thirty-nine minutes. All bomber aircraft would refuel and rearm after primary missions to be ready for other operations as directed.

Beginning at H-hour, fighter-bombers assaulted twelve artillery positions in the rear of the landing beaches while others waited in reserve for use against targets of opportunity or in answer to requests for air support from ground troops. Two light bomber squadrons could lay smoke screens during the assault, if needed.

P-38s, easily recognized by friend and foe, flew cover for the sea armada. Their greatest danger came from trigger-happy Allied naval gunners. They carried out these operations over the Channel all day long, from sunup till after dark, for ten days. When the time came for one squadron to return to base, another took its place. No enemy planes were sighted.

Allied tactical air forces harassed enemy reserves day and night; fighter-bombers disrupted rail and road transportation. Reconnaissance aircraft monitored enemy forces moving toward the lodgment area.[7]

Eighth Air Force was supposed to bomb beach fortifications as Allied landing craft approached the shore. The mission worried USSTAF; bombs could fall on friendly forces. Overcast skies magnified the danger. Employment of bombers in this kind of operation caused discord between air and ground forces. Many airmen believed it was a misuse of air power for heavy bombers to attempt to do a job that artillery could do better. If a battle situation was desperate enough to warrant such an operation, airmen wanted bomb lines to be set thousands of yards away from friendly forces. Ground commanders usually objected to such large safety zones; they wanted their troops to close with the enemy quickly after a bombardment. They accepted the risks of bombs falling on Allied soldiers, but this did not prevent some of them from disclaiming responsibility for mishaps or charging airmen with incompetence when accidents did happen.

Bad weather complicated Eighth Air Force D-Day missions. Three heavy bomber divisions comprising 1,361 aircraft assembled in the predawn hours. A force so large had to attack its targets in waves with precise timing. Bombing of fortified gun positions and strong points had to be completed not later than ten minutes before landing craft reached the beaches. Every air crew received stern warnings about the danger of bombing "short." Special orders forbade testing machine guns over the Channel; there would be no firing at aircraft. Takeoffs would be executed on schedule "or else."

Eighth Air Force had had little experience with constraints such as these on missions over Germany. Its heavy bombers flew 2,362 sorties in four attacks on targets near the beachhead on D-Day; Eighth Fighter Command flew patrols and fighter-bomber missions against ground targets.

GAF opposition was light; flak brought down five B-24s and twenty-six fighters. On their first D-Day mission, 659 B-17s and 418 B-24s dropped 2,851 tons of general-purpose bombs and 245 tons of fragmentation bombs on beachhead targets.

Thick cloud cover over the landing beaches made it extremely difficult for Eighth Air Force bomber crews to identify assigned targets, but no bombs fell on Allied troops; in fact, most bombs fell inland from the beaches, some as much as three miles. Airmen were exceedingly cautious. Few shore batteries could be destroyed by bombs regardless of accuracy; massive concrete structures protected them.[8]

Allied air forces battered rail centers, bridges, tunnels and railroad track to disrupt rail transportation. Leigh-Mallory believed strongly that a greater air effort should be made to interfere with German movements by road. He proposed bombing certain French towns — key road centers — to create rubble that would slow German moves. Spaatz and Tedder denounced the proposal, but Leigh-Mallory defended it with his usual tenacity: "That is a thing from which I personally will never be deflected," he wrote in his journal; "I have had all sorts of pressure put upon me to attack airfields and other targets.... My idea is to create blocks in towns and villages that form nodal points, and keep them blocked by repeated attacks."[9]

General Brereton also opposed the scheme, he recorded that "serious differences of opinion arose, when Leigh-Mallory outlined his plan ... to employ all the heavies of the RAF and Eighth [Air Force] as well as mediums in tactical area.... The allocation of the mass of bombers on the type of targets indicated for the purpose of attempting to block the roads and highways is also doomed to failure in my opinion."[10]

Discussion of the "chokepoints" plan generated heat at an AEAF meeting, and Leigh-Mallory lost his temper. After the meeting, he protested to Tedder about the latter's failure to support him in arguments with "Americans who have already shown themselves to be antagonistic to the Plan."[11]

When the issue came to Eisenhower for a decision, he supported Leigh-Mallory with the stipulation that warning leaflets be dropped on targeted towns in advance of bombing. Doolittle received permission to broadcast warnings to towns an hour before towns were to be bombed, a practice made feasible by the Allies' air supremacy.

During the Battle of Normandy, Allied air forces dropped more than forty million leaflets into the lodgment area; some of them warned inhabitants of ancient Norman towns to "Disperse out to the countryside. You do not have a minute to lose."[12]

The chokepoints offensive brought death and devastation to towns in the lodgment area. Bombers hit Caen repeatedly and demolished more than 75 percent of its buildings. Only ten residents remained in St. Lô when American forces entered it. Soldiers called it "the capital of ruins." Thousands of civilians died in these operations which were of doubtful value to Allied forces. Road and rail chokepoints close to the assault area were objectives of other missions of Eighth Air Force heavies on D-Day. In spite of overcast weather, it was considered imperative to block road and rail movements of the enemy. Leaflets warned residents of towns to be bombed of imminent danger. Targets included Thury-Harcourt, Vire, Lisieux, Falaise, Villers-Bocage, St. Lô, Coutances, Forêt de Cerisy, Caen and St. Sauvier. Thick cloud cover concealed most towns, and many bombers returned with their bombs or bombed secondary targets.

Rubble in a street of St. Sauveur, France. (U.S. Air Force Photo Collection [Neg. No. 73205 AC] courtesy of National Air and Space Museum, Smithsonian Institution.)

Caen, an important road and rail center, was near the beachhead; it was attacked repeatedly; seventy-three B-24s bombed the city, fifty-six of them through the overcast using radar. In Eighth Air Force's fourth mission of the day, 736 heavy bombers again attacked "chokepoint" towns." An operations report summarized the mission: "Results were good at Vire and Coutances, fair at St. Lô, Pont-l'Evêque, Argentan, and poor at Pontaubault and Thury-Harcourt."[13]

On D-Day, Eighth Fighter Command attacked 17 railway and road bridges, 10 marshaling yards, 4 railway junctions, a highway intersection, a tunnel and a dam; its score came to 21 locomotives destroyed and 34 damaged, damage to 216 trucks, 15 tank cars, 76 boxcars, 19 armored vehicles, 2 barges and 2 tugboats. Fighters strafed a wide range of targets including warehouses, radar towers, flak towers, barracks, troop concentrations, artillery positions and staff cars.

Interdiction increased in intensity after D-Day as the threat of compromising the secrecy of the landing beaches diminished. The Seine and Loire rivers were part of a ring of interdiction established by Allied air forces to seal off the battle area (see Map 3). In the "gap" between the two rivers, bridges were important interdiction targets at Cérisy, Nogent-le-Rotrou, Maintenon, Chartres, Cloyes and Beaugency. Bridges on the Loire between Nantes and Orléans were targeted for destruction. The list included bridges at Chalonnes, Port-Boullet, Angers, Cinq Mars, Tours, Montlouis and Blois. RAF Bomber Command damaged a tunnel at Saumur.

Loire bridges could not be attacked until D-Day for security reasons. The effort to cut them provided a partial test of the contention that air action could isolate a battlefield

Map 3: The Seine-Loire Line of Interdiction

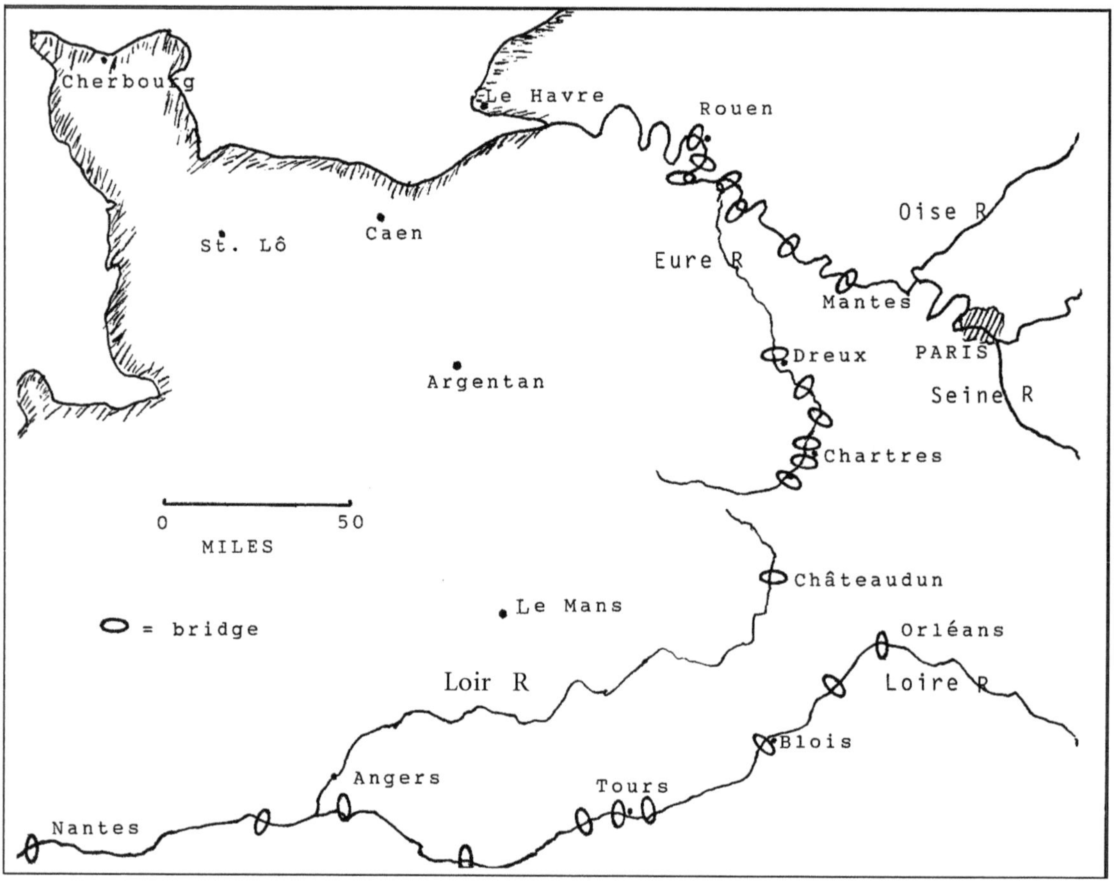

in a short period after the start of an invasion. Distances to Loire bridges from U.K. bases made it difficult for mediums or fighter-bombers to attack them. This, and the wide expanse of the river, made them appropriate targets for heavy day bombers. In anticipation, Spaatz alerted Doolittle early in May to be ready for this mission: "A task for which the entire Eighth Air Force will be prepared to accomplish on D-Day, or immediately thereafter, is the destruction of rail and road bridges of the Loire at least from Nantes to Tours inclusive."[14] Unfavorable weather delayed the campaign. As Leigh-Mallory had warned, bad weather could neutralize the Allies' great air power. Storms raged with a severity rarely seen in Europe at that time of year.

In spite of bad weather, Eighth Air Force attempted to bomb Loire bridges on June 7; one hundred aircraft returned without bombing. Next day, heavy bombers hit bridges at Tours, Nantes, Cinq Mars, Angers and Orléans. The Eighth continued to pound bridges on the Loire whenever weather permitted. On June 11, 640 heavies attacked bridges and airfields; some dropped bombs on alternate targets or returned with their bombs. They were able to make bomb runs with visual sighting at Beauvais and Blois. To execute some of these attacks, aircraft bombed from as low as 6,000 feet.[15]

B-24s of the 467th Bombardment Group attacked a bridge at Blois from an altitude so low that bombardiers could see the target; this was a challenging approach, as the Group's history recorded: "Hitting a bridge with heavy bombers who customarily drop

Cut railroad bridge at Tours. (U.S. Air Force photograph.)

from a high altitude and lay a large pattern is a difficult thing." At Blois the 467th "let down below the cloud deck and made a visual run in three ship elements. The bombing was excellent."[16]

Perseverance paid off for Eighth Air Force. Minutes of the AEAF commanders' meeting on June 16 record that Doolittle reported that his heavy bombers had "destroyed seven Bridges on the Loire ... upsetting the best theoretical thinking on this subject!"[17]

Ninth Air Force medium bombers attacked targets in the Utah Beach area on D-Day. Thick, low cloud blankets forced most of the B-26s to bomb from levels ranging from 3,500 to 7,000 feet. This made them vulnerable to flak, and losses were higher than expected.[18] Soon after D-Day, Ninth Bomber Command resumed interdiction operations by hitting bridges and embankments in the Paris-Orléans gap, on the Seine near Paris, and within the lodgment area. Medium bombers hit an important bridge at Pontaubault— gateway to Brittany— on June 8, but damaged only an embankment. The center span of the Coutances viaduct fell on June 10. An attack on a rail bridge at Chartres on June 15 blocked traffic. Allied fighter-bombers attacked a sturdy bridge at Oissel, near Rouen, repeatedly, but German repair crews kept it in service.[19] Energetic efforts by Germans to repair bridges testified to their importance. Allied air forces monitored bridges and attacked them again, if necessary, to keep them blocked. Two spans of a bridge at Maison Lafitte collapsed into the river after an attack by mediums on June 24. Next day, B-26s cut a viaduct at Chartres. Table 5 shows the scale of effort by Ninth Air Force in June.

Table 5: Ninth Air Force Operations, June 1944

Operation Type	Aircraft Attacking	Medium Bombers Lost	Fighter Bombers Lost
Marshaling Yards	2,357	5	3
Bridges	2,923	6	6
Rail Cutting	2,204	1	5

The Loire bridges were near the extremity of the tactical radius of the B-26 from the U.K., but they were such important interdiction targets that Ninth Bomber Command received orders to attack some of them as soon as possible. Between July 7 and July 31, General Anderson's mediums struck seven Loire bridges. Four attacks on a bridge at Nantes produced only minor damage, but the fifth attack holed its center. In a single attack, B-26s cut a bridge at Cinq Mars. Mediums hit a bridge at Tours four times in July causing substantial damage, but the enemy kept it in service by extraordinary efforts. Overall, Ninth Bomber Command cut or effectively blocked nineteen of the thirty-five bridges it attacked in July.

Fighter-bombers did most of the track-cutting. The effort on July 6 was representative of the period a month after D-Day: they executed twenty-three rail cuts and destroyed thirteen locomotives and fifty-one boxcars.[20]

Interdiction had to be coordinated with operations of the armies it was designed to assist. Indeed, this was one of its major strengths. When Allied forces broke through the German lines late in July and raced across France in pursuit of German forces in pell-mell retreat, Allied ground commanders requested a halt to attacks on bridges and some rail targets. Air attacks on Loire bridges ceased on August 2.

Planners tried to orchestrate interdiction so that it did not destroy installations that Allied armies were soon likely to need. German forces were in such disarray that their demolition efforts were erratic. Resistance fighters managed to de-arm some explosive charges set to blow up important installations.

Serious questions remained unanswered for decades about the effectiveness of various Allied air campaigns in support of the Normandy Invasion — the transportation campaign, interdiction, bombing towns to block their roads with rubble, bombing V-weapons launch sites, the oil offensive — but few observers, not even ground commanders, criticized the close tactical air support given by IX TAC and XIX TAC of Ninth Air Force starting on D-Day.

Chapter 12

Close Air Support for Invasion Forces

Interdiction and strategic air strikes at targets inside Germany gave crucial assistance to Overlord, but after D-Day the immediate needs of General Eisenhower's armies in Normandy took precedence over other air campaigns. The primary responsibility of Ninth Tactical Air Command (see Diagram 3) was to provide air support for General Bradley's First Army. Bradley rarely had a good word to say about Brereton, but he appreciated Quesada. Years later he remembered Quesada's success in air support:

> As a result of our inability to get together with air in England, we went into France almost totally untrained in air-ground cooperation. But we also went in with an offsetting advantage in a breezy young major general named Elwood P. Quesada....
>
> He succeeded brilliantly in a task where many airmen before him failed, partly because he was willing to dare anything once. Unlike most airmen who viewed ground support as a bothersome diversion to war in the sky, Quesada approached it as a vast new frontier waiting to be explored.[1]

Quesada *was* an innovator. He welcomed opportunities to use new equipment and tactics. IX TAC pioneered the use of napalm, airborne rockets and radar controlled dive bombing. Some of Quesada's approaches were unorthodox. Unable to acquire efficient radio gear through regular AAF channels, he sent a member of his staff to New York to buy FM radio equipment in the civilian market. His emissary returned with transmitters and receivers. "We tried them and, by God, they worked," Quesada told an interviewer, "So we had an FM communications net that was just unrivaled."[2]

An Army scientific advisor reported that "the benefits of Pete Quesada's inspired leadership are increasingly evident in the development of radar control in the IX TAC.... The flexibility of the system is such that any request from the ground forces can be acted on on very short notice and the fighter-bombers brought to the target area with a minimum of delay and confusion."[3] Quesada wrote to a friend about the radar: "We commandeered two MEWS [microwave early-warning sets] ... for control of our aircraft.... We lived off of that radar...."[4]

On D-Day, IX TAC and XIX TAC fighter-bombers of Ninth Air Force gave ground forces critical help. General Brereton recalled that "the Omaha Beach landings were in a critical state to the point of catastrophe."[5] Three fighter-bomber groups pounded enemy artillery positions throughout the daylight hours. Quesada, too, believed that fighter-

Diagram 3: Ninth Tactical Air Command

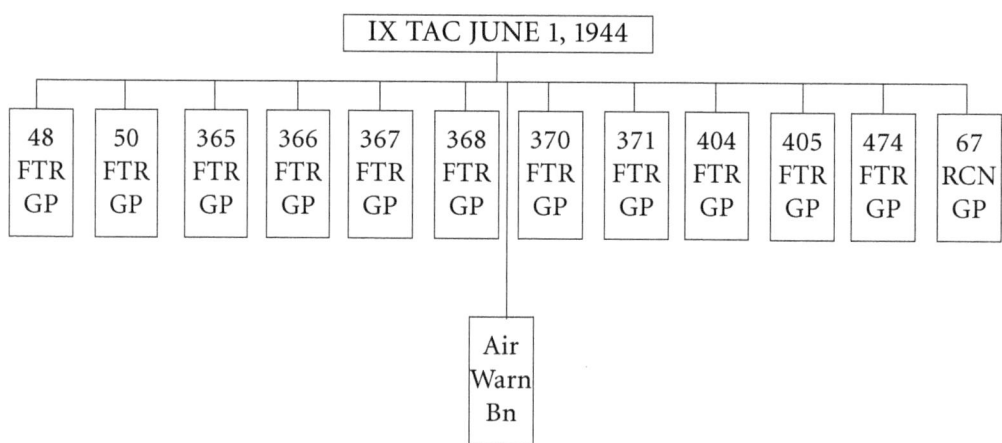

bombers were in large part responsible for the survival of troops on Omaha Beach on D-Day: "History may show they saved the day."⁶

Some of the troubles on Omaha Beach could be traced to AEAF neglect — at least General Vandenberg thought so. On D-Day, Vandenburg learned that the AEAF fighter-control center was not paying close attention to the needs of American forces. He noticed that the AEAF battle-room map had front lines marked for all British beaches "but that there was not a single mark on either of the American beaches." He later described how he went "over there and, as Deputy Commander AEAF, express[ed] forcibly my general disapproval at the way things were being handled." He got the attention of AEAF staff and "demanded more help for American soldiers."⁷

Quesada directed air support for First Army from Bradley's headquarters in the beachhead. Fighter aircraft employed rockets, bombs, napalm and machine-gun fire against a wide range of targets. They attacked mortar and artillery positions, fuel dumps, arms stockpiles, vehicle pools, tanks, railroad equipment, bridges, tunnels, ferries, barges, automobiles, trucks, horse-drawn vehicles and soldiers on foot and on bicycles. At all times, fighter-bomber groups had to be ready to engage GAF aircraft that intruded into the lodgment area. AAF engineers carved airfields out of Normandy's rich soil, often within range of enemy guns.⁸

Ninth Tactical Air Command's P-47s bombed from dives, glides or low-level, depending on the target, flak intensity and other conditions. Quesada described IX TAC operations in a letter to a friend: "We have sometimes carried two 1000-pound bombs plus extension tank [droptank] and on some occasions carried three 1000-pound bombs.... I am quite proud of our ability to cut railroad tracks and destroy bridges with a minimum of sorties. We can keep the rail-roads in any one area cut by dispatching small flights to various points and ramming bombs into the embankment from low level."⁹

Ninth Tactical Air Command fighters attacked railroad-repair equipment whenever it was spotted. They strafed and bombed trains ceaselessly; Quesada reported that strafing was effective and bombs dropped from low level made "a helluva mess that requires a long time to clean up. We throw the bomb into the locomotive as well as the trains...." He felt great pride in the armored-column cover technique IX TAC had developed from scratch. Its success depended on the installation of VHF radio sets in the tanks and putting Air Force officers in the leading tanks. As it turned out, the aircraft directed the tanks

Quesada and crewman pumping gasoline. (U.S. Air Force photograph.)

frequently; observers agreed that the improvised method contributed significantly to the rapid advances made by First Army in August.

Some doctrinaire AAF officers criticized Quesada for the intensive air support IX TAC gave ground forces. Table 6 gives a summary of this activity, adapted from an unpublished history of IX TAC.[10] "I was subjected to some ... ridicule for using air power for this purpose, Quesada revealed; "My answer was: this is where the fighting is.... I'm not willing to waste lives and use air power in an ineffective way, but this is effective...."[11]

Table 6: IX TAC Results, D-Day to December

Targets	Destroyed	Probably Destroyed	Damaged
Locomotives	835	39	215
Armored Vehicles	1,873	208	979
Motor Transports	1,234	626	2,939
Horse-drawn Vehicles	2,083	22	205
Barges	226	23	145
Railway Cars	6,712	463	5,178
Bridges	207	21	279
Supply Dumps	120	9	53
Track Cuts	1,685	—	—

Ninth Air Force was a powerful tactical air force with 1,098 medium and light bombers, 1,675 fighter-bombers, 202 reconnaissance aircraft and 1,295 troop-carrier transports.[12]

Brereton recalled some of the lessons Ninth Air Force had learned. Its education involved issues that had been hotly debated in the planning stages of Overlord. Combat experience proved that rail-cutting was effective. Bombing rail centers was wasteful, and if it delayed military rail movements at all it was only for brief periods. Armed reconnaissance "interferes seriously with the movement of even small bodies of troops and transport," Brereton recorded; "Bombing of towns does not constitute a reliable road block to enemy movements."[13]

At an AEAF commanders' meeting on June 29, Brereton denounced the bombing of towns. From his inspections of French villages, he concluded that their destruction to create road blocks was "ineffectual, producing no effective result beyond destroying property and killing friendly inhabitants." To clear a path through rubble the enemy "simply brings out a bulldozer...."[14]

Leigh-Mallory had forecast and prepared for a major air battle over the Normandy beachhead, but it did not happen. Few Allied pilots saw enemy aircraft over the Channel or the Normandy beachhead. P-38s flew cover for Allied ships. Their distinctive silhouette helped Allied naval gunners recognize them as friends, although some were fired on just the same. When it became clear that the GAF would not endanger the Allied landings, fighters providing the air umbrella received other, more useful, assignments.

Arnold was in the U.K. at the time of the landings in Normandy and heard many complaints about the waste of air power. He blamed it on the RAF. He wrote in his journal:

> German Air Force not so hot.... I have doubted R.A.F., G2 and A2 reports all along. Now it appears that:
> a. German Air Force does not have numbers.
> b. Does not have crews.
> c. Lacks training.
> d. Does not have will to fight.
> e. Has lost its morale.[15]

No one deplored the miscalculations of GAF strength more than Arnold. He had denied urgent requests from other theaters for desperately needed aircraft so that Overlord would have the air strength that intelligence estimates showed it needed. He suspected that the British doctored intelligence data for their own purposes. Arnold recorded a number of complaints about the RAF:

> We accept the R.A.F. estimate blindly.... What have the R.A.F. done to defeat the G.A.F. since Battle of Britain?
> Have they tried to increase range of their Fighters?
> Did they give us any encouragement when we said that we were going to force the G.A.F. to fight us and we were going to defeat and destroy them?
> Did they keep the belly tanks on the P-51s we gave them? No. Have they used any to penetrate into the heart of Germany? No.
> Could they put additional gas in their Spitfires? No... ... ...
> And yet they tell the world the strength of the G.A.F. and we accept their figures.[16]

The failure of intelligence agencies to accurately assess GAF strength is puzzling given the excellent source of data — Ultra — available to them. But Ultra was controlled by the British (who had developed it), which may be what reinforced Arnold's suspicions. Until D-Day, and even beyond, intelligence reports continued to warn of a serious enemy air menace in the west. On May 25, the Joint Intelligence Committee estimated that the GAF had 2,350 aircraft.[17] A report by GAF historians made soon after D-Day, however, claimed that Luftflotte 3 (the GAF force in the west) had only 319 aircraft available on June 6.[18]

For months before and after D-Day, Allied ships, supplies and equipment choked ports of England. Arnold called it "a bombardier's dream." As he flew over the beachhead, he saw hundreds of ships anchored offshore. "What a field day it would have been for the German Air Force," he wrote, "had there been one."[19] Some of Arnold's journal notes are intemperate — there was a GAF. The AAF had air supremacy, but the GAF could inflict painful losses at times. The experience of the 474th Fighter Group on August 25 is a case in point. Twenty-four P-38s went on a mission to attack airfields near Laon. More than forty German fighters bounced them. Eight Lightnings went down.[20]

Air supremacy brought priceless benefits to Allied forces, both air and ground. It permitted air forces to employ their power with optimum flexibility and effectiveness. It sharply restricted enemy ground forces and forced them to put enormous effort into activities designed to protect themselves against air attacks. In daylight hours on clear days, Allied fighter-bombers patrolled ceaselessly. German artillery and mortar units operated without air spotters and had to take elaborate precautions to protect their positions from Allied assaults. German vehicles moving in daylight were almost certain to be attacked. Many German soldiers were casualties of air attack, including Field Marshal Rommel. Army units could move only during hours of darkness or on overcast days. This drastically curtailed the ability of commanders to organize reserve forces for launching offensives and responding to crises. German forces had to expend large amounts of energy on construction of fortifications to protect important equipment and supply dumps from air attacks. Supplies had to be carried long distances at night, which consumed energy and gasoline. Frequent movements to disperse and conceal vehicles shortened their operational life and burned gasoline. Tracked vehicles suffered excessive wear from long road marches. The morale of German soldiers and their physical condition deteriorated from lack of sleep, tiring work on fortifications and the realization that they had virtually no air force to help them.

Allied troops dispensed with many routine safeguards against air attacks. The advantages that air supremacy gave them were opposite of the handicaps it inflicted on the Germans. A striking sign of Allied confidence in its immunity from air attack was the brightly colored tent near Bradley's headquarters that sheltered some of IX TAC's staff. The supreme commander gave his vote of confidence when he squeezed into a fighter piloted by Quesada for a flight over the beachhead. It was an incredibly foolish escapade for two generals acting like truants.

Ground-attack operations included Eighth Air Force fighters, although their primary obligation was strategic bombing. Eighth Fighter Command's history describes some of these activities during the invasion. On a "typical day," August 12, at the height of the Battle of France, Eighth Fighter Command flew 1,326 sorties on forty-six missions. Fighter-bombers, mostly P-51s, "burned, riddled with fifty caliber … 2,636 railroad cars, 359 locomotives, 112 ammunition cars, 464 trucks, 362 oil cars, 9 oil tanks, 9 oil barges, 306 vehicles, 15 bridges, 7 roundhouses, 13 buildings, 4 water towers, 19 aircraft, and many other targets."[21]

P-51s of the 4th Fighter Group attacked a truck convoy near Rouen on D-Day. Flak brought down four Mustangs. On June 7, the group, armed with 500-pound bombs, followed a rail line from Dieppe to Fougères until a bridge and four locomotives were sighted. The operations report claimed "there were two fair hits out of six on the bridge and one out of 12 on the locos. No question the boys were better fighter than bomber pilots." Flak knocked down one of the Mustangs on the flight home.[22]

The port of Cherbourg at the tip of the Cotentin Peninsula was a major objective of U.S. forces. SHAEF's planners hoped its docks, when captured, could be used to move some of the supplies needed by Allied armies pouring ashore in Normandy. Hitler ordered Cherbourg's commander to hold out to "the last cartridge." Strong fortifications protected German troops; artillery in concrete casemates could fire on every approach to the port.

On June 21, Major General J. Lawton Collins, Seventh Corps commander, ordered his forces to capture the port. He requested a powerful air bombardment and strafing assault to soften the enemy's resistance. There was hopeful talk of the air forces "pulverizing" the defenses. It would be the first large-scale, coordinated, air-ground operation in the Normandy campaign executed to capture a major strongpoint. It would test the ability of the air forces to provide massive close support on short notice.

Planning for the operation took place in England at various air forces headquarters. Collins did not send any staff officers to participate in the planning sessions. Commanders of U.S. divisions assigned to attack Fortress Cherbourg received copies of the air plan on June 22, a few hours before the start of the operation.

RAF rocket-firing Typhoons and Mustangs opened the air assault. Twelve groups of Ninth Air Force fighter-bombers attacked next. Ninth Bomber Command had a difficult assignment: its mediums tried to bomb eleven exceptionally strong fortified positions. Altogether, 557 fighter-bombers and 396 mediums participated in the operation. Thirty-eight Allied aircraft were lost in the effort, one of them a medium bomber. This ratio testified to the effectiveness of light flak against fighter-bombers.[23]

It was not likely that such an operation, carried out with forces inadequately trained for it, would be executed flawlessly. As it turned out, results fell far below expectations, which certainly had been too high. Only a small part of the area "pulverized" by the air attacks was in Allied hands by nightfall on June 22. Adding to the disappointment, Allied aircraft caused casualties in some Seventh Corps units. Angry air and ground commanders

Train under attack by the 363rd Fighter Group. (U.S. Air Force photograph.)

leveled charges of incompetence at each other. Airmen claimed that infantry did not follow up the bombardment promptly and aggressively.

Surveys of the Cherbourg campaign found little positive to report about the air attack; analysts concluded that its major achievement was to damage the morale of the defenders. Advocates of air power had often made this claim, and by now it had a hollow ring. However, the claim did receive backing from the enemy commander; after his capture he stated that confusion and panic hurt his defense more than the physical impact of bombing on defenses and personnel.[24]

General Collins's forces made only small gains on the day of the air assault on Cherbourg. Hard fighting continued during the next few days. On June 25, a naval armada pounded German positions. Not until June 29, did German soldiers in the last pockets of resistance surrender. Before surrender, German engineers thoroughly demolished the port's cargo-handling facilities; it was "a masterful job ... the most complete, intensive and best planned ... in history."[25] It took months of effort to clear the port, but by November more than half the cargo landed in France for American forces came through Cherbourg.

The primary objective of Overlord's air offensives in the period of January–July 1944 was to disrupt German anti-invasion efforts. No estimate of the effectiveness of these campaigns would be complete without testimony from German leaders who had to cope with Allied air power.

Chapter 13

Counter-Invasion and Resistance Operations

GAF plans to crush the invasion called for the transfer of fighter units swiftly from Germany to France soon after the first Allied troops landed. Those Luftwaffe fighters that attempted to execute this plan encountered, in the skies over Normandy, Allied fighters with overwhelming numbers and superior quality of equipment and pilots. The AAF had more than eight thousand aircraft assigned to Overlord.[1]

General Adolf Galland, commander of GAF fighters, later recalled how movements to Normandy worked out: "When the invasion finally came, the carefully made preparations immediately went awry. The entire transfer of the Fighter Arm into France was delayed 24 hours because Oberkommando West would not give the order; [this headquarters expected] a heavier landing attempt in the Pas de Calais." German pilots found themselves in a shambles during the move to the west as they attempted to operate out of inadequately prepared and poorly camouflaged airfields. Moreover, pilots had little experience in low-level, ground-attack operations and flew airplanes ill-equipped for it. Conditions were so bad that many units operated from airfields east of Paris, thus wasting gasoline on trips to and from the beachhead and shortening the time they could operate over it.[2]

During the eighteen months preceding D-Day, the AAF had attacked German industrial plants, forcing the GAF into combat that had caused it severe attrition. By June 1944, the GAF was not strong enough to seriously threaten invasion forces. Galland knew that the movement of his fighters into the west could not critically influence the Normandy battle and that it weakened German air resistance to Allied strategic air attacks.

Luftflotte 3 launched fewer than 100 sorties on D-Day. When GAF fighters were equipped with bomb racks and rocket launchers, this paraphernalia reduced aircraft performance and added to the GAF's qualitative inferiority. Soon after D-Day, GAF headquarters recognized this and ordered its fighter squadrons to remove bomb racks from aircraft.[3]

The GAF buildup in the west continued erratically. On June 30, Luftflotte 3 had only 233 fighters and 419 pilots. The GAF had lost almost half of the fighters that attempted to reach the front. In June, the Allies launched twelve times as many sorties as GAF air forces in the west.

Conditions for the GAF were not much better in July; in that month Galland inspected GAF fighter units in the west and compiled a long list of weaknesses, including lack of adequate ground facilities, poor communications systems, large numerical inferiority, inexperienced pilots, too many missions, inflexible tactics and inferior equipment.[4]

Galland's prediction that many of his fighter pilots would not survive in the west proved to be accurate; pilots that were desperately needed to oppose the Allied strategic air offensive did not return from futile anti-invasion missions.

Rail transportation in the west was chaotic by D-Day. A GAF intelligence officer reported that only a few ferries were in service to carry traffic across the Seine below Paris. Movement on roads in the lodgment area was full of danger for German forces. Officers carried aircraft spotters on their staff cars.[5] On June 6, when the German high command realized that an invasion of northern Europe had started, orders went out to various Wehrmacht units to move to the beachhead. The difficulty encountered in movement by these divisions in the next few weeks testifies to the effectiveness (or lack of it) not only of close air support but also of various Allied campaigns to disrupt transportation facilities controlled by the enemy.

Crack German panzer divisions in the vicinity of the lodgment area constituted a great danger to Overlord. They had elite troops, exceptional mobility and devastating fire power. One of these, Panzer Lehr, was equipped "like no other German armored division," in the words of its commander, General Fritz Bayerlein. From its station, only ninety miles south of Caen, Panzer Lehr moved toward the beachhead on D-Day. After his capture, Bayerlein told Allied interrogators that his division was alerted on the morning of June 6 at 2 a.m. and warned that it must move north at 1700 hours. Bayerlein requested that he be permitted to wait for twilight, but this was refused. Though it was rather late in the day when they started out, the division met severe air attacks almost immediately. The northward advance was further delayed by attacks on road junctions at Condé, Argentan, Falaise and Thury-Harcourt. These things did not delay the tanks very much, but they slowed up the speed of the lighter vehicles and supply columns. The main road Vire–Le Bény-Bocage was so bad that German troops called it a fighter-bomber racecourse. Bayerlein set the division's losses in the attacks of the late afternoon, night and day of June 6/7 at 84 half-tracks, prime movers and self-propelled guns out of approximately 700; 130 trucks; and 5 out 140 tanks. This, as he pointed out, was a serious loss of vehicles for a division not yet come into action, especially of fuel trucks of 2.5-ton capacity. During the night of 7/8 June, two combat commands were organized. There were fewer losses from air attack because previous losses had taught the men to respect march discipline, because they were moving at night and because they exercised better camouflage discipline. Every vehicle was covered with tree branches and made to hug the hedges or woods. Panzer Lehr was to attack on June 8 but was not yet strong enough, and this was postponed until the ninth.[6]

Panzer Lehr's movements on June 6–9 were not slowed by damaged rail centers, blocked bridges or Resistance actions. Its troubles came primarily from fighter-bombers. Operating with air superiority, tactical air forces demonstrated that they could disrupt movements of enemy forces during daylight hours in clear weather. (In fact, there was *little* clear weather in this period.) Bayerlein pointed out that German troops rapidly adapted to the menace of air attack, but the precautions they had to take caused delay and consumed materials and energy.

The impact of Resistance actions against German forces in the Battle of France was appreciable and far more significant than SHAEF had anticipated. Resisters crossed battle lines frequently to bring priceless information to invasion forces. Resistance leaders informed Allied commanders when Germans evacuated towns, thereby helping to prevent needless bombardments. They gave Allied forces crucial information about enemy strong points, stockpiles and troop movements.

The cost to the French was high. A history of the British SOE's assistance to the Resistance reported that over two hundred thousand French men, women and children died resisting the Germans; seventy-five thousand of these belonged to organized Resistance groups.[7] French civilians suffered from shortages of food, fuel and medicines; thousands were deported to Germany for labor or imprisonment. When captured, Resistance members could expect to be tortured brutally. Exposed to unspeakable treatment, some betrayed their comrades. The end for many captured Resistance members was a summary trial and execution or incarceration in a hellish concentration camp, which in most cases was equivalent to a death sentence.

The irregular character of the Resistance did not inspire confidence at SHAEF. General Morgan, who directed the initial planning for Overlord, told his staff to look on Resistance efforts as a bonus, but not to plan operations that depended on them.[8] SHAEF gave low priority to programs designed to support and encourage Resistance groups. Air force commanders considered the use of aircraft to supply the Resistance to be a diversion of resources from more important operations. The fear that supplies sent to the Resistance would fall into the hands of the Germans tended to dampen enthusiasm for such efforts.

The Resistance fought with whatever weapons it could acquire. Rail-cutting was widespread and effective. One historian of the French Resistance claimed, with some exaggeration perhaps, that sabotage by railway workers destroyed more rolling stock than the Allied air forces put out of action in four months of bombing.[9]

Sabotage often damages key installations with little wasted effort. A Resistance action involving two French schoolgirls, ages fourteen and sixteen, shows the potential effectiveness of sabotage. They helped an SOE agent replace axle oil in tank-transporter rail cars with abrasive, ground carborundum. This action put most of a Panzer division's transporters out of action — and did it at a crucial time.[10]

Resistance groups also destroyed communication lines and railroad equipment. They felled trees to block roads and railways. They blew up bridges. In some areas they engaged German troops in battle. The Allies gave them arms and supplies but not enough to enable them to operate with maximum effectiveness.

Security lapses plagued the Resistance. Time after time German security forces captured Resistance members and forced them to reveal vital information about their groups. The Allies generally tried to keep important information from the French, even from officers fighting alongside British and American forces and from officials of de Gaulle's organization.[11]

Throughout the German occupation, workers of the French communications and railroad industries engaged in espionage and sabotage. Communications workers operated radio networks to deliver information to London. They cut telephone and telegraph lines, forcing Germans to rely on radio communication which the Allies intercepted and decrypted.[12]

Some of the most effective Resistance sabotage was made to look like accidents or equipment breakdowns. Communications workers designed sabotage that could be repaired easily when an area was liberated. More than five hundred telephone and telegraph employees were executed by the Germans and fifteen hundred were deported.

Almost all French railway men actively opposed the Germans. They put locomotives and complicated switching mechanisms out of action in ways that did not appear to be sabotage. Railway workers helped Resistance fighters and Allied agents evade capture. They sent a steady stream of intelligence to Allied forces about German rail movements and other matters. Germans executed three hundred French railway workers and deported more than three thousand.[13]

The experiences of the 2nd SS Panzer Division, known as Das Reich, as it moved to the lodgment area, illustrate the effectiveness of Resistance actions. This crack armored division left the Toulouse area soon after D-Day and headed for Normandy. At a bridge over the Dordogne, Resistance forces delayed Das Reich for four hours. Numerous rail-track cuts forced the division's tanks to use roads. These heavy vehicles consumed great quantities of gasoline, and their treads suffered excessive wear moving by road. Saboteurs set fire to fuel dumps to aggravate Das Reich's fuel problems.

Das Reich inscribed its name on the rolls of infamy when it carried out a brutal atrocity in reaction to Resistance actions. As it moved near Limoges, the Resistance delayed it for the better part of forty-eight hours. In reprisal for the kidnapping of a division officer and to vent its fury, Das Reich rounded up the inhabitants of a village and shot the men. Soldiers herded women and children into a church and then set it afire. Over seven hundred residents perished.

The division sputtered to a halt repeatedly as it neared the Loire, where most of the bridges were down. As Das Reich came into the tactical radius of Allied warplanes, the Resistance reported its location, and air attacks disrupted the march. Das Reich straggled into its assigned sector in Normandy weary and disorganized, with its equipment badly worn, seventeen days after D-Day.[14]

German units moving to the front in Normandy required weeks to travel distances normally covered in days. An SS motorized division entrained near Troyes for a move to the beachhead. Rail lines to the west were blocked so extensively that the division had to backtrack repeatedly. It arrived in Normandy after a fortnight.

In the spring of 1944, the AAF increased its efforts to aid French Resistance groups. Eighth Air Force assigned forty B-24s to carry out supply missions; they dropped thousands of containers to the French forces of the interior. To be successful, these sorties required well-organized reception committees on the ground, ones not penetrated by German agents. Careful planning and effective communication with London were essential. Air crews involved in these efforts had to be exceptionally competent. Too often, drops turned into disasters if one or more of the elements necessary for a successful undertaking went wrong. Nevertheless, those supplies that did reach Resistance Fighters were put to highly effective uses. The French patriots created enormous problems for German forces. In recognition of this, SHAEF decided to give them more assistance. In June, Eighth Air Force assigned five wings of thirty-six aircraft each to deliver arms, munitions, sabotage materials, support personnel and supplies to Resistance Forces.[15]

A German division with the same numerical designation as Das Reich, the 2nd Panzer Division, was in northern France on D-Day. It started to move by rail to the lodgment area on June 9. Soon its tanks had to leave the trains stalled on blocked rail lines and take to the roads. Close to 40 percent of its tanks broke down during the march; it went into action in Normandy on June 20, too late to participate in an invasion-crushing counterattack.[16]

The 17th SS Panzer Grenadier Division, another elite mobile unit, received orders on June 6 to move from its station south of the Loire to a section of the front, a distance of two hundred miles. Allied fighter-bombers disrupted the march. Movement had to be limited to the hours of darkness and restricted to secondary roads. In daylight, the division huddled under trees. When German forces dispersed onto secondary roads, Resistance units often blew bridges, blocked roads and set up ambushes. The various routes of the 17th Division's units tended to converge on the bridges of the Loire; the scarcity of bridges in service aggravated the delay, congestion and confusion. After five days of harassment, the division reached its assigned sector near Périers.[17]

The major deterrent to German anti-invasion moves was, of course, the Allied air forces. Field Marshal Rommel commanded German forces in the west. One of his reports described the effects of Allied air power on his troops:

> During the day, practically our entire traffic — on roads, tracks and in open country — is pinned down by powerful fighter-bomber and bomber formations, with the result that the movement of our troops on the battlefield is almost completely paralyzed, while the enemy can maneuver freely. Every traffic defile in the rear area is under continual attack and it is very difficult to get essential supplies of ammunition and petrol up to the troops....
> All the reserves that came up arrived far too late to smash the enemy landing by counterattacks.[18]

Rommel concluded that German forces could not contain Allied armies in Normandy for long, but he was unable to convince Hitler to permit an orderly retreat.

Soon after D-Day, USSTAF's G-2 section issued a report that matched Rommel's estimate of the situation. It confirmed that the supply and reinforcement of German forces had been seriously delayed by the disruption of rail and road transportation, the destruction of bridges and the constant attacks on all movements upon highways and railways approaching the battle area. Long detours had been inevitable. Some equipment and troops had been destroyed before reaching the front lines. German commanders had experienced great difficulty making plans and concentrating reserves and equipment for offensive actions or as responses to crises.[19]

By the end of June 1944, it was evident that Allied air forces had achieved their major objectives in support of the Normandy invasion, as prescribed in AAF guidelines: (1) they had won air superiority; (2) they had isolated the battlefield; and (3) they had provided excellent air support to ground forces. In Leigh-Mallory's opinion, his tactical air forces had given ground forces superb support; but after a month of fighting on the beachhead, Allied armies had still not penetrated the German front. He believed strongly that the strategic air forces should be doing more to help ground forces, and he had a plan to employ them for that purpose. It called for an air action which became known as "carpet bombing." Spaatz, Tedder and many air commanders opposed Leigh-Mallory's proposal, but he persevered and gained Eisenhower's approval. A carpet bombing was planned for July 24 to begin a First Army offensive codenamed Cobra.

Chapter 14

Air Support for the Allied Breakout from Normandy

In the first month after D-Day, Allied armies in Normandy established a secure beachhead and captured the port of Cherbourg. U.S. forces then pushed south, but progress was slow and casualties were heavy. Bradley's First Army fought in the Bocage, an agricultural region with thousands of small pastures enclosed by hedgerows — embankments of earth matted with tough, twisted tree roots and covered by thick brush and profuse vegetation. Hedgerows provided extensive cover and concealment and excellent defensive positions; in fact, they were natural bastions for German soldiers, who knew how to use the terrain expertly. Movement of First Army units tended to be channeled onto sunken, unpaved roads. Marshes and streams limited the use of tanks.

It is often claimed that First Army had not anticipated the terrain obstacles found in hedgerow country. Actually, Allied photo-reconnaissance units produced excellent photographs of the area. One of Bradley's aides explained that there were advantages as well as disadvantages for First Army: "the area would not be an easy one for forces to advance through rapidly in the face of determined resistance, but it would likewise be most difficult for the enemy to prevent a slow and steady advance."[1]

In July, General Kepner visited the front in Normandy. His experience as a World War I infantry commander, followed by many years in the Army Air Corps — culminating in his present job as Eighth Fighter Command's commander — made him an acute observer: "These hedges are an impassable barrier for tanks," he wrote, "and perfect concealment for the foot soldier. There is a gully for drainage sometimes two or three feet deep. At its side, parallel, there is a bank of earth, often six or seven feet high, into which big trees are rooted." Kepner respected the German infantryman; he was "still very good. He has a lot of guts, too. When our infantry advances, he comes out of his hole to man mortars, automatic weapons, 37mm field guns and even 88mm artillery."[2] Kepner observed that flak was a "tremendous problem. There seems to be an unwritten rule that a fighter bomber mission is too dangerous from altitudes less than 3000 feet. Silhouetted against the overcast, the attacking aircraft make too good a target." The German 88mm guns fired with great effectiveness against both ground and air targets.

Allied aircraft attacked targets so close to the front that ground crews could often see the bombs fall. The location of airfields amazed Kepner. There were ten of them in the strip, eight miles wide, between Caen and the sea, "almost within range of enemy artillery." Air supremacy made it possible to use airfields so close to the front. Kepner reminded Spaatz that the situation was so "grotesquely in conflict with what the book prescribes that anyone would have been bounced out of Leavenworth [Army Command and General Staff School] for suggesting it as a possibility." Kepner observed at first hand the benefits of air supremacy. "The relatively unmolested landing of 200,000 vehicles and a million men in two weeks and the construction of a dozen air strips practically within sight of the front ... created advantages beyond the fondest dreams of the Army." Kepner reported that the engineers "had been tremendous."

The disappointing Allied progress inspired many complaints about Eisenhower and his commanders. His subordinates reacted by criticizing each other's performance. Tedder blamed General Montgomery for the failure of Allied forces to advance rapidly. He was too cautious, Tedder charged; his dilatory tactics gave Germans time to build up their forces and restore the transportation system that Allied air forces had wrecked at such a great cost. And Montgomery's forces failed to capture terrain needed for airfields. This handicapped some air units, especially RAF fighters; they were forced to operate from the U.K. In frustration, Allied air and ground commanders watched the best days of the year for mobile ground operations with close air support slip away as Allied forces remained mired in Normandy.[3]

Tedder's low opinion of Montgomery was reciprocated. Montgomery told associates that his "main anxiety these days was the possibility that we should not get the full value from our great air power.... The man who ought to keep the whole show on the rails is Tedder; but he is weak and does nothing about it."[4]

General Bradley tended to be exceptionally critical of the strategic air forces. In a postwar book he explained that "for untold years we infantrymen had been subjected to the glib, enticing arguments of strategic air power advocates, who unfailingly promised a quick-easy-cheap victory through air power.... Air power had not lived up to the glamorous advance billing."[5] Bradley's use of a theatrical metaphor was significant. Infantry soldiers resented airmen for the media attention they received and for benefits such as flight pay and comfortable living conditions behind front lines.

In an army dominated by ground officers, AAF regulars heard such complaints throughout their careers. In Spaatz's opinion, commanders like Bradley did not understand strategic air-war principles and certainly did not know how to use heavy bombers in a tactical role. Spaatz heard disturbing rumors of Leigh-Mallory's plan to use heavy bombers to attack targets close to the front line. He complained to Eisenhower that ground commanders could imagine no better use for heavy bombers than to "plow up several square miles of terrain in front of ground forces to obtain a few square miles of advance." He wrote a note in his diary: "Our forces now are superior to Germans opposing us in men and material. The only thing necessary to move forward is sufficient guts on the part of the ground commanders."[6]

Arnold shared Spaatz's concerns about SHAEF's use of air power. He reminded Spaatz that the AAF had come first in procurement of sparse resources and first in receiving the "cream of America's fighting men. The stupendous cost of this war, the tight ceiling we have reached in our Troop Basis, and the generally stable combat aircraft situation places full responsibility on you, me and our subordinates to exploit fully the air power we now possess in this war."[7]

The transfer of Eighth Air Force and RAF Bomber Command to SHAEF had given Leigh-Mallory a powerful voice in the tactical employment of heavy bombers. This worried Spaatz. Leigh-Mallory was known to have little faith in strategic bombing. His views on the issue were closely in tune with those of ground commanders. During the Battle of Normandy he complained endlessly about Eighth Air Force: "In view of the weakness of the German air force," he wrote, "to attack aircraft factories was a dangerous folly at a time when vital moves in the Normandy battle were in progress." He believed that Doolittle "had no real understanding of the military battle, and attacked tactical targets with a sense of conferring a favour." His journal recorded this observation: "The Americans are a strange lot. They are still obsessed with the notion that to bomb Germany in daylight is the proper course. I have to humour them."[8]

The proposal to use bombers to "plow up several square miles of terrain," as Spaatz derided it, came from Leigh-Mallory. To break the stalemate on the Normandy front, he proposed that an armada of heavy bombers drop an enormous number of bombs on a small section of the front. The resulting cataclysm, he believed, would permit Allied forces to break through the ruptured front and force a war of movement on the enemy. Leigh-Mallory recorded in his journal his determination to promote the proposal: "I maintain that ... heavy bombers can produce a concentration of high explosive infinitely greater than any which can be produced by any other means. Either I am to be allowed to direct, if necessary, the whole Air Forces available to the full and immediate support of the Army or I will resign on the issue. Some of the younger American Generals won't like it but they will have to lump it for Eisenhower is behind me."[9]

British as well as American airmen opposed the proposal. Portal and Tedder believed it would set an unhealthy precedent; it would encourage ground commanders to ask for support from heavy bombers whenever they faced tough obstacles. Anticipating this reaction, Leigh-Mallory bypassed Tedder, who "feels that the Army should be left to act on its own with ordinary air support. Naturally, his views are shared by the supporters of strategical bombing.... I believe that Ike will back me."[10] Leigh-Mallory was right: Eisenhower approved the proposal.

AEAF coordinated planning for the carpet bombing with First Army, 21st Army Group, and Eighth Air Force. The air assault would start Cobra, the powerful U.S. offensive that First Army planners hoped would lead to a breakout from the lodgment area.

Despite Tedder's antipathy to carpet bombing, his scientific advisor, Solly Zuckerman, participated in planning Cobra's air actions. In a paper he distributed in June, he asserted that the risk of bombs falling on Allied troops was acceptable "when one establishes rational bombing lines." He acknowledged that "there will always be a small chance that bombing will go wrong, and that bombs will fall amongst our own troops. But in general it must be remembered that ... the risk of disasters occurring from wide spills is very much less than the certain risk of heavy damage and casualties in the enemy whom we would be attacking."[11]

Zuckerman studied bombing records and recommended that troops be withdrawn about 1,250 yards from the target area in carpet bombings executed by Eighth Air Force day bombers. He estimated that a safety zone of this depth would make it unlikely that stray bombs would fall on Allied troops.

RAF Bomber Command carried out a carpet bombing on a section of the front near Caen on July 18, but the results were disappointing. German forces stoutly resisted the advance of British ground forces. German resistance was tougher than anticipated from troops subjected to such a bombardment. Nevertheless, plans went forward to try the tactic again on July 24 on a section of the German lines facing Bradley's forces.

Zuckerman visited First Army headquarters during the planning stage of Cobra and advised Quesada and Bradley about some of the complexities of carpet bombing by heavy bombers. He urged them not be conservative about fixing bomb lines.[12] It was important for infantry to close with the enemy promptly after the carpet bombing ended. Bradley

Map 4: Operation COBRA

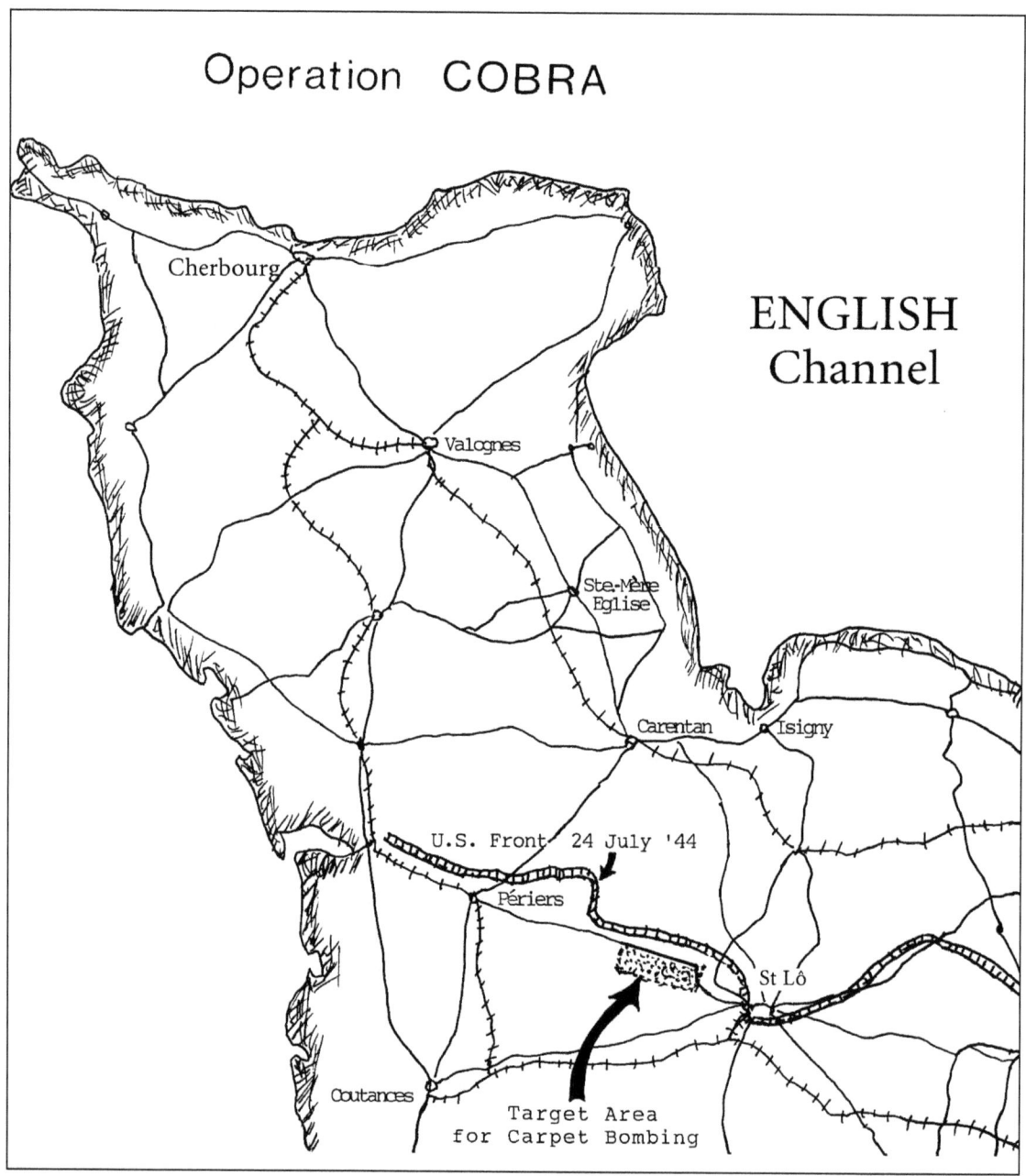

favored the use of fragmentation bombs so that deep bomb craters would be avoided which could delay the Allied advance.[13]

Cobra would start with an attack by fighter-bombers on the target area, a rectangular strip, one mile by five miles, just south of a ruler-straight stretch of the St. Lô–Périers road, a prominent landmark that would help aircraft crews identify targets (see Map 4). As fighter-bombers completed their attack, the lead formation of a force of 1,586 heavy bombers would arrive at the target area flying a north-south route at altitudes of not more than 15,000 feet. Eighth Air force heavies would attack in three waves, each wave taking fifteen minutes, with five minutes between waves. Fifty thousand bombs would create chaotic conditions in the target area. Planners debated about the size of the safety zone — an area from which First Army troops would withdraw to reduce the chance that stray bombs would fall on them — and concluded that they should move back 1,500 yards. Special enemy strongpoints would be marked with red smoke by artillery. Boxes of twelve to fourteen bombers would drop their bombs on signals of lead bombardiers. After heavy bombers finished their part of the operation, medium bombers would attack targets in the rear of the German front lines. Eighth Fighter Command would provide area cover.[14]

Eisenhower and Bradley hoped that Cobra would rupture the German front so that Allied forces could break out of the beachhead and force a war of movement in which their mobility and air power would create grave disadvantages for the enemy. Bradley later described the Allied command situation on the eve of Operation Cobra:

> Cobra thus assumed vast importance in my mind. If it succeeded, I was certain it would give everybody a much-needed shot in the arm. It would help eliminate the back-stabbing. It would put such momentum in the war that the very speed of it would heal the seams of our rupturing alliance. Conversely, if it failed, it could develop into much more than another military setback. It could bring on dangerous open warfare in the alliance that might lead to Monty's relief and perhaps Ike's and my own.[15]

Allied air forces started Cobra on July 24. Leigh-Mallory flew to First Army headquarters to observe the operation. He ordered the air operation to begin despite warnings of bad weather. Forecasts were accurate and weather worsened steadily during assembly of Eighth Air Force heavy bombers. As the lead groups approached the target area, Doolittle received word belatedly from Leigh-Mallory to abort the mission, but by then the bombers were only seven minutes from their targets; it would be difficult to recall them before they dropped their bombs. However, it was standard procedure for bombers to return with their bombs if their crews could not identify targets.[16]

Some bombers did not receive the recall message and released their bombs. A botched mission turned tragic when some bombs fell on First Army positions. The aborted operation alerted Germans that an Allied offensive was imminent. It was a depressing start to an operation upon which so many Allied hopes rested.[17] General Collins ordered Seventh Corps to take back some of the terrain it had relinquished to form a safety zone. More American casualties resulted from this effort, but it helped to mislead some German commanders into thinking they had repulsed an Allied offensive.[18]

Bradley was furious about the bombing casualties. He claimed that airmen had violated an agreement when they sent heavy bombers along a flight path perpendicular to the St. Lô-Périers road rather than parallel to it as he had recommended. He charged that this rejection of his advice was partly responsible for the bombing of American troops. On the evening of July 24, Bradley faced an agonizing decision. Despite his strong feelings about the flight path, he felt compelled to ask Eighth Air Force to carry out the carpet bombing next day even though it would have to be executed as planned.

Eighth Air Force carried out Cobra's carpet bombing on July 25. At 0614 the aircraft of the lead Eighth Air Force division began to assemble over England. A weather aircraft carrying an air commander, a meteorologist and a bombardier flew to Normandy to reconnoiter the target and prevent blunders like those committed the previous day. At 0800 the air commander reported that the target area was clear; but cloud cover with a base of 14,000 feet along the route forced many bombers to descend from planned altitudes. Bombardiers had to reset their bombsights hurriedly.[19]

At 0939, as fighter-bombers attacked enemy positions in the target area, heavy bombers of Eighth Air Force neared the St. Lô-Périers road. Air crews searched for landmarks which would identify targets, but this was difficult over an agricultural region. Exploding bombs sent great clouds of dust and smoke billowing up from the ground, making target recognition even more difficult. Cobra's plan required the air forces to complete the attack in one hour; this meant that bomber crews could not wait for smoke to clear before attacking.

General Vandenberg flew to Normandy in a P-38 to observe the air action. He observed that visibility was fairly good for the first twenty-five minutes. After that "a pall of smoke and dust crept slowly north and obscured ... any marks of identification of the front...." Near the end of the operation Vandenberg could not even see bomb blasts through the smoke.[20]

A large number of observers visited First Army positions to witness Cobra's air bombardments, including Lieutenant General Leslie McNair, former chief of the Army Ground Forces and now holding a position in Overlord. He wanted to observe the performance of troops whose training he had designed and directed. One of Bradley's aides described how the air assault appeared to those on the ground: "Soon the heavies came in, we heard them long before seeing them. Heavy roar up above the clouds which were now about 8,000 feet with small patches of blue beginning to show through...." When the bombs exploded, "angry black spirals of dirt boiled out of the ground." Soldiers who had been standing in the open watching the air spectacle now dove for ditches; for some it was too late.[21]

Bombs fell on First Army soldiers on July 25, too. The 30th Division was hit especially hard: 61 killed, 374 wounded, 60 missing and 164 cases of shock. These casualties exceeded those of any other single day in the history of this renowned division, one of Overlord's finest.[22] A history of the 30th Division's 120th Infantry Regiment describes the bombing tragedy: "Huge flights of planes ... Fascinated, we stood and watched this mighty drama.... The earth trembled and shook. Whole hedgerows disappeared and entire platoons were struck, huge geysers of earth erupted and subsided leaving gaping craters...."[23]

In spite of the battering it received from Allied bombers, Seventh Corps attacked and encountered surprisingly tough resistance from German troops, who had learned to protect themselves from air attacks. The aborted bombing of July 24 impelled German commanders to move their artillery to the rear. German casualties were not as high as Allied planners had expected. The enemy's dug-in tanks, machine guns and artillery exploited terrain features and covered approaches expertly.[24]

In the early evening of July 25, a discouraged Eisenhower returned to England fearful that Cobra had failed. Bradley felt angry and depressed. The operation seemed to be stalling, and bombs had killed American soldiers, including General McNair. First Army's headquarters' diary described the gloom that had settled over the U.S. forces: "This day, a day to remember for more than one reason, did not bring the breakthrough for which we had all hoped...."[25] Bradley relieved his feelings by dictating a memo that sharply criticized Allied airmen for their performance in Cobra.

General Collins was too busy on July 25 to worry about who would eventually get blamed for failures. He searched diligently for weak spots in the enemy's positions. Although his infantry divisions had met stubborn resistance and failed to capture their first-day objectives, Collins sensed that the enemy was seriously disorganized. On the

Bradley, Major General Leonard Gerow, Eisenhower, Collins. (Courtesy of the National Archives and Records Service.)

afternoon of July 25, he ordered his armor to attack on the next morning.[26] This decision led to the breakthrough that Cobra planners had hoped for. By late afternoon of July 26, American forces had penetrated the German line and were driving south. With the front crumbling, enemy forces could no longer hold static positions. Forced to move in daylight, German tanks, trucks, artillery vehicles and horse-drawn wagons became targets for ceaseless, devastating attacks by Allied fighter-bombers. Aerial reconnaissance provided a steady flow of useful information.

After his capture General Fritz Bayerlein described the condition of his division after the carpet bombing:

> Shelters were destroyed and the occupants were buried.... I also have the impression that a number of those who lived through the bombings surrendered quickly to the attacking U.S. infantry, or left their positions and withdrew to the rear.

The bombings demolished Panzer Lehr's forward positions The attacking U.S. infantry, nevertheless, encountered resistance; German reserves at battalion, regiment and division levels had been held in position immediately behind the main line of resistance. Bayerlein recalled that "particularly tenacious resistance was offered by anti-aircraft and other artillery batteries which had escaped destruction and were employed in infantry action."[27]

Seventh Corps tanks received highly effective air support as they drove south on July 26. In the lull periods of June and July, Quesada's IX TAC had developed the air-ground communications that sharply improved cooperation between fighter-bombers and

Seventh Corps soldiers digging out after the Allied air bombardment that started Operation Cobra. (Courtesy of the National Archives and Records Service.)

armored units. Quesada implemented an innovative system of air cover for armored columns, which put an airmen equipped with an air force-type VHF radio in each tank column to communicate with supporting aircraft. It became standard procedure for four-ship flights of fighter-bombers to cover each armored column to attack enemy units holding up the column's advance and to warn of enemy concentrations ahead.

General Collins's historic order of July 26 sent his armor charging through the German lines. Brigadier General Maurice Rose, commander of Combat Command A [CCA] of the 2nd Armored Division, received an order to "get moving." Rose's tanks crossed the St. Lô-Périers road through German positions in disarray. In mid-afternoon CCA's tanks roared through St. Gilles meeting only light, scattered opposition. Late in the afternoon Rose received an order to continue advancing through the night. CCA spearheaded Seventh Corps into the exploitation phase of Operation Cobra, the beginning of the end for German forces in Normandy.

A IX TAC air-support officer who rode in a CCA tank during its advance south from St. Lô described his experiences: "I was attached to the 2nd Armored Division from 22 July to 6 August…. I used an SCR 522 to communicate with the planes. Four fighter-bombers were assigned initially to cover each column. As each flight approached, the leader contacted me by radio giving his call sign. He remained with us until relieved, usually about thirty minutes. Column cover was maintained whenever we were moving in daylight."[28]

The success of Cobra exceeded even the hopes of optimists on Allied staffs. Allied forces raced across France in August and September in pursuit of German units fleeing in disorder.

Eisenhower and most of his staff believed that the carpet bombing was a crucial part of Cobra. Tedder and Spaatz tried to counter this assumption by claiming that Cobra would probably have succeeded without the heavy-bomber contributions. Ike told them he would never be able to make his ground commanders believe that. USSTAF received many requests for heavy bomber support in the coming months, and it executed some carpet bombings to help ground armies.

Leigh-Mallory's journal recorded satisfaction with his part in Cobra: "My main business was organizing this show and getting things going. I had to fight all the preliminary battles behind the scenes. Things are now in running order."[29]

Every German commander cited Allied air power as the major cause of their defeats in the west. Von Rundstedt's successor, Field Marshal von Kluge, warned Hitler that there was no way in which his troops could cope with the "all powerful enemy air forces" unless they surrendered territory. Allied air forces attacked with "terrific numbers of aircraft dropping carpets of bombs. ... bombs raining down with all the force of elemental nature...."[30]

On August 1, the U.S. Third Army became operational in France under the command of Lieutenant General George S. Patton, Jr. At the same time General Bradley took command of the U.S. 12th Army Group comprising the First and Third Armies. XIX TAC of Ninth Air Force, commanded by Brigadier General Otto Weyland, provided close air support for Third Army; IX TAC continued to support First Army. Patton, himself a pilot, later wrote that "it was love at first sight between the XIX Tactical Air Command and the Third Army."[31]

Patton's divisions squeezed through a narrow corridor near Avranches and moved south toward the Loire and west into Brittany. Patton asked Weyland to monitor his right flank as his armor moved ahead rapidly. "If I had worried about flanks," Patton wrote, "I could never have fought the war. Also I was convinced that our Air Service could locate any groups of enemy large enough to be a serious threat, and then I could always pull something out of the hat to drive them back while the Air Force in the meantime delayed their advance."[32]

To help XIX TAC carry out its wide-ranging missions, Ninth Air Force increased its strength to nine groups. It was now common practice to shift groups to cope with changing battle conditions.

Weyland later described his relationship with Patton: "I had full control of the air. The decisions were mine as to how I would allocate the air effort. He ran the ground, and I ran the air ... whether it would be close support, interdiction, something to do with air superiority, or perhaps helping out somebody else or doing something that General Eisenhower directed as a joint effort of all the air power."[33] In the Battle of France, XIX TAC employed the flexible operating tactics recommended by the AAF for years.

Weyland, like Quesada, encouraged innovations in tactical air warfare. He told an interviewer how fighter-bombers supported armored columns: "[Third Army would] run these armored columns into the Germans, and I'd violate what used to be a principle of tactical air power, 'Don't use air power against something that the artillery can hit.' Well, time was of the essence. So I said to hell with that. Here, they were moving, so by the time they'd stopped a column and deployed their artillery and what-not ... hell, it might take them an hour or two. I'd have fighter-bombers out in front, and we'd try to take care of anything out there."[34]

During the autumn collapse of German positions in the West, XIX TAC attacked troops fleeing from southern France. A German force, disrupted and demoralized by both

Patton and Weyland. (U.S. Air Force photograph.)

constant air attack and harassment by Resistance groups, surrendered to Allied forces. In recognition of XIX TAC's part in bringing about the German surrender, Weyland participated in ceremonies at a bridge over the Loire near Beaugency where nineteen thousand German soldiers laid down their arms.[35]

In July, General Brereton left Ninth Air Force and took command of the First Allied Airborne Army. During the period of his command, the Ninth had executed the most successful close tactical air support campaign in history. Vandenberg now took command of the Ninth and led it for the rest of the war in Europe.

General Patton was one of the first Allied commanders to request a moratorium on interdiction in France. On August 2, attacks on bridges and fuel dumps in the Third Army area were banned. An AEAF directive, dated August 17, ordered a general pause in interdiction: Allied air forces would not bomb bridges without express AEAF authorization. On September 20, AEAF decided to stop all attacks on bridges and rail yards and issued an injunction against rail-cutting except for immediate tactical purposes.[36]

SHAEF now realized that Allied forces, with their supply lines extending to the U.K. and the U.S., often derived more problems than benefits from promiscuous destruction of transportation facilities. With overwhelming air superiority, Allied air forces could often disrupt enemy movements by tactical air attacks without extensive bridge and railroad destruction.

As Allied armies raced toward the German frontier in the fall, they began to outrun their supply lines. Eisenhower now felt a dire need for some of the rail facilities his air forces had demolished in the spring. Overlord's planners had not anticipated the need to operate such long supply lines so soon. Lack of ports and railroads contributed to severe supply shortages. For months, most supplies for Allied forces came over Normandy beaches and were carried to the front by trucks and even airplanes. These stopgap measures themselves consumed vast quantities of gasoline, the commodity that was most crucial in maintaining the Allied offensive.

On August 29, General Patton saw nothing to his front able to stop Third Army except "imaginary enemies"—that is, excessive caution on the part of SHAEF. On that very day a shortage of gasoline began to immobilize Third Army tanks. Patton called this supply crisis the "momentous error of the war."[37] This judgment, coming from a commander of so much experience, should not be dismissed lightly. Third Army siphoned gasoline from trucks and jeeps to keep its tanks moving; some tanks received no fuel so that others could keep attacking. Spaatz ordered Eighth and Ninth Air Forces to use bombers and transports to carry gasoline to Third Army. Hopes were high for a German surrender before winter when bad weather would give the German air forces, industry and armies some relief from air attacks. If given time to recover and regroup, Germans could organize a fierce, effective defense of their homeland, one that would inflict heavy casualties on invading armies. Doolittle understood the importance of helping to supply Patton's tanks with gasoline, but he also felt uneasy about using bombers to transport gasoline during the good bombing weather of autumn; it diverted them from campaigns that could cripple the production resources that supported German armies.[38]

The fast-moving operations of Third Army strained XIX TAC's logistics. There were too few Air Liaison officers available to assign to armored columns. Communications were the key to effective operations, but equipment and trained personnel were scarce. Frequent changes of bases consumed valuable supplies and took squadrons out of operational status. Fighter-bomber operations were costly because of flak. P-51s were especially vulnerable because of their liquid-cooled engines.[39]

The winter campaign that followed the tragic failure to defeat Germany in the autumn brought alarming setbacks and severe losses to Allied armies in the west. Often it was not a lack of supplies but a lack of transportation that caused difficulties. This failure could be blamed in part on the transportation campaign which had caused widespread devastation: merely to clear rail installations of rubble required an enormous effort. Allied commanders could not be as ruthless as Germans had been in giving absolute priority to military trains. They had also to satisfy the needs of civilians for food and other essential commodities in winter.

Winter weather tended to neutralize air power, one of the Allies' greatest advantages. Air operations diminished sharply as the crucial year, 1944, ended. XIX TAC's sortie record testifies to a plummeting scale of operations:

August	12,292 sorties
September	7,791 sorties
October	4,790 sorties
November	3,509 sorties
December	2,563 sorties[40]

The dark skies of late autumn matched the mood of Allied forces as the realization sank in that Germany would not be defeated before winter. Bloody battles lay ahead against a tough enemy defending his homeland.

Chapter 15

Reorganization of Eisenhower's Air Command

In September 1944, General Eisenhower learned that the CCS intended to resume direction of the strategic air forces. He asked Marshall to delay the move: "I would urgently oppose any change in the U.S. Strategic Air Force control and I know Spaatz would do the same."[1] He also appealed to Arnold and expressed his appreciation for the help the air forces had given to Overlord: "The air has done everything we asked. It has practically destroyed the German Air Force. It disrupted communications, it neutralized beach defenses and it has been vitally helpful in accomplishing certain breakthroughs by ground forces. While all this was being done the strategic forces have been committed to the greatest extent possible on strategic targets...."[2]

Arnold appreciated the tribute to the AAF but felt uneasy about some of Eisenhower's comments, for example: "We are now stretched to the limit in maintenance of ground and air forces on the continent.... To help in this [supply crisis] we will have to use, over and above all other means, some of the heavies.... In preparation for such tasks Spaatz is now ready to use 200 bombers in transportation of troops and supplies and soon his whole force will be able to do so."[3] Arnold had supported Eisenhower throughout the war, but he could feel little enthusiasm for a proposal to use heavy bombers as transport aircraft.

Behind Eisenhower's concern for logistics was a supply crisis of major proportions, one that stopped Patton's army in its tracks. Overlord's plans specified that a balanced U.S. force of twenty-one divisions would be on the continent by the end of August. But the plans had not anticipated the rapid advances of August and September, so supply pipelines had not expanded enough to meet demands on them. A channel storm in June had wrecked an artificial harbor near Omaha Beach. Hitler had ordered commanders of ports to defend them to the last cartridge and to demolish cargo-loading facilities.

Eisenower's appeals did not convince the CCS to postpone its takeover of the strategic air forces. Marshall explained that the CCS did not believe that Eisenhower could direct strategic air forces based in the U.K. and Italy from headquarters on the continent.[4] Spaatz assured Eisenhower that USSTAF's heavy bombers would be available to support crucial ground efforts regardless of directives.

Eisenhower swallowed his disappointment and reported to Marshall: "The arrival of the Chiefs of Staff directive ... threw consternation into the headquarters. The most disturbed individual was Spaatz. However, I have calmed down everybody and I assure you that I can make the system work. I am absolutely certain of the good will of the key individuals involved, principally Harris and Spaatz...."⁵ Spaatz kept his word: AAF strategic bombers supported ground operations many times in the coming months.

The new directive gave Portal and Arnold authority over the strategic air forces operating in the European Theater of Operations [ETO], with Spaatz and Air Vice Marshal Norman Bottomley designated to provide day-to-day direction. Spaatz assured Arnold that he would not allow the British to exert undue influence on USSTAF's plans and operations.⁶

In September, Leigh-Mallory prepared to take a new job in the China-Burma-India theater, but Eisenhower delayed the move until mid-October. He explained to British authorities that Leigh-Mallory could not be spared until then: "He has gotten very intimately mixed up with a terrific battle we are fighting, particularly on our north flank."⁷

Eisenhower decided to eliminate AEAF after Leigh-Mallory's transfer. AAF leaders had never given whole-hearted support to the RAF-dominated organization. Spaatz often reminded Eisenhower that Americans disliked serving under British commanders, reminders that Eisenhower of all people did not need. Vandenberg drew up a list of reasons for removing Ninth Air Force from AEAF. He was the American commander most knowledgeable about AEAF, having served as its deputy commander. Quesada and Weyland backed Vandenberg completely. Henceforth, Overlord's air operations would be directed by a small group at SHAEF.

Arnold congratulated Eisenhower for his decision to terminate AEAF: "I concur heartily in the plan to do away with Hq. AEAF at the earliest possible moment. It appears to me that this intermediate headquarters no longer serves any useful purpose...."⁸ Eisenhower took exception to the smug tone of Arnold's letter and its explicit criticism of Leigh-Mallory. He responded with a sharp rebuttal:

> Through every day of this campaign Leigh-Mallory has proved his intense desire to cooperate and a very admirable grasp of the whole situation. Our plans for reorganization when and if he is detached will eliminate that headquarters and all the functions it has been performing will be centered right here at SHAEF. But you should not be under any misapprehension as to Leigh-Mallory's qualifications. ... he is one of the type that never ceases to develop and above all, he is a real fighter, which I like. He is an experienced and valuable officer.⁹

Leigh-Mallory never lacked for critics, but Eisenhower respected him. Leigh-Mallory had supported the campaign against rail centers. He had originated the plan to bomb towns to create road blocks, defended it against many opponents and guided its execution. He had commanded the tactical air forces as they gave close air support of unparalleled effectiveness to ground armies. Against intense, widespread opposition, he had defended AEAF's plan to use heavy bombers to lay carpets of bombs on sections of the front lines; he had coordinated the carpet bombing near St. Lô that started Operation Cobra. In disputes with other commanders over these and other Overlord programs, controversy swirled about him. He tended to disdain Americans assigned to his staff and humiliated many of them. Antipathy towards Leigh-Mallory among AAF officers is reflected in the official AAF history. It judged AEAF to have been "the least successful venture of the entire war with a combined Anglo-American command."¹⁰ The authors of this judgment may not have given sufficient consideration to the achievements of AEAF and its commander. Leigh-Mallory died when the aircraft in which he was flying to his new post crashed in the mountains near Grenoble.¹¹

The AAF had achieved its major objectives in support of the Normandy invasion, but it was far from clear just how effective the various air campaigns had been. Especially difficult to evaluate were those campaigns that helped bring about transportation chaos in the west. How effective had the transportation campaign been? Operation Pointblank? Bridge interdiction? The oil offensive? Bombing towns to create road blocks? Allied staffs evaluated these and other offensives continuously. The subsequent reports would be useful in other campaigns, especially in the war against Japan. They would also influence histories of Overlord if historians were able to consult them.

Part III
Evaluations of Overlord's Air Campaigns

Chapter 16

Surveys of the Transportation Campaign and Interdiction

Preliminary assessments of air campaigns evolved from reports of intelligence agents, photographic reconnaissance and debriefing of air crews. Air forces received information obtained from photographs of targets before and after attacks. Operational research sections manned by civilian scientists, for the most part, used statistical techniques and other scientific tools to evaluate tactics and equipment. They searched for ways to improve combat performance and sent their recommendations promptly to units that could implement them. It was crucial to evaluate current operations so that future campaigns, especially the invasion of Japan, would be carried out with maximum effectiveness.

After Allied armies had captured places that had been targets for air attacks, survey teams visited them to evaluate the effectiveness of weapons and tactics used. Inhabitants of towns and German prisoners gave evidence. Air force units that had carried out the attacks paid particularly close attention to reports of results.

Research scientists competent to evaluate air attacks were in short supply and great demand. Commanders tended to believe that only units that had planned or carried out operations could be competent to judge them, even though their objectivity would be questionable. Military discipline and loyalty to commanders sometimes inhibited subordinates from issuing candid reports that could be perceived as critical of a unit's performance.

Predictably, some of the survey reports of bombing campaigns issued by the same units that planned and executed them did vindicate the judgment and performance of their commanders and personnel. It would be a mistake, however, to conclude that all such reports were self-serving. ORS's, intelligence units, and survey teams often operated with independence and integrity; their reports expressed the best judgment of their analysts regardless of whose reputation might suffer.

The chief proponents of the transportation campaign—Eisenhower, Tedder and Leigh-Mallory—never conceded that it was anything but vitally necessary and completely effective despite much evidence to the contrary. In a report to the Allied chiefs of staff, Eisenhower gave his account of the campaign:

> By D-Day the Strategic Air Forces together with the Tactical Air Forces had so successfully performed their mission of disrupting enemy communications that there was a chronic shortage of locomotives and cars; repair facilities were inadequate, coal reserves reduced to six days supply and 74 bridges and tunnels leading

Devastated marshalling yard at Paris/Juvisy. (Library of Congress, Spaatz Collection 2-3260.)

to the battle area were impassable. The communications chaos thus produced had a fatal effect on the enemy's attempt at reinforcement to the threatened areas after our landing.

This carefully worded statement asserts that attacks on transportation were effective but avoids making claims about the respective effectiveness of the transportation campaign and of interdiction. Its statements about railway equipment are contradicted by surveys that found there was no shortage of locomotives, cars or servicing facilities for military purposes. Eisenhower also claimed that the transportation campaign had been necessary:

> I was aware that the attacks upon the marshaling yards and rail centers, by both the Strategic and Tactical Air Forces, would prove costly in French lives. In addition, a very important part of the French economy would for a considerable period be rendered useless.... Nevertheless, for purely military reasons, I considered that the communications system of France had to be disrupted. The fate of a continent depended upon the ability of our forces to seize a foothold and to maintain that foothold against everything we expected the enemy to throw against us.

This statement begs the question: could interdiction, executed primarily by the tactical air forces, have achieved the objective of the transportation campaign — disruption of the communications system of France? This question will be examined later in this chapter.[1]

Eisenhower only implied that the transportation campaign had been effective, but Tedder was far more explicit about it, especially about the RAF's contribution:

> The [transportation] attacks began on March 6 and were completed shortly before D-Day. Of a total of 67,000 tons [of bombs], 45,000 were dropped by Bomber Command in a series of highly concentrated and extremely accurate attacks.... The primary object of these attacks was the destruction of locomotive sheds and of maintenance and repair facilities, but it was calculated that in addition they would dislocate the marshaling yards, through lines, signaling equipment and destroy or damage locomotives and rolling stock.[2]

Tedder described RAF Bomber Command's operations as "extremely accurate;" this exaggeration is typical of Tedder's style. He asserted that attacks on rail centers had "achieved their objective ... and had virtually paralyzed the railway system in France and Belgium." Without mentioning interdiction, he conceded that the attacks "were, however, only a part, though it is now clear that they were the decisive part, of a wide pattern of operations...."[3]

Before he left AEAF, Leigh-Mallory wrote a report that echoed the assertions of Eisenhower and Tedder: "As it turned out, weather conditions allowed only a partial use of our air forces in the weeks following the assault, and had these preliminary operations not been started before D-Day the task of the air forces in interfering effectively with the enemy's movement within and to the battle area could not have been achieved in time to have directly influenced the land operations in the initial phases."[4]

Leigh-Mallory's premise that the possibility of bad weather during the invasion justified the assault on rail centers appears cogent, especially since fierce storms did indeed occur during the landings. Nevertheless, the argument is flawed. The possibility that air power might be handicapped by bad weather in June does not justify an ineffective, unnecessary campaign in April. Allied tactical air forces demonstrated that interdiction could disrupt German transportation to the necessary degree in operations beginning shortly before D-Day. Furthermore, tactical air forces could have executed interdiction with greater intensity in the months before D-Day if AEAF had given the campaign greater support. It is often pointed out that interdiction would threaten the secrecy of the lodgment area, but air attacks before D-Day on targets in Normandy were matched by attacks on targets away from Normandy, distracting attention from the future lodgment area. It should also be noted that bad weather handicapped tactical air forces less than heavy bombers.

The timing of the transportation campaign was one of its major weaknesses, which is often overlooked by both its defenders and critics. Damage done to railways months before D-Day could be repaired before the invasion started. Moreover, these untimely attacks demonstrated to the Germans the difficulties they would have to contend with during the invasion. They promptly devised compensatory stratagems to keep trains running and to make greater use of other means of transportation besides railways. Interdiction did not have these drawbacks for it began shortly before D-Day. The interdicted zone was small enough to permit Allied air forces to isolate it. Interdiction also afforded the enemy far less time to devise alternate transportation facilities.

When Eisenhower, Tedder and Leigh-Mallory wrote their justifications for the transportation campaign, the success of interdiction was evident. To justify the transportation campaign, they crafted the argument that interdiction's effectiveness was dependent on the prior destruction of rail centers. This claim was difficult to refute or to validate. Dissemination and acceptance of the thesis that the transportation campaign was necessary and effective was aided in no small measure by the power of commanders to stamp "SECRET" on documents that challenged it.

In fairness to SHAEF, it should be remembered that some of the reports critical of the transportation offensive came from its own G-2 section. A report, dated May 25, 1944, gave an unequivocal warning: "The program of rail center attacks has clearly not impaired the enemy's ability to move the necessary daily supply and maintenance tonnage by rail into the bridgehead area."[5] Thus, it was evident that the transportation campaign had failed *before* interdiction started in earnest.

The EOU also distributed a paper questioning the effectiveness of attacks on rail centers. This OSS group operated from the U.S. Embassy in London and assisted Allied air forces with target planning. The memo, "German Rail Movement in France in the First Ten Days After D-Day" by Major Charles P. Kindleberger, explained that only four of fourteen enemy divisions in the west had had to travel by rail any considerable distances to reach their battle stations. Bombing rail centers did not, of course, impede the other ten significantly. Interdiction and Resistance actions gave them their most serious problems while moving to their positions in Normandy.

With regard to German divisions outside the lodgment area, Kindleberger observed that "some part of the credit [for their delays] may be due to the line of interdiction along the Seine."[6] It is one of the first official statements claiming that bridge interdiction had been a crucial part of the campaign to delay German moves. The EOU report traced the routes of German divisions and concluded that "the pre–D-Day program of attacks on marshaling yards has had almost no effect on German rail movement, so far as it has been possible to observe it."[7] German forces had moved by rail through towns whose rail centers had been flattened by bombing — Ghent, Lille, Amiens, Aulnoye, Compiegne and Creil. "There is no evidence of which I am aware ... that the Germans have been handicapped by the attacks against locomotive servicing facilities; and the positive evidence that they run trains by routes through the heart of the 'railway desert' suggests that they have not been."[8]

Ninth Air Force was a component of AEAF and had participated fully in the transportation campaign. Its report concluded that "The campaign was well executed ... the bombing accuracy was high and on the whole the planned objective to destroy the engine and heavy servicing facilities of each target was accomplished. The damage to working sidings, cars, through tracks, junctions, warehouses must be regarded as a bonus to the primary objective."[9] Despite its part in the competent execution of the campaign, Ninth Air Force conceded that the transportation campaign had failed. The enemy kept vital rail lines open; traffic was usually moving through any bombed yard the Germans decided they needed in less than forty-eight hours after an attack.

The rail center in Trappes was one of the first to be bombed. Tedder had cited it to back up his claim that RAF heavy bombers had sufficient accuracy to demolish rail centers. Ninth Air Force reported that rail traffic through Trappes had not been delayed very long. "Photos taken twelve (12) days later showed through lines open and repairs to the sidings well under way."[10]

The Ninth Air Force report summarized the results of the transportation campaign:

> Great damage has been done to the heavy facilities and marshaling yards of the railway systems of France and Belgium. The damage has caused distress and hardship to the civilians rather than the Germans and it is too early to determine what the long term effects will be. While the rail operations may have contributed in some degree to delays in enemy movement it in no way compares with that caused by the bridge interdiction program on the Seine and Loire. So far the enemy has been free to use the rails at will with little evidence that the attacks have caused more than local diversions. The effort to destroy the [railway] facilities was long and costly and to date it does not appear justified by the results obtained.[11]

Bridge cutting, attacks on rolling stock and the bombing of railway tracks were major elements of the interdiction campaign. Ninth Air Force investigators concluded that "bridge attacks and rail cutting have achieved their primary purpose — interdicting of enemy movement, with the result that [German] reserves and supplies have reached the battle area late and in disorder."[12]

Reports such as these may have motivated the RAF to conduct its own evaluations of Allied air campaigns. Tedder nominated his scientific advisor, Solly Zuckerman, to organize and direct the British Bombing Analysis Unit [BAU]. Critics of the transportation campaign must have wondered about the decision to appoint Zuckerman to evaluate it; no one could consider him unbiased about a campaign he had planned and promoted. In any case, a SHAEF directive made it unmistakably clear that BAU was "a purely R.A.F. body, and ... the conclusions drawn in its Reports are those of the R.A.F. and not necessarily those of SHAEF."[13]

BAU investigators examined rail-transportation records and visited target sites in France and Belgium. Tedder advised Zuckerman that it was highly important to be "first in the field." Zuckerman concentrated on rail centers. He believed that flawed research methods and the preconceived opinions of the transportation campaign's opponents were responsible for disparaging reports. During his investigations Zuckerman received a message from a staff officer of SHAEF, a unit he believed had "consistently denigrated the results of the bomber offensive against the railways...."[14] He was therefore amazed to be given some records SHAEF had acquired that dealt with railroad traffic in France during the German occupation. It was the kind of data he prized. These documents showed that the volume of railway traffic in northern France had started to fall about the middle of March. In his memoirs, Zuckerman wrote that by May 26, "that is to say, *before* the destruction of the Seine bridges, [it] had fallen to 20 per cent of its previous peak level. By D-Day the level was 13 per cent. It was this region that had received the heaviest share of the [transportation] attacks."[15]

Zuckerman was jubilant, as was Tedder when shown the rail records. On the basis of this data, Zuckerman emphasized that —*before* the beginning in earnest of the interdiction campaign — the transportation offensive had had a tremendous impact on rail traffic. The records were particularly precious to Zuckerman because they constituted evidence which could not be challenged as having been influenced by preconceived ideas.[16] Zuckerman, then and for the rest of his life, attached the highest importance to the reductions in rail traffic. To him they were proof that the transportation campaign had succeeded. His critics, however, had never denied that massive bombing of rail centers would cut rail traffic, and they were not overly impressed to learn that it had apparently done so.

Tedder's advice to be first in the field meshed neatly with Zuckerman's determination to be first in print with a transportation-campaign report based on evidence not conjectures. BAU Report No. 1, labeled "preliminary," was dated November 4, 1944. It claimed that the railroad network needed by anti-invasion forces had been paralyzed by early May. The emphasis on May was significant. It called attention to the claim that the transportation campaign had achieved its goals before bridge interdiction began. The report employed the scientific jargon Zuckerman customarily used, buttressed with tables, graphs, data from railway records and summaries of interviews with railway officials, captured Germans, and French and Belgian civilians. It asserted that "a precipitous fall" [had occurred] in French and Belgian rail traffic by the beginning of March. "The fall was well advanced before the Seine Bridge attacks began on May 7." To insure that no reader missed the main point, the report explained that "attacks on rail centers were responsible for by far the larger part of the overall decline in the traffic originating in France."[17]

Eisenhower and Tedder welcomed this "preliminary" report. It vindicated their decisions. Its conclusions appeared in many SHAEF official reports and in virtually all histories of Overlord. Nevertheless, its veracity is highly questionable, and its conclusions were contradicted by other investigators who had much less reason than Zuckerman to justify past decisions. Unfortunately, their reports were often given security classifications and filed away.

The validity of BAU assertions that the transportation campaign had been effective relied heavily on reductions in rail traffic. There can be no doubt that blasted rail centers caused large reductions, but even deep cuts did not necessarily delay German military rail movements.

SHAEF parroted BAU's conclusions. One report stated that "by the end of the last week on which the Seine rail bridges were open traffic entering from outside France was barely 20% of its previous peak level in February."[18] This statistic does not prove what it purports to prove. German forces could meet their essential needs with 20 percent of the "previous peak level in February." Furthermore, any conclusions about German military rail traffic before D-Day are nebulous, for the Germans had not yet put their full energies into sending reinforcements to Normandy.

The success of the bridge offensive, however, could not be denied, not even by BAU. BAU Report No. 4 conceded that "the existence of a barrier of impassable bridges on the upper [sic] Seine at the beginning of June and ... of similar barriers in the Mantes-Orleans gap and along the Loire, must have seriously interfered with traffic in the Ouest and the Northern part of the Sud Ouest."[19] Other BAU reports repeated the claim that the bombing of rail centers, not interdiction, brought about most of the chaos in the transportation system and delayed German forces critically after D-Day. BAU reports disparaged interdiction. A history of BAU stated that fighter attacks on trains "produced small [results] compared with the results of attacks on locomotive depots...."[20]

The antipathy of BAU to interdiction, as well as its defense of the transportation campaign, never slackened. BAU Report No. 6 denied that it was relatively easy to repair tracks in rail centers as so many had claimed.[21] This strange assertion was followed by another: "Track-cuts in the open usually represent single cuts.... Track-cuts in railway centres, on the other hand, as a rule represent major damage to track against a background of devastation in the whole area of which they form a part."[22] This statement ignores the distinct possibility that "single cuts" may be more effective in stopping rail traffic than a pulverized rail center. BAU Report No. 7 continued the anti-interdiction theme. It asserted that damage to locomotives by machine gun or cannon fire is "relatively less serious than that caused by bombing."[23]

Bridge interdiction remained a tender subject at AEAF. Leigh-Mallory had accepted Zuckerman's opinion that it was too difficult and costly. Though Allied bomb groups had demonstrated the falsity of this claim, AEAF remained unenthusiastic about the tactic. Some of SHAEF's efforts to justify AEAF's policy surpassed even those of the BAU in absurdities. A draft history of SHAEF declared that "destruction of the Seine bridges was expected and the enemy had provided alternate crossing methods which handled troop movements efficiently. Movements were slowed but not below pre-attack plans."[24] The report did not explain how trains can cross rivers by alternate means "efficiently" when bridges are down. Other studies contradicted this assertion.

Leigh-Mallory prepared a "despatch" summarizing AEAF's campaigns. He commended the tactical air forces; they had performed brilliantly. He also showered praise on the transportation campaign: "If they had not been aided by the heavy blows which had already been delivered by heavy bombers on the key points in the railway systems the tactical air forces could hardly have played the successful part they did in bringing organized rail movement to a virtual standstill; nor could the isolation of the battle field have been subsequently achieved as rapidly as it was."[25] Leigh-Mallory probably believed this

Top: Collapsed bridge at Pontaubault. (U.S. Air Force photograph.) *Bottom:* Destroyed railroad bridge at Mantes-Gassicourt. (U.S. Air Force photograph.)

Bombed bridge at Rouen and nearby section of the city. (U.S. Air Force Photo Collection [Neg. No. 54053 AC], courtesy of National Air and Space Museum, Smithsonian Institution.)

proposition; he died before the mountain of evidence contradicting it had been thoroughly sifted.

The striking success of the attack on the bridge at Vernon on May 7 had undermined AEAF's opposition to bridge bombing and had led to a bridge offensive that got underway in earnest on May 24. By D-Day Allied aircraft had cut eight of ten rail bridges and ten of fourteen highway bridges on the Seine downstream from Paris, as well as two rail bridges on the Oise. By June 12 all rail and highway bridges over the Seine west of Paris had been cut or rendered impassable. By June 18 nine of eleven rail bridges on the Loire between Orléans and Nantes were cut. Medium bombers and fighter-bombers did most of the damage to Seine bridges; heavy bombers participated in the Loire campaign. Reconnaissance aircraft monitored the status of bridges. Those that the Germans restored to service were often struck again.[26]

In spite of general satisfaction felt by AAF units about the bridge offensive, ORS analysts sharply criticized its execution. Their investigations showed that unsuitable tactics or weapons had been employed often in bridge attacks. Already far less costly than AEAF's staff predicted, the bridge campaign could have been even more economical had AAF planners better understood bridge bombing. Ninth Tactical Command ORS's Report No. 60 contained many criticisms of bridge attacks. At Orival the piers and abutments were "perfect aiming points but 500-pound bombs only scarred the bridge." Three missions by fighter-bombers and medium bombers were required to knock down a rail bridge at Rouen. "Strangely enough the fuzing was correct only in the last fighter-bomber bomber attack." Fighter-bombers carried out three missions against a bridge at Le Manoir without success. "The abutments are so heavy that the explosion of a 1000-pound bomb against them would be of doubtful value. The type and strength of the bridge clearly make it a target for the mediums."[27]

After the liberation of France and Belgium, ORS analysts gathered data from on-site studies of bridge targets. This information helped them sharpen their judgments. In an introduction to IX TAC ORS Report #90, General Quesada admitted that "many of our Seine River bridge attacks were improperly carried out both as to planning of bombs and mode of attack.... There is usually *only one* best method and that can only be arrived at after careful study." Quesada felt bitter about the failure of AEAF to develop efficient procedures for planning and executing bridge attacks. "Instructions related to attacks on the Seine bridges were issued often from hour to hour," he recalled.[28]

Thirteen of the Seine bridges attacked were through-types requiring instantaneous fuses, but of the 1,401 bombs dropped on them only 232 had the correct fusing.[29] The bomb size and fuse settings needed to destroy a bridge often determined the type of aircraft assigned to do it. P-47s could carry 1,000-pound bombs, but many bridges required heavier bombs, which meant that light, medium and sometimes even heavy bombers had to attack them. The importance of the Loire bridges in the interdiction plan and their distances from the U.K., made it necessary for heavy bombers to attack some of them.

Teams from the AAF Evaluation Board surveyed damage and evaluated AAF air campaigns. They found that bombs which hit concrete piers often caused only superficial damage. "To achieve its maximum effect," a report advised, "a bomb must detonate as close to the vital supporting members as possible, and the selection of the fuze which determines the point of detonation, is of great importance."[30]

Findings of Evaluation Board teams generally confirmed ORS findings: bomb size and fuse settings had often been inappropriate. The AAF Evaluation Board prepared booklets with specific recommendations for bombing the various types of bridges, with illustrations (as shown by Diagram 4). The June 1945 Evaluation Board report, from which this diagram is taken, explained that "when ... [bombs] strike the floor of a through-type bridge and penetrate before detonation, the blast and fragmentation are dissipated in the open area below the bridge. The attacks on highway bridges at Vernon and Rouen, in which bombs fuzed .025-second tail-delay detonated harmlessly in the river, are typical of what may be expected when delay fuzes are used on through-type bridges. The fuzing found to produce the greatest amount of destruction on this type of bridge is either instantaneous nose or non-delay tail."

An AAF official history pointed out without elaboration that "those who had sponsored the rail center bombings in the first place generally thought they had been right, and the champions of interdiction continued to argue their side of the case."[31]

One of the groups that continued to argue its side of the case was the Enemy Objectives Unit. It prepared and distributed an "Interdiction Handbook," that became a "best seller at SHAEF," according to one of its authors.[32] The handbook called for strikes on supply depots, oil and motor transport pools and cuts in railway lines. The EOU recommended the establishment of rings of interdiction to isolate the battle area, the first along the Seine, Loire and Paris-Orléans gap, the second along the Albert Canal and the Meuse. It specified that "the First and Second Ring targets consist almost exclusively of bridges."[33]

AEAF and SHAEF reports usually reflected the convictions of their commanders — but not always. In August, a group calling itself "The American Contingent at AEAF" issued a paper that differed sharply with Leigh-Mallory's proclamations. It noted that

Diagram 4: AAF Evaluatioin Board Bridge Diagram

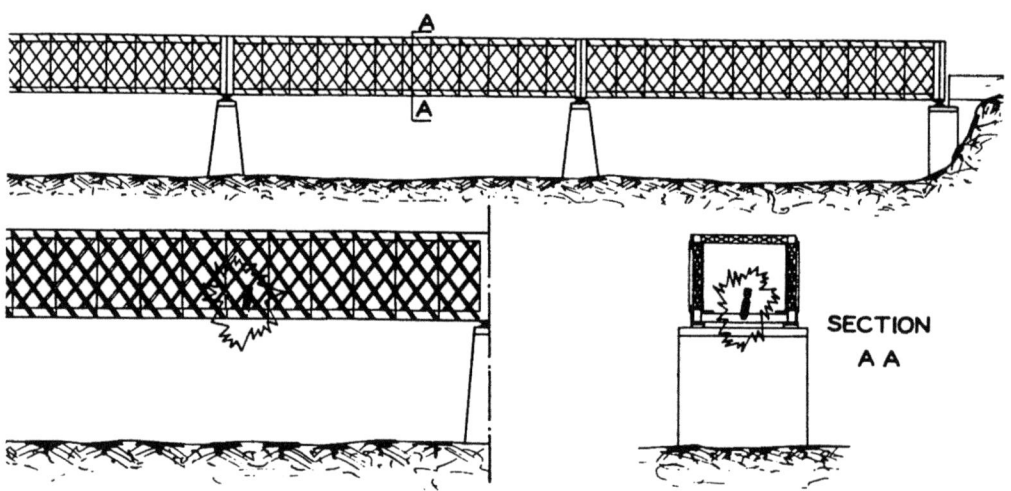

AAF Evaluation Board, report, "Effectiveness of Air Attack Against Rail Transportation in the Battle of France," June 1945.

two methods of preventing the flow of enemy rail traffic had been tried: "The first was to bomb rail centers and marshaling yards. The second was to bomb rail bridges, viaducts and tunnels. Bridge interdiction was the better method. Military trains and trains carrying enemy goods are not found in marshaling yards or rail centers. Usually only civilian trains and supplies are found in these areas. This has been found to be true in France as well as Italy."[34]

This group — whose members were staff officers of the organization that had planned and directed the transportation campaign — concluded, as have so many others, that to disrupt military transportation by bombing rail centers required first the virtual obliteration of a large part of the railroad network serving the civilian economy. Only then would the military forces begin to feel a pinch.

Ninth Air Force had contributed to both the transportation campaign and interdiction. As noted above, it reported that the assault on French and Belgian rail centers had not produced results commensurate with the weight of attack. Interdiction, however, received high marks:

> The periodic and systematic cutting of rail lines supplemented the attack on bridges.... Railroads leading into the battle area from both the north and south of the LOIRE and east and west of the SEINE were continuously attacked. ... rail movement was hazardous and very often impossible. Enemy troops and armor in many cases were forced to de-train and proceed to the battle area by road. This is believed to have caused a considerable reduction in serviceability of heavy armor.[35]

In the planning stage of Overlord, AEAF's staff had disparaged track-cutting as wasteful and ineffective. Investigators from IX TAC ORS found that "the tactic was productive if not sufficient unto itself. The enemy was forced to revamp procedures and reroute traffic over circuitous routes. The resulting disruption often led to bottlenecks and traffic congestion which could be exploited by fighter-bombers."[36]

The EOU's report of its investigation of Allied air offensives received high praise from a Ninth Air Force historian. He wrote in an introduction: "This report should be preserved with the greatest care. It constitutes the best evidence derived from enemy sources as to the effects produced by the Interdiction Program of the Ninth Air Force in the period prior to and during the battles in Normandy and Northern France." The report traced the progress of twenty-three German divisions as they moved to the Normandy beachhead. The first major obstacle met by German troops moving from the south was the "persistent cutting of lines by the Maquis [French Resistance fighters]." The Loire constituted a formidable barrier with many of its bridges down. More than half of the troops detrained at the Loire and marched six to twelve days to reach their battle stations. No evidence was found of any delay in troop movements resulting from attacks on eastern marshaling yards. Some German units coming from the north crossed the Seine by ferry: "The delay imposed by this method was approximately the same as the delay to those elements which moved around the impassable Seine bridges by rail to Paris."[37]

In June 1945, the AAF Evaluation Board issued the comprehensive report of its investigations of Allied air campaigns. The report acknowledged that the results of the transportation campaign and interdiction had been "thoroughly intermingled." Nevertheless, the Board addressed the crucial question: "How much of the decline in traffic was due to attacks on rail centers: how much to attacks on bridges, track and trains?"[38]

A tabulation of rail traffic in France military and non-military (see Table 7) showed the anticipated sharp decline in the latter. As also anticipated, the transportation campaign did not prevent the Wehrmacht from getting essential trains to the front.

The number of available locomotives declined by one-third. This presented little hardship to the Germans. The number of usable freight cars was cut by only 18 percent. AAF Evaluation Board investigators concluded that blocked Seine bridges, track cuts and air attacks on operating trains gave the greatest transportation problems to German divisions—in a word, interdiction. Divisions coming from the south met the same obstacles, and Resistance actions were more aggressive there.

Many air and railway experts predicted that track-cutting would be uneconomical. The AAF Evaluation Board reported that 150 line cuts had been made in the two and a half weeks prior to the invasion on lines serving the lodgment area (see Table 8). Immediately after D-Day, track-cutting became widespread in Normandy, not executed according to a master plan but on the pragmatic basis of cutting lines observed to be in use by German forces. In all, Allied air forces expended 7,000 tons of bombs to execute 1,000 line cuts. The report offered a startling conclusion: "The saturation of cuts in the Ouest was sufficient by itself to account largely for the decline in post–D-Day traffic, and if attacks had been more systematic, the same results could have been achieved for less tonnage." This remarkable statement raises questions about the transportation campaign and interdiction actions other than track-cutting.

The AAF Evaluation Board agreed with other surveys about locomotives: attacks on rail centers had not reduced their numbers to levels which hampered German forces significantly. Moreover, "all available evidence indicates that interference with servicing facilities had only an insignificant effect on train movement...." As the amount of civilian rail traffic decreased, the burden on servicing centers decreased proportionally, with priority given to military trains.

The AAF Evaluation Board strongly endorsed cutting rail lines at bridges and other chokepoints to form lines of interdiction. It endorsed track-cutting. Its investigations were thorough, and its survey teams visited targets to analyze bombing results. The Board arrived at the following conclusions about Overlord's campaigns against railroads:

Table 7: Freight Traffic, Jan.–July 1944

	French Freight	Wehrmacht and Supply
Jan.	218	29
Feb.	214	32
Mar.	210	34
Apr.	178	30
May	117	26
June	56	20
July	30	21

*Millions of gross tons hauled per kilometer each day.

Table 8: Selected Attacks on French Rail Bridges

Rail Section	Fighter-Bombers		Mediums		Day-Heavies	
	Cuts	Tonnage	Cuts	Tonnage	Cuts	Tonnage
Rouen to Mantes	4	130	8	196	1	239
Mantes to B'gency	4	102	13	164	0	—
Blois to Nantes	3	48	11	114	9	322

Even without the tonnage dropped on French rail centers before D-Day, as great a degree of interference with tactical traffic could have been achieved [by interdiction] as was actually achieved. Hence if this degree of interference is considered adequate, the pre-D-Day attacks against French rail centers were not necessary, and the 70,000 tons involved could have been devoted to alternative targets.

The reports cited in this chapter were produced by groups actually involved in the campaigns being evaluated. No independent, unbiased agency analyzed bombing results and evaluated air campaigns that supported the Normandy invasion. However, a thorough study of U.S. and British documentary materials related to World War II air campaigns uncovered no evidence that American air forces, the EOU, or the AAF Evaluation Board attempted to doctor evidence or gloss over mistakes. As will be shown in the next chapter, the same cannot be said about SHAEF.

Chapter 17

German Opinions of Allied Air Campaigns

Captured German soldiers, officials and records provided Allied investigators with valuable sources of information about the effectiveness of air offensives. German commanders invariably identified air power as the most important reason for their defeats in the west. Field Marshal von Rundstedt remembered that all his preparations "came to nothing" because of the transportation chaos; "it was impossible to move anyone at all by day whether a column or an individual vehicle ... [to] carry fuel or ammunition."[1]

The commander who replaced Von Rundstedt in the west died during the Normandy battle; but before his death, Field Marshal von Kluge sent a message to Hitler: "In the face of the total enemy air superiority, we can adopt no tactics to compensate for the annihilating power of air except to retire from the battlefield...."[2]

The capture of Colonel Hans Hoeffner, who had directed German railway operations in the west, inspired intense interest at various Allied headquarters. Here was a source of information of the highest quality. Allied intelligence officers interrogated Colonel Hoeffner for months. His testimony about the bombing of transportation targets would exert a profound influence on evaluations of Overlord's air campaigns. But some interrogators blatantly twisted his testimony to make it more pleasing to SHAEF. The following excerpt from a verbatim account illustrates the approach:

> RAF Officer:
> Which events did you dread most during the bombing offensive before the invasion? What did you fear most as regards its effects after the invasion?
>
> Hoeffner:
> We dreaded attacks on bridges most, and they actually proved extremely serious, and secondly attacks on workshops and coaling plants, that is, attacks on communications centers, owing to their effect on repair and coal installations.
>
> RAF Officer:
> As regards bridges, what I meant by my last question was not so much which causes did you dread most but which effects did you fear most of all before the invasion?[3]

This attempt and others to put words in Hoeffner's mouth failed. He never recanted his statement: "We dreaded attacks on bridges most."

Hoeffner's testimony contradicted claims disseminated by SHAEF about the transportation campaign. To cope with this awkward development, SHAEF G-2 prepared a carefully worded summary of the testimony to make it appear that Hoeffner believed the transportation campaign had been effective — a claim that he had categorically denied. The following is an excerpt from SHAEF's summary of Hoeffner's interrogations:

> The attacks on the French railways between March and May 1944 reduced the capacity of the network so seriously that in addition to the practically total elimination of French civilian and economic traffic, German economic, armaments and fortification traffic was progressively abandoned. In addition military supply traffic to Paris and beyond, which had previously totaled 60 to 70 trains a day, was eventually cut down to a bare 20.[4]

Bearing a top-secret classification, copies of the stenographic record of Hoeffner's interrogations circulated among intelligence officers at various Allied headquarters. They quickly perceived that his comments did not support the conclusions SHAEF purported to draw from them. Furthermore, other Allied organizations had interrogated Hoeffner and detected discrepancies between his statements and SHAEF's summary of them.

A report by G-2 (Air), 12th Army Group, is especially significant because this ground-forces headquarters, with little responsibility for air campaigns, had nothing it would be inclined to gloss over. The report opened with a sharply worded rebuke of SHAEF in capital letters:

> THIS SUMMARY IS A DIGEST OF FOUR DIFFERENT IPW [interrogations of a prisoner of war] REPORTS. IT HAS BEEN PREPARED BY THE TARGET INTELLIGENCE SECTION, G-2 (AIR), HQ. 12th ARMY GROUP, AND DIFFERS MARKEDLY FROM AN EARLIER SUMMARY OF THESE SAME INTERROGATIONS PREPARED BY G-2 SHAEF.

This opening salvo was followed by another which charged that the SHAEF report contained "a number of *obiter dicta*" attributed to Hoeffner but not supported by his comments.[5]

Principally, intelligence analysts at 12th Army Group denied that Hoeffner had said that the transportation campaign had been effective; quite the contrary:

> Military railroading did not require the extensive facilities built for the French economy; in the lull between the end of April and 10 May, Hoeffner had sufficient time to remedy some of the most pressing deficiencies by setting up auxiliary installations which were used to a considerable extent. Available locomotives had been decreased by destruction, delay in repair at the French roundhouses, lengthened running time, and by French trickery in concealing locomotives. Military requirements were guaranteed, however, by the addition of 200 locomotives which Hoeffner imported from Germany about the first of June. Damage to locomotive servicing facilities was countered by the use of small station installations, and by shifting locomotive factories over to repair. Damage to through lines, particularly by the destruction of bridges, had so reduced over-all traffic that there was a surplus of railroad cars.... Track capacity was the limiting factor; and Hoeffner feared that this would be more fully exploited by Allied aircraft. It was because he expected 4,000 American and 4,000 British planes to be used against the rail system after D-Day, and not because of any catastrophic damage existing in May, that he advised von Rundstedt to expect no scheduled troop movements by rail for the first two weeks, and no movements of supplies for the first 10 days.[5]

The 12th Army Group's report of Hoeffner's interrogations leveled a serious charge of duplicity against SHAEF. A report which disseminated false conclusions from intelligence data could cause a misdirection of future air efforts, including those against Japan.

Hoeffner's assessment of the transportation campaign differed from SHAEF's. Moreover, he declared that interdiction had given him insurmountable problems. Destruction of rail and road bridges over the Seine forced unloading north of the Seine upon all trains arriving to take up position on the front. Only eight trains could get across the river each night (by barges and ferries) so it would have been futile to bunch up trains at the river in excess of this number. The same kind of chaotic conditions on the Loire restricted traffic substantially.

Hoeffner's remarks conformed closely with predictions and evaluations made by EOU and other groups critical of the transportation campaign. Blocked bridges sharply limited the number of trains dispatched across the Seine and Loire. Interdiction operations, primarily track-cutting and attacks on trains, severely reduced the number of trains that could operate inside the lines of interdiction. These conditions accounted for most of the reductions in rail traffic that Zuckerman attributed to bombed rail centers. As Hoeffner explained, it made no sense to send trains to the Seine and Loire if they could not cross them.

Hoeffner's testimony is unambiguous on two major issues.

1. The transportation campaign had little effect on military rail traffic.
2. Demolished bridges on the Seine and Loire, track-cutting and attacks on running trains in the lodgment area brought about a critical reduction in military rail transportation.

The 12th Army Group report contained this important statement: "It is HOEFFNER's view that even greater difficulties would have been occasioned for the Germans if a lesser effort had been made against marshaling yards and the whole fury of the Allied attack concentrated on rail lines with emphasis on the bridges."

Hoeffner stated that fighter-bomber attacks on running trains gave him serious problems. They were particularly upsetting when they stranded a train on an open stretch of track. He worried much less about track cuts in rail centers; they were usually repaired quickly, often in less than twenty-four hours. Hoeffner explained: "There was no difficulty in commandeering emergency labor for the roadbed repair in thickly-populated industrial regions. There, when necessary, factories were closed down partly or entirely until track repairs had been carried out. In thinly-populated agricultural regions it was difficult to get sufficient workmen quickly." This statement refuted Zuckerman's strange assertion that it was easier to repair track in open country than in urban areas. During interrogations by Ninth Air Force, Hoeffner described track and bridge cuts as a "first-class calamity even though loss of those on the Seine had been anticipated and ferries had been provided."[6]

Field Marshal Erhard Milch had been a top-level Luftwaffe officer and one of Hitler's key industrial coordinators. He had occupied positions which gave him a broad perspective on military-supply problems. After his capture Milch was asked "What caused greatest damage: attacks on stations, marshaling yards etc., or bridges? He replied without hesitation, "Bridges of course."[7]

In postwar books Tedder and Eisenhower claimed that the casualties and devastation inflicted on France and Belgium by the transportation campaign had been necessary to bring about the defeat of Germany. This assertion is refuted by virtually every survey of Overlord's air campaigns except those of the British Bomb Analysis Unit, whose investigations and reports were tightly controlled by Zuckerman and Tedder. Hoeffner's interrogation, Ninth Air Force studies, EOU investigations and other bomb-damage surveys confirmed the conclusion of the AAF Evaluation Board: "The pre–D-Day attacks against rail centers were not necessary and the 70,000 tons [of bombs] involved could have been devoted to alternative targets."

The transportation campaign and interdiction were major Overlord air offensives executed by Allied air forces to give direct assistance to General Eisenhower's invasion forces. Other Allied air efforts produced significant impacts on the Normandy invasion and deserve examination.

Chapter 18

Evaluations of Allied Air Offensives: Oil, V-Weapons, Aircraft, Road Junctions, Carpet Bombing

Spaatz and Arnold recognized a need for thorough evaluations of Allied strategic air campaigns by impartial investigators. Arnold wanted the job done by civilians, people of eminent status in their fields, competent to assess evidence objectively. They would not be suspected of glossing over mistakes or of making prejudgments. Arnold opposed a joint U.S.-British survey: "We alone are engaged in daylight precision bombing," he wrote to Spaatz, "and we must have our own critical appraisal of our efforts for use in the strategic bombing of Japan."[1]

With the approval of President Roosevelt and Secretary of War Stimson, the United States Strategic Bombing Survey [USSBS] was established with a force of 350 civilians, 350 officers and 500 enlisted men. USSBS examined several hundred German industrial plants, studied production records and interviewed thousands of military and civilian authorities. It eventually issued more than two hundred detailed, documented reports.[2]

The Allied oil offensive had started slowly in May 1944, gathering momentum in the fall. By March 1945, the German synthetic-fuel industry was virtually inoperative. Monthly production of crude oil had dropped from 167,000 tons to 40,000 tons.[3] Fuel shortages handicapped every part of the German war machine. Throughout the winter of 1944–45, Hitler's brilliant industrial coordinator, Albert Speer, directed a high-priority effort to maintain a minimum quantity of liquid fuels for German industry and armed forces.

USSBS reports on the oil offensive contained some sharp criticism of Allied errors of omission and commission. Bombing accuracy had been poor: only 15 percent of the bombs hit their targets and only 3 percent actually struck critical, damagable parts. Allied air forces dropped too few incendiary bombs; many bombs were too small; too many were duds. They had bombed some plants too often, and others not often enough.[4]

The oil campaign against synthetic-fuel plants hurt the GAF both in fighters lost defending the plants and in fuel shortages which limited operations. Aviation gasoline was a major product of synthetic-fuel plants; the per monthly production fell from 170,000 tons to 52,000 tons during the oil offensive. Fuel shortages handicapped all GAF efforts, but the effect on pilot training was catastrophic (see Table 9). Pilot skill depends in large measure on the quality of training. Because of fuel shortages, the number of hours devoted to GAF training flights plummeted.[5]

The Allied air offensive against oil installations is often cited as the most effective strategic-bombing campaign of World War II. It was the pride of USSTAF, and many AAF airmen believed that it vindicated the doctrine of strategic bombing. Some of them criticized Eisenhower and Portal for not allowing it to begin sooner. Spaatz did not support this complaint. He explained to a USSTAF historian: "The oil enthusiasts get a little bit off base in what they say about it [the oil campaign]. In my opinion our Air Force would not have attacked them any oftener than we did if oil had been selected as first priority...." Spaatz pointed out that the primary objective of the oil offensive in the pre-D-Day period was to force the GAF to fight and to win air supremacy. He also cited the impact of weather on operations: "We attacked oil targets just about as often as we would have if oil had been first priority ... [considering] weather conditions in the various areas of Germany."[6]

General Eisenhower once considered issuing a citation to honor the people of London, "who had never asked him to divert resources from Overlord to their defense." It was Eisenhower at his most diplomatic. Actually an enormous amount of effort went into the defense of the U.K. against V-weapons. During the V-1 assault, the RAF transferred 800 anti-aircraft guns, served by 23,000 men and women and 60,000 tons of supplies and ammunition to the U.K. coast to be used in defense against flying bombs.[7] The campaign consumed vast amounts of ammunition, including scarce proximity-fused shells. Much radar equipment, a large number of Allied aircraft and a vast photo-reconnaissance effort went into the fight against V-weapons. The effort continued for many months during Overlord's buildup period. Crossbow consumed artillery and air matériel at a time when Allied forces were battling to consolidate a beachhead in Normandy. Shortages of artillery shells hindered Bradley's troops at the time.

One of Churchill's most trusted scientific advisors, a man who directed the intelligence effort against V-weapons, recalled that the V-1 provoked a "great expenditure of effort ... [despite being] a simple, inexpensive weapon to produce."[8] Was the effort to blunt the V-weapon offensives commensurate with the danger? Speer calculated that 5,000 V-2s could have delivered only 3,750 tons of explosive, less than half the tonnage dropped on Germany in a single day by Allied bombers.[9] (1,190 V-2s were launched against England.)

V-weapon installations were exceedingly difficult to destroy. Brereton visited captured V-1 sites. One of them near Valognes was "a tremendous installation," he recorded: "The concrete cover was at least 20 feet thick and absolutely bombproof."[10]

Crossbow did produce some benefits to Overlord; it delayed the V-weapon offensives until after D-Day. Moreover, Germany diverted thousands of laborers from construction of anti-invasion obstacles to work on launch sites.

Between January and June 1944, Allied air forces dropped twenty thousand tons of bombs at V-1 sites, many of which the Germans had abandoned. In his book about V-weapons, Basil Collier described the counter-V-1 offensive as "illogical and extravagant to an almost incredible degree." Between June 13 and September 1, the Allies expended seventy-four thousand tons of bombs to counter the V-1 offensive, but many of the targets were of "doubtful relevance," in Collier's words.[11]

Spaatz and his air force commanders strongly opposed the bombing of French towns

Table 9: Flight Hours* of Pilots in Training

Time Period	GAF	RAF	AAF
Oct. '42–June '43	220 (55)	360 (75)	300 (100)
July '43–June '44	175 (30)	360 (75)	340 (140)
July '44–May '45	125 (35)	360 (75)	400 (200)

*Total Hours (Hours in Combat Types)

in the lodgment area to block highways with rubble of demolished buildings. But Eisenhower approved Leigh-Mallory's proposal to conduct such an offensive.

Allied investigators studied bombed towns to evaluate these operations. Local inhabitants and officials gave evidence and town engineers helped in the assessment of any transportation disruption these operations had caused. Eighth Air Force teams concluded that bombing towns to create road blocks produced few serious obstacles to German forces. "In some towns, no through-routes had been blocked; and in one small town all routes were blocked but by-pass routes were available outside town. ... the bombing of towns is an ineffective method of blocking roads and is extremely costly both from the standpoint of effort involved and the property destroyed."[12] Armored vehicles could force their way through streets covered with rubble. Equipment and labor to clear streets were readily available.

Although Leigh-Mallory's journal recorded his fervent support for a campaign of bombing towns to block roads, he later claimed that it had been requested by ground forces. Ninth Air Force investigators disputed this claim. They learned that First Army did not favor or request the bombing of towns to create road blocks "and was of the opinion that it delayed and hindered Allied troop movements ... more than it hampered the enemy."[13]

ORS teams also concluded that bombing towns did not delay German forces significantly. Numerous possibilities existed for detours; rubble could be cleared quickly. They recommended bombing roads outside of towns at places where they crossed bridges, gullies, marshes and wooded areas.

W. Messerschmitt headed one of Germany's major aircraft-manufacturing companies. In a postwar interview he stated that Allied attacks on oil were "the principal cause of Germany's collapse." The Pointblank offensive against aircraft installations had been less effective in his opinion. Neither high explosive nor incendiary bombs did much damage to machine tools even when buildings collapsed on them. After workers cleared the machines of rubble, they stretched a tarpaulin over the rafters and production continued. USSBS investigators generally agreed with Messerschmitt.[14]

USSTAF's bombing offensive against the aircraft industry in the first half of 1944 did not cause a deep cut in fighter production, but it did bring about massive attrition in the GAF fighter arm. In its defense of the aircraft industry, the GAF lost many experienced pilots and leaders. This permitted the Allies to achieve air supremacy in time for the Normandy invasion. Furthermore, attempts to maintain aircraft production required extraordinary efforts which were negated when the aircraft produced could not fly for lack of pilots and fuel. Problems created by bombing forced aircraft manufacturers to concentrate on output at the expense of quality. USSBS concluded that this failure was as "injurious as if aircraft plants had been damaged or destroyed."[15]

As part of the campaign to emasculate the GAF, USSTAF and AEAF attacked airfields in the west. Not all airmen believed that it was worthwhile to bomb airfields. Craters in runways could be repaired quickly. Many bombs caused no damage at all to working facilities. Fighters comprised the primary GAF threat, and they could operate from rudimentary air strips and be serviced in the field without elaborate equipment. AEAF designated about one hundred airfields in the west for attack prior to D-Day. Allied fighter-bombers frequently struck airfields when returning from escort missions. Mediums and heavy bombers attacked them occasionally when their primary objectives were covered by clouds. Deadly anti-aircraft artillery protected most airfields, and it took a heavy toll of Allied aircraft. Eighth Air Force carried out large-scale operations against airfields on May 9 and May 23. Ninth Air Force mediums started an offensive against airfields on May 11. As with all pre–D-Day operations, some targets outside the lodgment area had to be hit to preserve the secrecy of the landing beaches. By D-Day, Allied air forces had dropped 6,717 tons of bombs on airfields in an area 130 miles around Caen.[16]

After the Battle of Normandy, USSTAF's intelligence section investigated the impact of heavy bombers on airfields. The report pointed out that there had been substantial waste of effort. Heavy bombers destroyed few aircraft on the ground and "little was accomplished by destruction of facilities [which] are rarely indispensable to fighter operations." Moreover, airfields returned to operation quickly after bombing attacks. "St. Dizier was successfully attacked twice in 1944 and was heavily damaged by the second attack on May 9, 1944. Its serviceability was restored within a week and despite damage to installations the field apparently resumed full activity." GAF defensive measures improved continuously, "and they now scatter their fighters over many small airfields and landing strips, disperse them widely, and hide and conceal them with great care." USSTAF's evaluators concluded that airfields were usually not a suitable objective for heavy bombers except "where counter air force operations are integrated with a ground offensive. Here the objective is to neutralize the enemy air force for *a limited period of time and within a limited area.*" Fighters in low-level attacks destroyed aircraft on the ground most efficiently. In summary the report stated that "destruction of repair facilities, post-holing runways, and blitzing housing certainly slows up operations and the efficiency and morale of air crews inevitably suffer. This is certainly a worthwhile by-product of bombing, but it is hardly considered adequate in itself to justify attacks on airfields [by heavy bombers.]"[17]

Operation Cobra led to a great Allied victory in France. The bright glow of success tended to obscure errors that had been made in its execution. Spaatz and Tedder tried to convince Eisenhower that Cobra would have succeeded without the carpet bombing, but their arguments did not convince the supreme commander.

It was obvious, however, that Cobra's carpet-bombing techniques had been tragically flawed. Eighth Air Force bombs fell on First Army positions on both July 24 and July 25, killing 128 U.S. soldiers including General McNair. Investigations of air support for Cobra showed that both air and ground forces had made mistakes.[18]

On July 24, some of the bombers did not receive Leigh-Mallory's order to abort the mission. The communications system was inadequate. Eighth Air Force recommended that in future operations of this kind one of its officers should be at Army headquarters with communications equipment to enable him to contact bombers when emergency instructions had to be broadcast.

The depth of a safety zone — the distance friendly troops should withdraw from a carpet-bombing target area — was the subject of much discussion during the planning of Cobra. Too far back, the infantry would be unable to reach enemy positions in time to exploit the chaos produced by the bombs. But the closer troops were to the bomb line, the higher was the probability that they would be hit by the bombardment. Airmen who investigated the Cobra bombings recommended that in future, troops be withdrawn at least three thousand yards from bomb lines.[19] Gross bombing errors would still be possible, however. This was one of the reasons why airmen lacked enthusiasm for the tactic.

One of the investigators of Cobra's carpet bombing searched through the evidence so thoroughly that he was able to name individual bomb groups and even airmen whose mistakes caused the short bombings: "Bombing errors can be attributed to personnel errors and malfunctioning of equipment," he reported; "The majority of personnel errors were caused by bad judgment, not identifying the target properly [and] wrong data set up in the bombsight which was caused by lowering the altitude on the bombing run making it impossible for the bombardiers to reset their bombsights in time."[20]

Not all mistakes in the Cobra bombing were made by airmen. Many U.S. ground soldiers failed to take standard precautions against air attack. Allied air superiority had made them careless, and many did not protect themselves in foxholes, trenches, bunkers or ditches.

Weather reconnaissance was poor on July 24, but steps were taken to improve it for the mission next day. It was immensely wasteful and hazardous to assemble more than a thousand heavy bombers and then to recall them because of bad weather.

During the air overture for Cobra, artillery smoke shells marked important targets, but air crews could not always distinguish between red smoke from shells and smoke from bomb blasts or fires. Smoke and dust concealed targets. Fighter-bombers attacked first, and their bomb explosions increased sighting problems for heavy bombers. Eighth Air Force reported that "These operations made it evident that a satisfactory system of target marking would be of material assistance.... Experiments were therefore undertaken at once and radio, radar, pyrotechnic and other devices were tested. A technique was subsequently developed which represented a vast improvement over the colored smoke marking employed during the subject [Cobra] mission."[21]

Cobra's carpet bombing was one of many cases in which the AAF had failed to prepare for future needs but, when forced to deal with them, did so with dispatch. Throughout the war, air and ground crews developed solutions to many problems that arose during combat operations. SHAEF's staff criticized Doolittle severely for Eighth Air Force mistakes in Cobra. He responded by seeking ways to improve carpet-bombing techniques. He informed Spaatz of new developments: "We have ... developed a very efficient type of anti-aircraft marking. Twelve [anti-aircraft] guns can mark a straight line something over two miles long with about a 400-yard interval between bursts. This will be ideal for marking front line troops."[22]

In his books about his army service in World War II, General Bradley excused himself from blame for Cobra bombing mishaps. Airmen were at fault, he charged; they failed to live up to agreements made in planning the operation, primarily by not taking his advice about certain crucial operational matters. Bradley's charges have been repeated in many written accounts of Cobra, but they are laced with prevarications. He distorted one major fact and ignored another. Bradley neglected to mention that the depth of the safety zone had been fixed at 1,500 yards at his insistence. He had initially recommended 800 yards! Eighth Air Force planners had asked for 3,000 yards, a depth that would have made bombing casualties among U.S. soldiers highly unlikely. The record of a Cobra planning conference attended by Bradley states that he was aware of the risk that gross bombing errors could cause casualties to his troops and agreed to accept it.[23]

Bradley also claimed that air planners agreed with his suggestion that heavy bombers approach the target area on flightpaths parallel to the St. Lô–Périers road. This a false claim. It is also not true that such flightpaths would have prevented bombing errors. The minutes of Cobra air-planning meetings do not record Bradley's claims. To airmen, it was obvious that parallel flightpaths were not possible if the mission was to be completed in one hour, as Bradley had specified. A force of fifteen hundred heavy bombers could not complete the mission in one hour on flightpaths that funneled it into a corridor only one mile wide. One investigator explained that such an approach would have required the bombers to line up and "enter the Continent at Holland ... in order to space all combat wings in column to avoid congestion."[24]

There were other considerations in favor of perpendicular flightpaths. They would tend to minimize bombing errors. As Spaatz explained to Eisenhower, "all our bombing experience shows that lateral error is greater than range error."[25] Had the bombers attacked along a path parallel to the highway, some of the "lateral errors" would have fallen on First Army positions, and bomb explosions would have created target-identification difficulties infinitely greater than those caused by the perpendicular approach. Bradley charged that airmen had favored the perpendicular approach because it minimized exposure to flak. Of course it is standard procedure for airmen to take flak into consideration, but there is no evidence to indicate that it was a primary reason for the choice of flightpaths.

The sincerity of Bradley's protests about the Cobra carpet bombing is doubtful. On July 24, even though some of his soldiers had been killed by stray bombs in the aborted mission, he requested that a carpet bombing be carried out next day as planned. He later claimed that he had no choice, that the carpet bombing was essential and had to be executed as planned. The latter part of this claim is true. Parallel flightpaths were not feasible. However, Bradley could have deepened the safety zone. This was entirely under his control. He did not do so. The truth is that Bradley wanted his soldiers to be near enough to the bomb line to be able to reach enemy positions before German soldiers recovered from the effects of the bombing. It was unworthy of Bradley to blame airmen for mishaps in an operation that his demands had done so much to shape.

Chapter 19

Postwar Debates About Allied Air Campaigns

For many years after World War II, General Eisenhower's claim that the bombing of rail centers in France and Belgium was an essential part of the effort to defeat Germany remained virtually unchallenged. But in 1978, Solly Zuckerman's book about his wartime experiences started a public debate about the transportation campaign and interdiction. Zuckerman excoriated people who had opposed the bombing of railroad centers. He denigrated their motives and competence. He reminded readers that he was a scientist who based decisions on evidence, whereas his critics were mere "theoreticians" who lacked experience in planning and evaluating bombing campaigns. He referred scathingly to the Enemy Objectives Unit of the Economic Warfare Division, manned by a staff of "young and enthusiastic economists" who based conclusions on "*a priori*" reasoning.[1]

Zuckerman often attributed ulterior motives to opponents. He suggested that their antipathy to his proposals stemmed from self-interest or some trivial slight they had received. He recalled that C. P. Kindleberger of the EOU, one of his pesky critics, resented being made to wait "in an empty office" until Zuckerman found time to see him. Zuckerman recalled that Leigh-Mallory had barred General Cabell from attending a conference, a slight which supposedly inspired his antipathy to AEAF. Kindleberger and his associates, according to Zuckerman, were typical of his opponents, "not one of whom had the slightest practical experience of the issues involved."[2]

Zuckerman's book was so one-sided that Kindleberger, then a professor of economics at the Massachusetts Institute of Technology, felt compelled to challenge some of its claims. He sent a note to *Encounter*, a scholarly journal that had reviewed Zuckerman's book, in which he defended the work of EOU in planning air support for Overlord. Kindleberger recalled that AEAF opposed bridge bombing, whereas EOU had proposed, as an alternative to the transportation campaign, an offensive to destroy railroad and road bridges in a circle around the Normandy lodgment area. "We believed that bridges could be destroyed with a moderate concentration of aircraft...." Kindleberger was not impressed by Zuckerman's data which purported to prove that the transportation campaign had been effective. Zuckerman's evidence, according to Kindleberger, was "thoroughly unpersuasive to this partisan." Referring to reductions in rail traffic in France and Belgium, Kindleberger explained that while Zuckerman found it "very exciting," it was merely what the economists had claimed all along: "French civilian traffic was a cushion which would protect German military traffic."[3]

Encounter soon received a note from Zuckerman in reply to Kindleberger's criticisms.

He defended the transportation campaign and denied that he or AEAF had been opposed to bridge bombing. He claimed that Kindleberger was mistaken about the reason why attacks on bridges were not started until shortly before D-Day. The delay had been ordered to protect the secrecy of the invasion beaches, not because Zuckerman thought it was impossible to destroy bridges.[4]

Zuckerman returned to a favorite theme in his note: "What Dr. Kindleberger has written only served to reinforce my view that there is a wide difference between recommendations on military planning made *a priori* by economists, and those that are based on evidence from previous experience." Zuckerman expressed regret that "theoreticians" like Kindleberger had rejected his recommendations without even studying the empirical evidence he had provided to support them.[5]

Kindleberger replied to Zuckerman's broadside with another note to *Encounter*. It made no sense to an economist to say that bridges were expensive and bombing railroad yards does damage "without some more precise comparison of costs and benefits, including especially that bridges take three weeks to repair for through-traffic, and railway yards at most four hours." Kindleberger asked: "Am I to understand ... that Zuckerman now claims that his side recommended the bombing of bridges which led to the attack on Vernon? This is difficult to square with my memory of the period, or with [Zuckerman's] autobiography."[6]

W. W. Rostow, a wartime associate of Kindleberger's at EOU, entered the debate with a note to *Encounter*. He challenged some of Zuckerman's prized "empirical evidence," specifically some computations Zuckerman had included in a paper on bridge bombing in Sicily. That report influenced decisions at AEAF. Rostow analyzed the data in the Sicily report and found that they did not show what Zuckerman claimed they showed, that bridge attacks were costly and difficult.[7]

Zuckerman answered Rostow on the pages of *Encounter*. He reiterated that "attacks on bridges had from the start been an integral part of the plan that was adopted." He claimed that there was something "radically wrong" with Rostow's calculations, probably the result of relying too heavily on "regression methods which are frequently adopted by economists [and] uncritical use of computers." Clearly, Zuckerman had lost none of his zest for argument.[8]

This re-enactment of wartime controversies among Allied target planners encouraged re-examination of issues of the highest significance. It probably motivated Rostow to write a book, *Pre-Invasion Bombing Strategy,* that explores the issues from the point of view of EOU, a viewpoint that has not received much attention from historians. It is a valuable source of information about air campaigns in support of Overlord.

Epilogue

The issues debated so heatedly at SHAEF in 1944 continued to perplex U.S. leaders during wars in Korea, Vietnam and the Persian Gulf. Military commanders still tend to want to use air weapons against inappropriate targets. Military forces and civilians still come under unintentional or unwarranted air assaults.

Eisenhower often received contradictory recommendations from his air advisors. Spaatz would make one proposal, Tedder another, Leigh-Mallory a third. Complicating all such issues was the incipient air-ground hostility that made each side suspicious of the other's intentions. Eisenhower was not as hostile to airmen as his chief of staff, who had been heard to say, "We will have an independent air force over my dead body"; but he could not fail to be influenced by his many years in the Army's ground forces. General Bradley's books expressed negative feelings about airmen that were common in the Army.

Airmen had their long-term grievances, too. They often complained that high-ranking Army leaders did not know how to direct air operations. Spaatz and Arnold, West Pointers both, did not place a high value on their peacetime experience at the U.S. Army's command and general staff school, where both the curriculum and the administration favored ground officers. (Eisenhower graduated there near the top of his class.)

Criticism of the transportation plan cannot be dismissed as merely the product of hindsight; hundreds of experts warned *at the time* that it was unnecessary and that it would be ineffective, as well as devastating to civilians. With overwhelming air supremacy, it should have been evident long before D-Day that German military movements could be disrupted sufficiently by interdiction alone. Indeed, the tactical air forces did demonstrate the truth of this judgment in the Battle of Normandy. That it was not evident to everyone raises questions about the ways intelligence data were handled during World War II. Arnold and others believed that the British distributed intelligence information selectively to further their aims. Unfortunately, fifty years after the end of World War II, Winston Churchill's papers (a major source of information on this point) at the Churchill College Archives Center are "closed," and only a few approved researchers may consult them.

Why did Eisenhower authorize the bombing of rail centers in France and Belgium when so many advisors predicted that it was unnecessary and would fail to achieve its objectives, kill many civilians and devastate many towns? The reasons he gave to Churchill and to posterity do not constitute the whole truth. He behaved as commanders often do; he demanded the right to use the weapons he believed could improve his chances to defeat the enemy, regardless of their effect on the nation's other military campaigns or on its long-range interests. This happened again in Korea and Vietnam. Eisenhower's principal concern was to control the strategic air forces. To do so he had to offer a suitable program for their employment, one that would be directed by SHAEF. The Transportation Plan, despite its substantial drawbacks, satisfied these criteria, more or less. Interdiction, on the other hand, was obviously not appropriate employment for strategic air forces and, in any case, could not be started until shortly before D-Day. Eisenhower wanted the heavy bombers, and he wanted them long before D-Day. Air commanders and many railway experts warned SHAEF that interdiction could achieve the objectives of the Transportation Plan without its terrible costs. Subsequent events showed that they were right.

The Allies' combined Chiefs of Staff had responsibility to direct strategic air offensives. They understood the severe drawbacks of the Transportation Plan. One of their most important duties was to reject unwarranted or counterproductive requests from field commanders. In this case they failed to overrule Eisenhower. General Marshall made a strong appeal to President Roosevelt to support Eisenhower's position when it was challenged by Churchill. It was an unusual failure for the CCS; for most of the war, it prudently retained control of strategic air forces in recognition of the evident fact that they should not be controlled by a commander preoccupied with a ground campaign.

Guerrilla warfare, so poorly understood by SHAEF in 1944, disturbs current international relations despite intensive efforts to cope with it. Some scholars of the French Resistance believe it deserves far more credit than it has been given. Writing about harassment of German forces in Normandy, M. R. D. Foot states: "Credit for this is usually given to the photogenic allied air forces. More of it belongs ... to the obscure, devoted French saboteurs who blew up points, damaged bridges, misrouted trains ... sowed tyre-bursters, misdirected motor cyclists, and generally made the Germans' life unbearable...." Shortly before D-Day the French made 950 blockages of the railway system, "considerably more," Foot claimed, "than the RAF and USAAF had secured with Zuckerman's transport interdiction program over the previous two months."[1]

Allied air forces under SHAEF's direction continued to bomb rail centers in the winter of 1944-45. Most of the targets were in Germany. Tedder believed that the German railroad system could be paralyzed by bombing, and that its paralysis would help bring about a collapse of the German war machine. Tedder now had firm control of Overlord's air plans. USSTAF and Bomber Command, now directed by the CCS, promptly answered Eisenhower's requests for help. Fewer protests came to SHAEF about killing civilians by bombing; they were, after all, enemies. Spaatz consistently opposed bombing targets other than Germany's industries or those whose destruction would assist Allied ground forces, but he did not rule out massive attacks on civilian centers such as Dresden when such attacks might help topple a Nazi regime on the verge of collapse.

The military effectiveness of the air assault on German railroads is a question outside the scope of this book. It is obvious, however, that the transportation campaign in France and Belgium should not be cited either to justify or condemn the bombing of German rail centers. The two campaigns were utterly dissimilar. Most of the impact of the transportation campaign in France was absorbed by the civilian economy, although this was not one of its objectives. But paralysis of the German economy *was* a major goal of Allied air forces.

Fifty years ago the official Army Air Forces history stated that:

> Long after D-day, there remained the sobering question as to whether the results

of the [transportation] plan were commensurate with the cost in air effort and the ruin inflicted on French and Belgian cities.

The AAF history did not answer this question definitively, nor did it answer an even more sobering question: aside from its wastefulness and its destructive impact on French and Belgian towns, did the transportation campaign even achieve its primary objective — to disrupt German anti-invasion railroad movements significantly?

Was the transportation campaign necessary? Was it effective?

The answer to both questions is no.

Notes

In the notes, frequently cited archives have been identified by the following abbreviations:

LOC — Library of Congress, Manuscripts Division;
NARS — United States National Archives;
PRO — British Public Record Office;
USAFHRA — U.S. Air Force Historical Research Agency.

In citing works, short titles have generally been used after the first incident.

Preface

1. Henry H. Arnold, *Global Mission* (New York: Harper, 1949), p. 377.
2. W. F. Craven and J. L. Cate, ed.; *Europe: ARGUMENT to V-E Day, January 1944 to May 1945*, vol. 3 of *The Army Air Forces in World War II* (Chicago: The Univ. of Chicago Press, 1951), p. 620.

Chapter 1: Overlord's Air Command

1. Dwight D. Eisenhower, *Crusade in Europe* (Garden City, N.Y.: Doubleday, 1948), pp. 206–207.
2. Gordon A. Harrison, *U.S. Army in World War II: Cross-Channel Attack* (Washington, D.C., office of the Chief of Military History, 1951), p. 457.
3. W.F. Craven and J.L. Cate, eds. *Europe: TORCH to Pointblank, August 1942 to December 1943*, vol. 2 of The Army Air Forces in World War II (Chicago: The Univ. of Chicago Press, 1951), p. 494.
4. Arnold to Eisenhower, August 20, 1943, box 5, Personal Files of Dwight D. Eisenhower, Eisenhower Library.
5. Alfred D. Chandler, Jr., ed., *The War Years*, vol. 3 of *The Papers of Dwight D. Eisenhower* (Baltimore, Md.: The Johns Hopkins Univ. Press, 1970), p. 1479 (hereafter cited as *Papers*, vol. 3).
6. Arnold, *Global Mission*, p. 17.
7. Summary of Spaatz's military career, n.d., U.S. Air Force Office of Public Affairs.
8. Edgar F. Puryear, Jr., *Stars in Flight* (Novato, Calif.: Presidio Press, 1981), p. 94.
9. Spaatz, Report from England, August 27, 1940, box 7, Spaatz Papers, LOC.
10. Ruth Spaatz, oral history transcript, n.d. USAFHRA.
11. Arthur William Tedder, *With Prejudice* (Boston: Little, Brown, 1966), p. 404.
12. Harold Macmillan, *War Diaries* (New York: St. Martin's Press, 1984), p. 151.
13. Churchill to Portal, December 21, 1943, AIR 8/1153, PRO.
14. Tedder to Portal, March 26, 1943, *With Prejudice*, by Tedder, p. 406.

15. Eaker to Haywood S. Hansell, November 16, 1943, box 324, Spaatz Papers, LOC.
16. Marshall to Eisenhower, cable, December 23, 1943, box 66, Marshall Papers, George C. Marshall Foundation.
17. Spaatz, diary entry, December 25, 1943, box 12, Spaatz Papers, LOC.
18. Eisenhower, *Crusade in Europe*, p. 56.
19. Puryear, *Stars in Flight*, p. 94.
20. Eisenhower to Spaatz, May 12, 1943, *Papers*, vol. III, p. 1125.
21. Robert H. Ferrell, ed., *Eisenhower Diaries* (New York: W. W. Norton, 1981), p. 91.
22. Ibid.
23. Forrest Pogue, *Ordeal and Hope*, vol. 3 of *George C. Marshall* (New York: Viking Press, 1966), pp. 290–291.
24. Dwight D. Eisenhower, *At Ease*, (Garden City, N.Y.: Doubleday, 1967), p. 10.
25. Spaatz to Arnold, March 7, 1943, box 104, Arnold Papers, LOC.
26. Harry C. Butcher, *My Three Years with Eisenhower* (New York: Simon and Schuster, 1946), p. 484.
27. Kay Summersby Morgan, *Past Forgetting* (New York: Simon and Schuster, 1975), p. 33.
28. Eisenhower to Bedell-Smith, cable, January 5, 1944, *Papers*, vol. III, p. 1651.
29. Craven and Cate, *Argument to V-E Day*, p. 305.
30. Arnold, foreword to a report on the Combined Bombing Offensive, December 10, 1943, box 67, Spaatz Papers, LOC.
31. USSTAF directive, January 11, 1944, box 17, Spaatz Papers, LOC.
32. Eisenhower, diary entry, March 22, 1944, *Papers*, vol. 3, p. 1785.
33. Smith to Eisenhower, cable, December 31, 1943, *Papers*, vol. 3, p. 1648.
34. Eisenhower to Marshall, December 25, 1943, *Papers*, vol. 3, p. 1611.
35. Churchill to Portal, memo, January 9, 1944, AIR 8/1185, PRO.
36. Eisenhower, diary entry, March 22, 1944, *Papers*, vol. 3, p. 1784.
37. Eisenhower to Tedder, memo, March 9, 1944, *Papers*, vol. 3, p. 1765.
38. Charles Messinger, *Bomber Harris* (New York: St. Martin's Press, 1984), p. 157.
39. Charles Webster and Noble Frankland, *The Strategic Air Offensive against Germany, 1939–1945*, vol. 3 (London: Her Majesty's Stationery Office, 1961), p. 80.
40. Portal to Harris, January 3, 1944, AIR 8/1187, PRO.
41. Eisenhower, diary entry, February 29, 1944, *Papers*, vol. 3, p. 1756.
42. Statement of an agreement between Portal and Eisenhower, n.d., box 93, Personal Files of Dwight D. Eisenhower, Eisenhower Library.
43. Tedder to Portal, February 22, 1944, AIR 8/1185, PRO.
44. Eisenhower to Marshall, March 21, 1944, *Papers*, vol. 3, p. 1781.
45. Eisenhower, diary entry, March 22, 1944, *Papers*, vol. 3, p. 1786.

Chapter 2: Eighth Air Force Operations, 1942–43

1. Haywood S. Hansell, Jr., *The Air Plan That Defeated Hitler* (Atlanta, Ga.: Higgins-McArthur/Longino and Porter, 1972), p. 72.
2. Ibid., p. 104.
3. Ibid., p. 106.
4. W. F. Craven and J. L. Cate, *Men and Planes*, vol. 6 of *The Army Air Forces in World War II* (Chicago, The Univ. of Chicago Press, 1951), pp. 206–209.
5. Eaker, "Report of Lt. General Ira C. Eaker on U.S. Army Air Forces Activities in United Kingdom covering period from February 20, 1942, to December 31, 1943," box 323, Spaatz Papers, LOC.
6. G. Baley Price, "A Mathematician Describes His Work as Operations Analyst with the VIII Air Force," n.d., 520.310-7, USAFHRA.
7. Eisenhower to Marshall, December 25, 1943, *Papers*, vol. 3, p. 1612.
8. Hansell, *Air Plan*, p. 139.

9. MacKinlay Kantor, *Mission with Le May* (Garden City, N.Y.: Doubleday, 1965), pp. 231–232.
10. Minutes, Eighth Air Force commanders' meeting, June 7, 1943, 850.4, USAFHRA.
11. James Phinney Baxter III, *Scientists against Time* (Boston: Little, Brown, 1946), p. 53.
12. Hansell, *Air Plan*, p. 118.
13. Minutes, Eighth Air Force commanders' meeting, December 6, 1943, box 20, Eaker Papers, LOC.
14. H. M. McClelland to Eaker, February 15, 1943, box 323, Spaatz Papers, LOC.
15. Dennis Richards, *Portal of Hungerford*, (London: Heinemann, 1977), p. 314.
16. Portal to A. Sinclair, memo, September 26, 1942, AIR 8/833, PRO.
17. Churchill to Portal, Note, Dec. 16, 1942, PREM 3/483/1, PRO.
18. Allan A. Michie, *The Air Offensive against Germany* (New York: Henry Holt, 1943), p. 29.
19. Ibid., p. 90.
20. Ibid., p. 93.
21. Alexander De Seversky, *Victory through Air Power* (New York: Simon and Schuster, 1942), p. 206.
22. Ibid., p. 208.
23. Churchill to Portal, note, September 27, 1942, AIR 8/833, PRO.
24. Portal to Churchill, note, October 13, 1942, AIR 8/711, PRO.
25. See note 16 above.
26. Arnold to Eaker, message, December 23, 1942, box 322 Spaatz Papers, LOC.
27. Arnold to G. Stratemeyer, memo, February 26, 1943, box 48, Arnold Papers, LOC.
28. C. B. Overacker and F. H. Robinson, report on Eighth Air Force, February 15, 1943, box 92, Spaatz Papers, LOC.
29. Eaker to Spaatz, January 29, 1943, box 323, Spaatz Papers, LOC.
30. Eaker to Arnold, June 29, 1943, box 323, Spaatz Papers, LOC.
31. Winston S. Churchill, *The Hinge of Fate* (Boston: Houghton Mifflin, 1950), p. 678.
32. Albert C. Wedemeyer, *Wedemeyer Reports* (New York: Henry Holt, 1958), p. 192.
33. Sinclair to Churchill, memo, January 12, 1943, AIR 8/711, PRO.
34. Churchill, *Hinge of Fate*, p. 679.
35. Hansell, *Air Plan*, p. 63.
36. Eaker to Stratemeyer, January 30, 1943, box 17, Eaker Papers, LOC.
37. Craven and Cate, *Torch to Pointblank*, pp. 681–705.
38. Arnold to Portal, October 14, 1943, box 105, Arnold Papers, LOC.
39. Portal to Arnold, October 24, 1943, AIR 8/1108, PRO.
40. Leigh-Mallory to Portal, note, October 31, 1943, AIR 8/1108, PRO.
41. Eaker to ETOUSA's chief of staff, July 10, 1943, box 323, Spaatz Papers, LOC.
42. Craven and Cate, *Torch to Pointblank*, p. 680.

Chapter 3: Eighth Air Force Fighter Problems

1. V. Bush to Marshall, August 26, 1943, box 41 Arnold Papers, LOC.
2. Craven and Cate, *Torch to Pointblank*, p. 231.
3. Eaker to Arnold, February 15, 1943, box 323, Spaatz Papers, LOC.
4. Eaker to Eugene Eubank, March 12, 1943, box 322, Spaatz Papers, LOC.
5. Craven and Cate, *Men and Planes*, p. 216–217.
6. Charles Webster and Noble Frankland, *The Strategic Air Offensive against Germany, 1939–1945*, vol. 1 (London: Her Majesty's Stationery Office, 1961), p. 239.
7. C. C. Chauncey to F. M. Andrews, report, April 24, 1943, box 104, Arnold Papers, LOC.
8. B. E. Meyers to Arnold, report, April 9, 1943, 452.1 England, Arnold Papers, LOC.
9. Minutes, Eighth Air Force commanders' conference, July 20, 1943, box 20, Eaker Papers, LOC.

10. H. J. Knerr to Eaker, memo, October 12, 1943, box 324, Spaatz Papers, LOC.
11. Eaker to R. A. Lovett, June 14, 1943, box 323, Spaatz Papers, LOC.
12. Wilfred R. Freeman to Eaker, October 15, 1943, 520.13-2, USAFHRA.
13. Freeman to Henry F. Miller, February 18, 1943, box 109, Spaatz Papers, LOC.
14. Minutes, Eighth Air Force droptank committee, October 1943, box 109, Spaatz Papers, LOC.
15. Arnold to commanding general Eighth Air Force, cable, January 11, 1944, box 109, Spaatz Papers, LOC.
16. Arnold to Andrews, quoted in *Hap*, by Thomas M. Coffey (New York: Viking, 1982), p. 311.
17. Arnold's advisory committee to Arnold, memo, June 12, 1943, box 39, Arnold Papers, LOC.
18. Ibid.
19. Eaker to Hunter, memo, July 14, 1943, box 323, Spaatz Papers, LOC.
20. Ibid.
21. Hunter to Eaker, memo, July 20, 1943, item 159, Hunter Papers, Georgia Historical Society.
22. Report to General Hunter, "Brief Chronological Record of VIII Fighter Command from June 1942 to August 1943," n.d., 520.309-4, USAFHRA.
23. Arnold's advisory committee to Giles, report, June 17, 1943, 520.164, USAFHRA.
24. Report of the AAF Evaluation Board, "Tactical Employment Trials on the Republic Airplane P-47-C," February 16, 1943, box 49, Spaatz Papers, LOC.
25. Memo from headquarters Eighth Air Force to commanding general North African Air Force, "Tactical Employment of P47 Airplane," July 29, 1943, box 49, Spaatz Papers, LOC.
26. F. Anderson to G. E. Stratemeyer, letter, July 21, 1943, box 105, Arnold Papers, LOC.
27. Interview by USSTAF historian, box 136, Spaatz Papers, LOC (hereafter cited as "USSTAF interview").
28. Minutes, Eighth Air Force commanders' meeting, September 10, 1943, box 20, Eaker Papers, LOC.
29. Eaker to Arnold, June 29, 1943, box 323, Spaatz Papers, LOC.
30. Eighth Air Force ORS, report, n.d., 520. 310 v-4, USAFHRA.
31. AAF Proving Ground Command, report, "Tactical Suitability of the P-38F Type Aircraft," March 6, 1943, box 48, Spaatz Papers, LOC.
32. Narrative of operations, 55th Fighter Group, November 29, 1943, 168.60050-55, USAFHRA.
33. Kepner, USSTAF interview (see note 27 above).
34. Doolittle to Spaatz, memo, March 1, 1944, box 19, Doolittle Papers, LOC.
35. Robert W. Gruenhagen, *Mustang: The Story of the P-51 Fighter*, rev. ed. (New York: Arco Publishing, 1976), pp. 33–47.
36. David Birch, *Rolls-Royce and the Mustang* (Derby, England: Rolls-Royce Heritage Trust, 1987), p. 84.
37. Ronald J. Harker, *The Engines Were Rolls-Royce* (New York: Macmillian Publishing, 1979), p. 69.
38. Ronald Schlaefer and S. D. Heron, *Development of Aircraft Engines and Fuels* (Boston: Harvard Univ. Graduate School of Business Administration, 1950), p. 310.
39. John Morton Blum, *From the Morgenthau Diaries*, vol. II (Boston: Houghton Mifflin, 1964) p. 147.
40. Some biographical information concerning Hitchcock on these pages is taken from *Tommy Hitchcock: An American Hero*, by Nelson W. Aldrich, Jr., (Gaithersburg, Md.: Fleet Street, 1985).
41. Henry L. Stimson, undated note, Stimson Papers, Yale University.
42. Hitchcock to Lovett, June 5, 1942, RG 10738, Papers of the Assistant Secretary of War for Air, NARS.
43. B. E. Meyers to Lovett, memo, June 10, 1942, RG 10738, Papers of the Assistant Secretary of War for Air, NARS.

44. Lovett to Hitchcock, June 15, 1942, RG 10738, Papers of the Assistant Secretary of War for Air, NARS.
45. Roosevelt to Arnold, note, November 12, 1942, box 45, Arnold Papers, LOC.
46. Arnold to Roosevelt, memo, November 12, 1942, box 45, Arnold Papers, LOC.
47. James H. Kindelberger to Arnold, November 2, 1942, box 15, Arnold Papers, LOC.
48. Hitchcock, report on visits to aircraft factories, "Some Comments on American Fighter Planes," February 2, 1943, box 131, Arnold Papers. LOC.
49. Charles A. Lindbergh, *The Wartime Journals of Charles A. Lindbergh* (New York: Harcourt Brace Jovanovich, 1970), p. 630.
50. Hunter to Eaker, February 26, 1943, box 127, Arnold Papers, LOC.
51. AAF Pursuit Board, report, October 27, 1941, box 54, Eaker Papers, LOC.
52. Lovett to Arnold, memo, June 19, 1943, box 127, Arnold Papers, LOC.
53. Arnold to Lovett, memo, July 10, 1943, Papers of the Assistant Secretary of War for Air, RG 10738, NARS.
54. Arnold to Giles, memo, June 22, 1943, box 127, Arnold Papers, LOC.
55. Giles to Arnold, memo, July 5, 1943, box 127, Arnold Papers, LOC.
56. General Grandison Gardner to Giles, August 17, 1943, box 12, Spaatz Papers, LOC.
57. Giles to Spaatz, September 9, 1943, box 12, Spaatz Papers, LOC.
58. AAF Proving Ground Command, report, "Test to Determine the Effect of an Additional 85 Gallons of Internal Fuel on Performance and Handling of the P-51B Airplane," December 22, 1943, serial 4-43-23-, Eglin AFB Library.
59. Mark E. Bradley, "P-51 Over Berlin," *Aerospace Historian*, vol. 21, no. 3 (Fall 1974): p. 128.
60. Giles to B. N. Chidlaw, memo, September 9, 1943, box 131, Arnold Papers, LOC.
61. Kepner to Giles, July 15, 1944, box 105, Arnold Papers, LOC.
62. H. A. Craig to Arnold, memo, January 7, 1944, box 124, Arnold Papers, LOC.
63. Meyers to Giles, memo, November 25, 1943, box 124, Arnold Papers, LOC.
64. AAF Intelligence Section, report of an interview of Hansell, August 9, 1943, box 213, Spaatz Papers, LOC.
65. Winant to Hopkins, July 9, 1943, box 13, Map Room Papers, Franklin D. Roosevelt Library.
66. Winant to Hopkins, October 16, 1943, box 13, Map Room Papers, Franklin D. Roosevelt Library.
67. Quesada to E. Bowles, January 20, 1944, box 105, Arnold Papers, LOC.
68. James H. Howard, *Roar of the Tiger* (New York: Orion Books, 1991), p. 195.
69. Ibid., p. 233.
70. Chidlaw to O. P. Echols, memo, April 17, 1944, box 105, Arnold Papers, LOC.
71. AAF Proving Ground Command, report, "Tactical Trials of P-51-B," January 1944, 240.04-12, USAFHRA.
72. Hitchcock to Lovett, quoting Eaker, November 22, 1943, Papers of the Assistant Secretary of War for Air, RG 10738, NARS.
73. F. L. Anderson to Eaker, report, containing a comment by Kepner, December 12, 1943, box 327, Spaatz Papers, LOC.
74. Eighth Air Force, report, "Discussion of Fighter Employment," December 12, 1943, box 327, Spaatz Papers, LOC.
75. Kepner to Giles, December 27, 1943, box 105, Arnold Papers, LOC.

Chapter 4: The Allied Expeditionary Air Forces

1. Craven and Cate, *Torch to Pointblank*, p. 531.
2. Ibid., p. 737.
3. William O. Butler to Giles, November 13, 1943, box 105, Arnold Papers, LOC.
4. Grandison Gardner to Arnold, report, April 1944, 168.7016-22, USAFHRA.
5. Tedder, *With Prejudice*, p. 564.

6. E. J. Kingston-McCloughry, *The Direction of War* (New York: Frederick A. Praeger, 1955), p. 121.

7. Spaatz, diary entry, January 3, 1944, box 14, Spaatz Papers, LOC.

8. F. Anderson to Spaatz, memo, February 14, 1944, box 17, Spaatz Papers, LOC.

9. Ibid.

10. Spaatz to Arnold, February 1, 1944, box 14, Spaatz Papers, LOC.

11. Lovett to Spaatz, December 28, 1943, box 14, Spaatz Papers, LOC.

12. Kepner, USSTAF interview (see chapter 3, note 27).

13. Spaatz, diary entry, January 24, 1944, box 14, Spaatz Papers, LOC.

14. Tedder, *With Prejudice*, p. 508.

15. Spaatz, diary entries, February 19, 1944, box 14, Spaatz Papers, LOC.

16. AEAF directive, "Policy Governing Attacks on Railway Centers by U.S. IX Air Force," March 10, 1944, 533.314, USAFHRA.

17. Spaatz to Leigh-Mallory, memo, March 15, 1944, box 17, Spaatz Papers, LOC.

18. Eisenhower, memo for his diary, March 20, 1944, *Papers*, vol. 3, p. 1776.

19. Bernard Boylan, "Development of the Long-Range Escort Fighter," USAF Historical Study, (Maxwell AFB, Ala.: n.d.) p. 183.

20. Eisenhower to Marshall, March 1, 1944, box 17, Spaatz Papers, LOC.

21. Hoyt S. Vandenberg, diary entry, March 24, 1944, box 1, Vandenberg Papers, LOC.

22. Craven and Cate, *Men and Planes*, p. 200.

23. Arnold, *Global Mission*, p. 259.

24. Carroll V. Glines, *Jimmy Doolittle* (New York: Harper and Brothers, 1949), p. 125.

25. Minutes, Eighth Air Force commanders' meeting, April 26, 1943, box 20, Eaker Papers, LOC.

26. Roger A. Freeman, *B-26 Marauder at War* (New York: Charles Scribner's Sons, 1978), p. 49.

27. Eaker to Arnold, June 29, 1943, box 323, Spaatz Papers, LOC.

28. Idwal Edwards, report on Eighth Air Force, November 19, 1943, box 18, Eaker Papers, LOC.

29. F. Anderson to Eaker, note, December 20, 1943, 519.1612, USAFHRA.

30. F. Anderson to Spaatz, memo, February 4, 1944, box 17, Spaatz Papers, LOC.

31. Spaatz to Portal, February 11, 1944, box 14, Spaatz Papers, LOC.

32. Portal to Spaatz, February 15, 1944, box 14, Spaatz Papers, LOC.

33. Minutes, Ninth Air Force commanders' meeting, February 23, 1944, 533.06, USAFHRA.

Chapter 5: USSTAF's Campaign to Weaken the German Air Force

1. Craven and Cate, *Argument to V-E Day*, p. 8.

2. Spaatz to Portal, January 31, 1944, box 17, Spaatz Papers, LOC.

3. Craven and Cate, *Torch to Pointblank*, p. 638.

4. Spaatz to Doolittle, memo, January 26, 1944, box 143, Spaatz Papers, LOC.

5. Eaker to his staff, memo, September 18, 1942, box 322, Spaatz Papers, LOC.

6. Robert E. Lyons, "Report to the Surgeon, Headquarters USAAF in the UK," n.d., box 14, Spaatz Papers, LOC.

7. James H. Doolittle, *I Could Never Be So Lucky Again* (New York: Bantam Books, 1991), p. 387.

8. Spaatz to Arnold, March 7, 1944, box 17, Spaatz Papers, LOC.

9. Spaatz, diary entry, January 25, 1944, box 14, Spaatz Papers, LOC.

10. Lowell Thomas and Edward Jablonski, *Doolittle* (Garden City, N.Y.: Doubleday, 1976), p. 263.

11. Spaatz, diary entry, February 9, 1944, box 14, Spaatz Papers, LOC.

12. Minutes, Eighth Air Force commanders' meeting, January 24, 1944, 520.141-1, USAFHRA.

13. Headquarters Eighth Bomber Command, report, "Tactical Employment of Heavy Bombardment Aircraft in the European Theater of Operations," November 22, 1943, box 213, Spaatz Papers, LOC.
14. Doolittle to Arnold, memo, February 14, 1944, 519.1612, USAFHRA.
15. Spaatz to Arnold, February 18, 1944, 519.1612, USAFHRA.
16. Henry C. Martin, report to staff at AAF headquarters, November 17, 1943, 248.531-18, USAFHRA.
17. Kepner, USSTAF interview (see chapter 3, note 27).
18. Spaatz to Arnold, February 11, 1944, box 14, Spaatz Papers, LOC.
19. Doolittle, *Never Be So Lucky,* p. 380.
20. Minutes, Eighth Air Force commanders' meeting, March 15, 1944, box 6, Le May Papers, LOC.
21. Statement by prisoner of war Oberstleutnant Kogler, January 1, 1945, 168.6007-36, USAFHRA.
22. Adolf Galland, *The First and the Last: The Rise and the Fall of the German Fighter Forces, 1938–1945.* (New York: Henry Holt, 1954), p. 264.
23. Craven and Cate, *Argument to V-E Day,* pp. 50–51.
24. Ibid., pp. 52–53.
25. Ibid.
26. Record of the interrogation of prisoner of war Adolf Galland, May 5, 1945.
27. Stephen L. McFarland and Wesley P. Newton, *To Command the Sky* (Washington, D.C.: Smithsonian Institution Press, 1991), p. 52.
28. Erhardt Milch, address to a conference of aircraft-production officials, February 23, 1944, K-512 621 VII/140, USAFHRA.
29. Headquarters VIII Fighter Command to Doolittle, memo, "Tactics and Technique of Long-Range Fighter Escort," 524.454, USAFHRA.
30. Wladyslaw Kozaczuk, *Enigma* (Frederick, Md: University Publications of America, Inc., 1984).
31. Spaatz to commanders of Eighth and Fifteenth Air Forces, memo, "Necessity for Intensified Operations," March 2, 1944, box 17, Spaatz Papers, LOC.
32. J. E. Johnson, *Wing Leader* (New York: Ballantine Books, 1957), p. 152.
33. Spaatz to commanders of Eighth and Fifteenth Air Forces, memo, "Exploitation of Air Supremacy," memo box 14, Spaatz Papers, LOC.
34. Kepner, USSTAF interview (see chapter 3, note 27).
35. Lynn Farnol, "To the Limit of Their Endurance," unpublished history of Eighth Fighter Command, 168.6005-63A, USAFHRA.
36. Eighth Fighter Command, bulletin, "Down to Earth," n.d., 524.454, USAFHRA.
37. Ibid.

Chapter 6: The Plan to Bomb French and Belgian Rail Centers

1. Tedder, *With Prejudice,* p. 503.
2. Sir Solly Zuckerman, *From Apes to Warlords* (London: Hamish Hamilton, 1978), p. 216.
3. Tedder, proposal, "Employment of Allied Air Forces in Support of Overlord," March 24, 1944, box 144, Spaatz Papers, LOC.
4. E. J. Kingston-McCloughry, unpublished report, "The Transportation Plan," box 414, Kingston-McCloughry Papers, Imperial War Museum, p. 9.
5. E. D. Brant, report, "Air Attack on Communications," August 20, 1942, 506.425C, USAFHRA.
6. Zuckerman, paper, "Alternative Plans for Employment of Strategic Bombing Forces," March 5, 1944, Box SZ/AEAF/10, folder F1.2, Zuckerman Papers, East Anglia University.
7. "Air Plan for Overlord," n.d., box 179, Spaatz Papers, LOC.
8. Ibid.

9. Craven and Cate, *Torch to Pointblank.*
10. USSTAF report, "Review of Oil and Transportation Target Systems," June 6, 1944, Charles P. Cabell Papers, 168.7026-6, USAFHRA.
11. Zuckerman, *From Apes to Warlords*, p. 237.

Chapter 7: Opposition to the Transportation Plan

1. Martin Gilbert, *Winston S. Churchill: Road to Victory, 1941–1945* (Boston: Houghton Mifflin, 1986) p. 739.
2. Doolittle to Spaatz, memo, February 14, 1944, box 17, Spaatz Papers, LOC.
3. Ibid.
4. Harris to Portal, March 24, 1944, Portal Papers, Christ Church College Library, Oxford University.
5. Martin Middlebrook and Chris Everitt, *The Bomber Command War Diaries* (New York: Viking Penguin, 1985), p. 479.
6. Cabell, report, "Review of Oil and Transportation Target Systems," Charles P. Cabell Papers, 168.7026-6, USAFHRA (hereafter cited as "Review of Oil").
7. R. D. Hughes to F. Anderson, memo quoted in Cabell, "Review of Oil" (see note 6 above).
8. Anderson to Spaatz, memo, February 28, 1944, box 143, Spaatz Papers, LOC.
9. Cabell, "Review of Oil" (see note 6 above).
10. EOU/EWD paper, "Critical Analysis of 'Delay and Disorganization of Enemy Movement by Rail'" February 7, 1944, box 143, Spaatz Papers, LOC.
11. AEAF proposal, presented by Tedder for the March 25 meeting, "Employment of Allied Air Forces in Support of Overlord," March 24, 1944, box 144, Spaatz Papers, LOC.
12. Zuckerman, *From Apes to Warlords*, p. 228.
13. Eaker to J. Devers, April 1, 1944, box 22 Eaker Papers, LOC.
14. Sir John Slessor, *The Central Blue* (London: Cassell, 1956), p. 572.
15. Ibid.
16. Draft history of the Mediterranean Allied Air Forces, box 27, Eaker Papers, LOC.
17. Ibid.
18. Ibid.
19. Harris to Portal, March 24, 1944, AIR 8/1188, PRO.
20. Minutes, CCS meeting, March 21, 1944, AIR 8/1188, PRO.
21. Tedder to Portal, March 13, 1944, AIR 8/1188, PRO.
22. Cabell, "Review of Oil" (see note 6 above).
23. Tedder's paper, mentioned throughout this discussion, is the AEAF proposal, "Employment of Allied Air Forces" (see note 11 above).
24. The USSTAF paper, mentioned throughout this discussion, is the USSTAF report, "Employment of Strategic Air Forces in the Support of Overlord," March 24, 1944, box 144 Spaatz Papers, LOC.
25. Eisenhower, *Papers*, vol. 3, p. 1784.
26. Spaatz to Arnold, cable, March 17, 1944, box 146, Spaatz Papers, LOC.
27. Richards, *Portal*, p. 22.
28. All of the following accounts of words spoken at the meeting are taken from the report, "Minutes of a Meeting Held on Saturday, 25 March 1944 to Discuss the 'Bombing Policy in the Period Before Overlord,'" box 14, Spaatz Papers, LOC.
29. Portal to Sinclair, memo, September 27, 1942, quoted in Webster and Frankland, *Strategic Air Offensive*, vol. 1, p. 359.
30. Spaatz to Portal, memo, March 30, 1944, box 144, Spaatz Papers, LOC.
31. Spaatz to Eisenhower, March 31, 1944, box 110, Personal Files of Dwight D. Eisenhower, 1916–1952, Eisenhower Library.
32. Spaatz to Eisenhower, April 22, 1944, box 14, Spaatz Papers, LOC.
33. Cabell, "Review of Oil" (see note 6 above).

Chapter 8: Air Preparations to Support Invasion Forces

1. Lewis Brereton, *The Brereton Diaries* (New York: William Morrow, 1946), p. 237.
2. Arnold to Spaatz, April 24, 1944, box 14, Spaatz Papers, LOC.
3. Arnold to Brereton, February 26, 1944, box 105, Arnold Papers, LOC.
4. Idwal Edwards, report on Eighth Air Force, November 19, 1943, box 18, Eaker Papers, LOC.
5. AAF Pursuit Board, report, March 1941, box 54, Eaker Papers, LOC.
6. De Seversky, *Air Power*, p. 242.
7. Daniel Mortensen, *A Pattern for Joint Operations: World War II Close Air Support, North Africa* (Washington, D.C.: Office of Air Force History and U.S. Center of Military History, 1987), p. 18.
8. Giles to Spaatz, September 10, 1943, box 12, Spaatz Papers, LOC.
9. Glenn Duncan to commanding officer of the 66th Fighter Wing, memo, September 19, 1943, 524.454, USAFHRA.
10. F. L. Martin to Frank M. Andrews, June 20, 1938, box 5, Andrews Correspondence, Tennessee State Historical Archives.
11. 353rd Fighter Group historian, unpublished history of 353rd Fighter Group, reporting an interview of Glenn Duncan, GP353-HI(FI), USAFHRA.
12. Ibid.
13. Lynn Farnol, "To the Limit of Their Endurance," unpublished history of Eighth Fighter Command, 168.6005-62, USAFHRA.
14. Ken C. Rust and William N. Hess, *The Slybird Group* (Fallbrook, Calif.: Aero Publishers, 1968), p. 21.
15. Gilbert W. Wymond, report on P-47s in ground attack, January 25, 1944, 168.6007-23, USAFHRA.
16. Ibid.
17. "The Development and the Technique of Low Level Bombing with P-47 Type Aircraft," draft history of IX TAC, box 4, Quesada Papers, LOC.
18. Arnold to director of air support, memo, December 28, 1942, box 38, Arnold Papers, LOC.
19. Quesada, oral history transcript, n.d., U.S. Army Military History Institute.
20. Mortensen, *Joint Operations*, p. 78.
21. Ibid.
22. Omar N. Bradley, *A Soldier's Story* (New York: Henry Holt, 1951), p. 249.
23. Brereton to Spaatz, memo, February 24, 1944, 533.14, USAFHRA.
24. Headquarters Air Force Accident report #44-4-18-506, n.d., Department of the Air Force.
25. Draft history of IX TAC (see note 17 above).
26. SHAEF G-2, report, May 21, 1944, 506.451-313A, USAFHRA.
27. IX TAC ORS, report, "The Paralyzation of a Railroad System by Fighter-Bombers," May 9, 1944, 533.310, USAFHRA.
28. Ibid.
29. Brereton, *Diaries*, p. 273.
30. Ibid., pp. 265–268.

Chapter 9: Attacks on Rail Centers, Oil Plants, and V-Weapons Before D-Day

1. Middlebrook and Everitt, *Bomber Command War Diaries*, pp. 479–493.
2. Arthur Harris, *Bomber Offensive* (New York: Macmillan Publishing, 1947), p. 266.
3. Webster and Frankland, *Strategic Air Offensive*, vol. IV, p. 205.

4. Ibid., Annex I.
5. Ibid.
6. Middlebrook and Everitt, *Bomber Command War Diaries*, pp. 493–494.
7. Portal to Churchill, memo, March 29, 1944, Portal Papers, Christ Church College Library, Oxford University.
8. Winston S. Churchill, *Closing the Ring* (Boston: Houghton Mifflin, 1951), p. 528.
9. Eisenhower to Churchill, April 5, 1944, *Papers*, vol. 3, p. 1809.
10. Minutes, meeting of War Cabinet, April 26, 1944, AIR 8/1190, PRO.
11. Ibid.
12. Webster and Frankland, *Strategic Air Offensive*, vol. 3, p. 39.
13. Tedder, *With Prejudice*, p. 518.
14. War Office, report, March 26, 1944, WO 205/532, PRO.
15. British Directorate of Intelligence, report, April 25, 1944, AIR 37/1072.
16. F. H. Hinsley, *British Intelligence in the Second World War*, vol. 3, (New York: Cambridge Univ. Press, 1988), p. 114.
17. Protest by bishops of Lille, Paris, Lyons, Cambrai, May 15, 1944, AIR 37/1050, PRO.
18. Churchill to Eisenhower, April 29, 1944, box 414, Papers of Kingston-McCloughry, Imperial War Museum.
19. Hinsley, *British Intelligence*, vol. 3, p. 7.
20. Minutes, of War Cabinet, April 29, 1944, AIR 8/1190, PRO.
21. Cabell to Spaatz, memo, "Proceedings of Overlord Air Support Advisory Committee, 10 April 1944," April 11, 1944, box 17, Spaatz Papers, LOC.
22. Eisenhower to Churchill, May 2, 1944, *Papers*, vol. 3, p. 1842.
23. Ibid.
24. Eisenhower, directive to Montgomery, Ramsey, Leigh-Mallory, and Bradley, May 26, 1944, *Papers*, vol. 3, p. 1891.
25. SHAEF G-2, memo to Group Captain C. W. B. Urmston, May 25, 1944, 506.425E, USAFHRA.
26. Ministry of Economic Warfare, report, May 12, 1944, box 137, Spaatz Papers, LOC.
27. Eisenhower to Marshall, April 12, 1944, *Papers*, vol. 3, p. 1817.
28. SHAEF, report, May 2, 1944, box 203, Spaatz Papers, LOC.
29. Craven and Cate, *Argument to V-E Day*, pp. 154–162.
30. Middlebrook and Everitt, *Bomber Command War Diaries* pp. 502–524.
31. SHAEF, report, May 25, 1944, 506.425D, USAFHRA.
32. Middlebrook and Everitt, *Bomber Command War Diaries*, pp. 502–524.
33. Churchill to Roosevelt, *Churchill and Roosevelt, the Complete Correspondence*, Vol. III, ed., Warren F. Kimball, (Princeton, N.J.: Princeton Univ. Press, 1984), p. 138.
34. Ibid., p. 129.
35. Eisenhower, *Papers*, vol. III, p. 1904.
36. Charles de Gaulle, *Unity: 1942–44*, vol. 2 of *War Memoirs of Charles de Gaulle* (n.p., 1959), p. 241.
37. Minutes, Allied Air Force Bombing Committee, January 18, 1944, 505.26-19, USAFHRA.
38. W. B. Smith to Marshall, quoting Koenig, May 17, 1944, *Papers*, vol. 3, p. 1810.
39. Minutes, meeting no. 6 of the War Cabinet Defense Committee, April 13, 1944, Cabinet Papers, 69/6, PRO.
40. Churchill, *Closing the Ring*, pp. 528–530.
41. "Economic Outpost with the Economic Warfare Divisions," vol. 5 of the OSS history, n.d., RG 226, NARS.
42. Craven and Cate, *Argument to V-E Day*, pp. 175–178.
43. Robert Goralski and Russel W. Freiburg, *Oil and War: How the Deadly Struggle for Fuel in World War II Meant Victory or Defeat* (New York: William Morrow, 1987), p. 246.
44. Hinsley, *British Intelligence* p. 502.
45. Ibid., p. 503.
46. Ibid.

47. Craven and Cate, *Argument to V-E Day*, p. 281.
48. Spaatz, diary entry, April 19, 1944, box 14, Spaatz Papers, LOC.
49. Craven and Cate, *Argument to V-E Day*, p. 98.
50. 365th Fighter Group, report, "Experimental Attack on Noball Targets by the 365th Fighter Group," n.d., 524.454, USAFHRA.
51. R. V. Jones, *The Wizard War* (New York: Coward, McCann and Geoghegan 1978), pp. 403–405.
52. USSTAF intelligence, report, September 8, 1944, 520.310, USAFHRA.
53. John T. Godfrey, *The Look of Eagles* (New York: Random House, 1958), p. 145.

Chapter 10: Attacks on Bridges and Airfields Before D-Day

1. Brereton, *Diaries*, p. 237.
2. S. E. Anderson, oral history transcript, n.d., K239.0512-904, USAFHRA.
3. Ninth Air Force, booklet, "Bombing Procedures," n.d., 534.310, USAFHRA.
4. Ninth Air Force ORS, report, "Major Changes of Tactics and Technique within Ninth Air Force," January 22, 1945, 533.549-1, USAFHRA.
5. Report, "Ninth Air Force: April to November 1944," n.d., 519.041-1, USAFHRA.
6. AEAF, report, April 30, 1944, AIR 37/519, PRO.
7. Minutes, AEAF meeting, February 29, 1944, AIR 37/732, PRO.
8. Cabell, "Notes on a meeting at SHAEF," May 6, 1944, box 15, Spaatz Papers, LOC.
9. Minutes, Frederic H. Smith, Jr. at SHAEF, May 3, 1944, 505.26-18, USAFHRA.
10. F. H. Smith, oral history transcript, n.d., K239.0512-903, USAFHRA.
11. Mission report of 365th Fighter Group, May 7, 1944, in appendix D of *Pre-Invasion Bombing Strategy*, by W. W. Rostow (Austin: Univ. of Texas Press, 1981).
12. Brereton, *Diaries*, p. 263.
13. Charles Johnson, *History of the Hell Hawks*, p. 80.
14. Craven and Cate, *Argument to V-E Day*, p. 159.
15. C. G. Peterson to D. M. Schlatter, memo, May 13, 1944, 505.26-35, USAFHRA.
16. Brereton, directive to Ninth Air Force, May 7, 1944, 533.314, USAFHRA.
17. Zoekler to Brereton, memo, May 13, 1944, 533.314, USAFHRA.
18. Johnson, *Hell Hawks*, pp. 101–105.
19. Ninth Air Force ORS, report no. 77, "Analysis of Weapon Effectiveness of Seine River Bridge Operations," n.d., 533.310, USAFHRA.
20. Junior G. Ziegler, *Bridgebusters* (New York: Gannis and Harris, 1949), p. 38.
21. British Air Ministry, report, "Recent Attacks on Railway Bridges in Northwest Europe," June 3, 1944, 534.309-1, USAFHRA.
22. Ninth Air Force ORS, report no. 77 (see note 19 above) 533.310, USAFHRA.
23. IXth TAC ORS, report no. 39, "Bridges of the Seine, Loire, and Somme Rivers," June 3, 1944, 533.310, USAFHRA.
24. IXth TAC ORS, report no. 60, "An Analysis of Fighter Bomber Attacks on Bridges During the Period 7 May 1944–4 June 1944," 533.310, USAFHRA.
25. Craven and Cate, *Argument to V-E Day*, p. 178.
26. Allan Healy, *The 467th Bombardment Group, September 1943–June 1945* (Privately printed, 1947; reprint, North Tonawanda, N.Y.: Enterprise Printing, 1980), pp. 50–59.
27. SHAEF G-2, report, "The Use of Air Power Against Transport and Military Supplies," June 7, 1944, 505.26-28, USAFHRA.
28. Ibid.

Chapter 11: Air Support for the Landings in Normandy

1. Eisenhower, *Crusade in Europe*, p. 246.
2. Clay Blair, *Ridgway's Paratroopers* (Garden City, N.Y.: Dial Press, 1985), p. 222.

3. Harrison, *Cross-Channel Attack*, p. 304.
4. John M. Taylor, *General Maxwell Taylor: The Sword and the Pen* (New York: Doubleday, 1989), p. 92.
5. James M. Gavin, *On to Berlin* (New York: Viking Press, 1978), p. 102.
6. Matthew Ridgeway, "Report on the Normandy Operations of the 82nd Airborne Division," n.d., 533.451-16, USAFHRA.
7. Unpublished history of SHAEF, box 212, Spaatz Papers, LOC.
8. Craven and Cate, *Argument to V-E Day*, p. 192.
9. Notes on an interview of Leigh-Mallory, June 5, 1944, AIR 37/1007, PRO.
10. Brereton, *Diaries*, p. 270.
11. Leigh-Mallory to Tedder, June 3, 1944, AIR 16/614, PRO.
12. USSTAF G-2, leaflet, June 5, 1944, box 204, Spaatz Papers, LOC.
13. USAF, Historical Study no. 70, "Tactical Operations of Eighth Air Force, 6 June 1944–8 May 1945," n.d., 101-70, USAFHRA.
14. Spaatz to Doolittle, memo, May 10, 1944, 168.6005-72, USAFHRA.
15. Craven and Cate, *Argument to V-E Day*, p. 215.
16. Healy, *467th Bombardment Group*, p. 59.
17. Minutes, AEAF commanders' meeting, June 16, 1944, AIR 37/1007, PRO.
18. Craven and Cate, *Argument to V-E Day*, pp. 210–211.
19. AAF, Historical Study no. 36, "Ninth Air Force: April to November, 1944," 101.36, n.d., USAFHRA.
20. Ibid.

Chapter 12: Close Air Support for Invasion Forces

1. Bradley, *Soldier's Story*, p. 249.
2. Quesada, oral history transcript, n.d., U.S. Army Military History Institute.
3. David T. Griggs to Edward L. Bowles, February 22, 1945, 519.161-7, USAFHRA.
4. Quesada to W. W. Momeyer, August 22, 1944, box 1, Quesada Papers, LOC.
5. Brereton, *Diaries*, p. 281.
6. Ibid., p. 282.
7. Vandenberg, diary entry, June 6, 1944, Vandenberg Papers, LOC.
8. Craven and Cate, *Argument to V-E Day*, p. 204.
9. Quesada to Momeyer (see note 4 above).
10. Draft history of IXth TAC, box 5, Quesada Papers, LOC.
11. Minutes, AEAF commanders' meeting, July 15, 1944, AIR 37/1126, PRO.
12. AAF Historical Study no. 36 (see chapter 11, note 19).
13. Brereton, *Diaries* pp. 265–258.
14. Ibid., p. 297.
15. Arnold, journal entry, June 10, 1944, box 272, Arnold Papers, LOC.
16. Ibid.
17. Hinsley, *British Intelligence*, vol. 3, p. 104.
18. GAF historical study, "The Normandy Invasion," August 6, 1944, part III/31, 512.621, USAFHRA.
19. Arnold, journal entry, June 10, 1944, box 272, Arnold Papers, LOC.
20. Donald L. Caldwell, *JG 26* (New York: Orion Books, 1991), p. 278.
21. Eighth Fighter Command booklet, "Down to Earth," n.d., 168.6005-63, USAFHRA.
22. Garry L. Fry and Jeffrey L. Ethell, *Escort to Berlin* (New York: Arco Publishing, 1980), pp. 58–59.
23. Harrison, *Cross-Channel Attack*, p. 426.
24. Craven and Cate, *Argument to V-E Day*, pp. 199–200.
25. Brereton to Arnold, report, July 20, 1944, 533.4501-4, USAFHRA.
26. Harrison, *Cross-Channel Attack*, p. 441.

Chapter 13: Counter-Invasion and Resistance Operations

1. Paul Carell, *Invasion—They're Coming* (New York: E. P. Dutton, 1963), pp. 74–75.
2. Adolf Galland, "The Birth, Life and Death of the German Fighter Arm," n.d., 168.6007-19, USAFHRA.
3. Caldwell, *JG 26*, p. 257.
4. Galland, "German Fighter Arm" (see note 2 above).
5. GAF historical study, "The Normandy Invasion" (see chapter 12, note 18).
6. Report of an interrogation of General Bayerlein, n.d., box 134, Spaatz Papers, LOC.
7. M.R.D. Foot, *S.O.E. in France* (London: Her Majesty's Stationery Office, 1966), p. 424.
8. Harrison, *Cross-Channel Attack*, p. 203.
9. Ladislas Farago, *Burn After Reading* (New York: Walker, 1961), pp. 250–251.
10. Foot, *S.O.E. in France*, p. 397.
11. Robert Aron, *France Reborn* (New York: Charles Scribner's and Sons, 1964), p. 152–154.
12. Ibid.
13. Ibid.
14. Ibid.
15. Craven and Cate, *Argument to V-E Day*, pp. 498–500.
16. Enemy Objectives Unit, report, "Movement of German Divisions into the Lodgment Area: Overlord, D to D+50," October 3, 1944, 533.454-1, USAFHRA.
17. B. H. Liddell-Hart, *The Rommel Papers* (London: Collins, 1953), pp. 476–483.
18. USSTAF G-2, report, July 12, 1944, box 204, Spaatz Papers, LOC.

Chapter 14: Air Support for Allied Breakout from Normandy

1. Arthur Nevins papers, U.S. Army Military History Institute.
2. All quotations of Kepner to follow are taken from his report to Spaatz, July 24, 1944, Kepner Papers, 168.60005, USAFHRA.
3. Tedder, *With Prejudice*, p. 507.
4. Nigel Hamilton, *Master of the Battlefield* (New York: McGraw-Hill, 1983), p. 593.
5. Bradley, *Soldier's Story*, p. 228.
6. Spaatz diary entry, June 15, 1944, box 14, Spaatz Papers, LOC.
7. Arnold to Spaatz, June 29, 1944, box 14, Spaatz Papers, LOC.
8. Leigh-Mallory, entry in "Daily Reflections of Air Chief Marshal Sir Trafford Leigh-Mallory," June 27, 1944, AIR 37/784, PRO.
9. Ibid.
10. Ibid.
11. Zuckerman, report, "On Density of Attack in Relation to Air Support for Operation Overlord," n.d., AIR 37/1057, PRO.
12. Zuckerman, *From Apes to Warlords*, pp. 278–279.
13. Bradley to Leigh-Mallory, July 23, 1944, AIR/37/762, PRO.
14. Walter E. Todd, "Report of Operations 24 and 25 July 1944," n.d., box 71, RG 243, NARS.
15. Omar Bradley and Clay Blair, *A General's Life* (New York: Simon and Schuster, 1983), p. 278.
16. Minutes, AEAF commanders' conference, July 24, 1944, box 9, Spaatz Papers, LOC.
17. Craven and Cate, *Argument to V-E Day*, pp. 231–232.
18. J. Lawton Collins, *Lightning Joe* (Baton Rouge, La.: Louisiana State Univ. Press, 1979), p. 238.
19. Craven and Cate, *Argument to V-E Day*, pp. 232–233.
20. Vandenberg, diary entry, July 25, 1944, box 1, Vandenberg Papers, LOC.
21. Chester Hansen, diary entry, July 24, 1944, Hansen Papers, U.S. Army Military History Institute.

22. Robert L. Hewitt, *Workhorse of the Western Front* (Washington, D.C.: Infantry Journal Press, 1946), p. 35.
23. Officers of the regiment, *History of the 120th Infantry Regiment* (Washington, D.C.: Infantry Journal Press, 1945), pp. 36–37.
24. Craven and Cate, *Argument to V-E Day*, p. 234.
25. Hansen, diary entry, July 25, 1944 (see note 21 above).
26. Martin Blumenson, *The U.S. Army in World War II: Breakout and Pursuit* (Washington, D.C.: Center for Military History, 1961), p. 246.
27. Report of an interrogation of General Bayerlein, n.d., 519.511-1, USAFHRA.
28. Report of an air liaison officer with an American corps in France, "Air Support of Armoured Columns," n.d., 168.6007-26B, USAFHRA.
29. Leigh-Mallory, "Daily Reflections" (see note 8 above).
30. Bodo Zimmerman, *The Fatal Decision*, ed. Seymour Freiden and William Richardson (New York: William Sloan Associates, 1956), p. 209.
31. George S. Patton, Jr., *War as I Knew It* (Boston: Houghton-Mifflin, 1947), p. 99.
32. Ibid., p. 113.
33. Otto Weyland, oral history transcript, n.d., USAFHRA, p. 143.
34. Ibid.
35. Craven and Cate, *Argument to V-E Day*, p. 266.
36. Hugh M. Cole, *The U.S. Army in World War II: The Lorraine Campaign* (Washington, D.C.: Center for Military History, 1950), p. 599.
37. Patton, *War as I Knew It*, pp. 119–120.
38. Doolittle to Spaatz, September 23, 1944, box 19, Doolittle Papers, LOC.
39. XIXth TAC report, "Twelve Thousand Fighter-Bomber Sorties," n.d., 537.02, USAFHRA.
40. Cole, *Lorraine Campaign*, p. 599.

Chapter 15: Reorganization of Eisenhower's Air Command

1. Eisenhower to Marshall, cable, September 2, 1944, *Papers*, vol. 4, p. 2111–2112.
2. Eisenhower to Arnold, cable, September 14, 1944, *Papers*, vol. IV, p. 2112.
3. Ibid.
4. Marshall to Eisenhower, cable, September 15, 1944, *Papers*, vol. 4, p. 2159.
5. Eisenhower to Marshall, cable, September 18, 1944, *Papers*, vol. 4, p. 2157–2158.
6. Spaatz to Arnold, October 4, 1944, box 48, Arnold Papers, LOC.
7. Eisenhower to A. Sinclair, September 22, 1944, *Papers*, vol. 4, p. 2180.
8. Arnold to Eisenhower, September 6, 1944, box 5, Personal Files of General of the Army, D. D. Eisenhower, 1916–1942, Eisenhower Library.
9. Eisenhower to Arnold, cable, September 14, 1944, *Papers*, vol. IV, p. 2112.
10. Craven and Cate, *Argument to V-E Day*, p. 620.
11. Notes for the AEAF war diary, n.d., AIR 37/784, PRO.

Chapter 16: Surveys of the Transportation Campaign and Interdiction

1. Eisenhower to the CCS, report, box 104, Spaatz Papers, LOC.
2. Sir Arthur Tedder, *Air Power in War* (London: Hoddard and Stoughton, 1948), p. 116.
3. Ibid, p. 112.
4. Leigh-Mallory, summary of his report to Eisenhower, November 1944, box 104, Spaatz Papers, LOC.

5. SHAEF G-2, report, "Effects of Recent Attacks on Rail Centers in FRANCE, BELGIUM AND WESTERN GERMANY," May 25, 1944, 506.425E, USAFHRA.

6. Kindleberger, report, in Appendix F of Rostow, *Bombing Strategy*, pp. 122–137.

7. Ibid.

8. Ibid.

9. Headquarters Ninth Air Force, report, "Results Attained by the Destruction of Railway Transportation Centers," July 22, 1944, 505.78-3, USAFHRA.

10. Ibid.

11. Ibid.

12. Ibid.

13. Draft history of the Bombing Analysis Unit, n.d., 505.54-2, USAFHRA.

14. Zuckerman, *From Apes to Warlords*, pp. 298–299.

15. Ibid.

16. Ibid.

17. Bombing Analysis Unit, report No. 1, "The Effects of the Overlord Air Plan to Disrupt Enemy Rail Communications," November 4, 1944, 506.551-1, USAFHRA.

18. SHAEF, report, "Survey of Attacks on the French Railway Centers," November 12, 1944, 506.55C, USAFHRA.

19. BAU, report no. 4, November 4, 1944, AIR 37/1261, PRO.

20. Draft history of the Bombing Analysis Unit, n.d., 505.54-2, USAFHRA.

21. BAU, report No. 6, November 24, 1944, 506.551-6, USAFHRA.

22. Ibid.

23. BAU, report No. 7, AIR 37/1261, PRO.

24. SHEAF, draft history of Overlord, n.d., 142.042-14, USAFHRA.

25. Leigh-Mallory to Eisenhower, report, November 1944, box 104, Spaatz Papers, LOC.

26. SHAEF, draft history of Overlord, n.d., 142.042-13, USAFHRA.

27. IXth TAC ORS, report No. 60, "An Analysis of Fighter Bomber Attacks on Bridges during the Period 7 May–4 June 1944," July 30, 1944, 533.310, USAFHRA.

28. IXth TAC ORS, report No. 90, "Fighter-Bomber Attacks on the Seine River Bridges," February 10, 1945, 533.310, USAFHRA.

29. IXth TAC ORS, report No. 60 (see note 27 above).

30. AAF Evaluation Board, report, "AAF Evaluation Board in ETO," n.d., 138.4-10, USAFHRA.

31. Craven and Cate, *Argument to V-E Day*, p. 160.

32. Rostow, *Bombing Strategy*, pp. 72–73.

33. OSS, report, "Economic Outpost with the Economic Warfare Division," n.d., RG 226, NARS.

34. AEAF, memo, "Bridge Interdiction," August 10, 1944, 505.26-36, USAFHRA.

35. Headquarters Ninth Air Force, report, "Results Attained by the Destruction of Railway Transportation Centers," July 22, 1944, 505.78-3, USAFHRA.

36. IXth TAC ORS, report No. 67, November 28, 1944, 533.310, USAFHRA.

37. Economic Objectives Unit, report, "Movement of German Divisions into the Lodgment Area: Overlord, D to D+50," October 3, 1944, 533.454-1, USAFHRA.

38. AAF Evaluation Board, report, "Summary Report: Effectiveness of Air Attack Against Rail Transportation in the Battle of France," June 1945, 138.4-37A, USAFHRA.

Chapter 17: German Opinions of Allied Air Campaigns

1. Report of interrogations of von Rundstedt, n.d., box 134, Spaatz Papers, LOC.

2. Blumenson, *Breakout and Pursuit*, p. 213.

3. Report, "Interrogation of Oberst Hoeffner by a Senior RAF Officer," box 134, n.d., Spaatz Papers, LOC.

4. SHAEF, report, "A German Transport Officer's Views on the Results of Air Attacks on Railways," April 24, 1945, 506.619-2, USAFHRA.

5. The report, quoted here and extensively in this chapter, is "Summary of the Views of Oberst I. G. Hoeffner, General Des Transportwesens (Abt V), OB West, On the Effects of Air Attack Against the French Railroad System, Mar.–Sept. '44," by Headquarters 12th Army Group G2, May 11, 1945, 506.619-2, USAFHRA.

6. Ninth Air Force (Advanced), report of an interrogation of Hoeffner by an AIR P/W interrogation unit, March 6, 1945, 506.619-2, USAFHRA.

7. Report of an interrogation of Milch, n.d., box 134, Spaatz Papers, LOC.

Chapter 18: Evaluations of Allied Air Offensives: Oil, V-Weapons, Aircraft, Road Junctions, Carpet Bombing

1. Arnold to Spaatz, June 1944, box 15, Spaatz Papers, LOC.
2. Craven and Cate, *Argument to V-E Day*, p. 790.
3. USSBS, report no. 109, *Oil Division — Final Report* (Washington, D.C.: USSBS, 1947), p. 23.
4. Ibid, p. 122.
5. Table adapted from John Ellis, *Brute Force* (New York: Viking, 1990), p. 205.
6. USSTAF historian, report of an interview of Spaatz, n.d., box 136, Spaatz Papers, LOC.
7. Jones, *The Wizard War*, p. 428.
8. Ibid., p. 459.
9. Ibid.
10. Brereton, *Diaries*, p. 297.
11. Basil Collier, *The Battle of the V-Weapons, 1944–1945* (New York: William Morrow, 1965), p. 148.
12. Eighth Air Force ORS, report, "Bomb Damage Survey of Road Interdiction in French Towns," August 16, 1944, 520.310, USAFHRA.
13. Ninth Bomber Command ORS, report no. 49, "Road Interdiction Within Towns," 533.310, USAFHRA.
14. Report of an interview of W. Messerschmitt, n.d., box 134, Spaatz Papers, LOC.
15. USSBS Aircraft Division, report, p. 88.
16. Craven and Cate, *Argument to V-E Day*, p. 164–166.
17. USSTAF G-2, report, "An Appreciation of Heavy Bomber Attacks on Airfields in Germany," October 25, 1944, box 17, Doolittle Papers, LOC.
18. Craven and Cate, *Argument to V-E Day*, p. 237.
19. Harold W. Ohlke, "Report of Investigation of Bombing, July 24–25," n.d., box 168, Spaatz Papers, LOC.
20. Walter E. Todd, "Report of Operations 24 and 25 July 1944," box 168, Spaatz Papers, LOC.
21. Ibid.
22. Doolittle to Spaatz, memo, August 10, 1944, box 18, Doolittle Papers, LOC.
23. John H. de Russy, "Summary of Planning and Execution of Missions 24 and 25 July 1944," n.d., 520.453A, USAFHRA.
24. Ohlke, "Investigation of Bombing" (see note 19 above).
25. Spaatz, diary entry, July 26, 1944, box 15, Spaatz Papers, LOC.

Chapter 19: Postwar Debates About Allied Air Campaigns

1. Zuckerman, *From Apes to Warlords*.
2. Ibid., p. 237.

3. Charles P. Kindleberger, note in *Encounter*, vol. 51, no. 5, November 1978, pp. 39–40.
4. Zuckerman, note in *Encounter*, vol. 52, no. 6, June 1979, p. 87.
5. Ibid., p. 89.
6. Kindleberger, note in *Encounter*, vol. 52, no. 6, June 1979, p. 89.
7. W. W. Rostow, note in *Encounter*, vol. 55, nos. 2–3, August–September 1980, p. 100.
8. Zuckerman, note in *Encounter*, vol. 55, nos. 2–3, August–September 1980, p. 101.

Epilogue

1. Foot, *S.O.E. in France*, p. 225.

Glossary

AAF Army Air Forces
AEAF Allied Expeditionary Air Forces
AFB Air Force Base
Anvil codename for Allied landings in southern France
Argument coordinated attacks of Eighth and Fifteenth Air forces against aircraft factories
AWPD Air War Plans Division
BAU Bombing Analysis Unit
CBO Combined Bombing Offensive
CCS Combined Chiefs of Staff committee
Cobra codename for First U.S. Army offensive, July 1944
CCA Combat Command A
Crossbow codename for the offensive against V-weapons.
Enigma complex electrical machine used by Germans to encipher and decipher messages
EOU Enemy Objectives Unit
GAF German Air Force
G-2 headquarters intelligence section
NAA North American Aviation
MAAF Mediterranean Allied Air Forces
mission an operation to accomplish a specific objective
Noball codename for V-weapons targets
Neptune codename for the assault phase of Overlord
ORS Operational Research Section
OSS Office of Strategic Services
Overlord codename for the invasion of northwest Europe
Pointblank codename for the strategic bombing offensive against Germany
RAF Royal Air Force
SHAEF Supreme Headquarters Allied Expeditionary Forces
sortie a single operation of a single aircraft
SOE Special Operations Executive
TAC Tactical Air Command
Ultra codename for Allied program of interception and decryption of German radio communications
USSBS United States Strategic Bombing Survey
USSTAF United States Strategic Air Forces

Bibliography

Aldrich, Nelson W., Jr. *Tommy Hitchcock: An American Hero*. Gaithersburg, Md.: Fleet Street, 1985.
Arnold, Henry Harley. *Global Mission*. New York: Harper, 1949.
Aron, Robert. *France Reborn*. New York: Charles Scribner's Sons, 1964.
Baumbach, Werner. *The Life and Death of the Luftwaffe*. New York: Coward-McCann, 1949.
Baxter, James Phinney, III. *Scientists against Time*. Boston: Little, Brown, 1946.
Bennett, Ralph. *Ultra and Mediterranean Strategy*. New York: William Morrow, 1989.
_____. *Ultra in the West*. New York: Charles Scribner's Sons, 1979.
Birch, David. *Rolls-Royce and the Mustang*. Derby, England: Rolls-Royce Heritage Trust, 1987.
Blair, Clay. *Ridgeway's Paratroopers*. Garden City, N.Y.: Dial Press, 1985.
Blum, John Morton. *From the Morgenthau Diaries*. Vol. II. Boston: Houghton Mifflin, 1964.
Blumenson, Martin. *The U.S. Army in World War II: Breakout and Pursuit*. Washington, D.C.: Center for Military History, 1961.
Blumentritt, Gunther. *Von Rundstedt, the Soldier and the Man*. London: Odhams Press, 1952.
Boylan, Bernard. *Development of the Long-Range Escort Fighter*. Maxwell AFB, Al.: USAF Air University, 1955.
Bradley, Omar N. *A Soldier's Story*. New York: Henry Holt, 1951.
Bradley, Omar and Clay Blair. *A General's Life*. New York: Simon and Schuster, 1983.
Brereton, Lewis. *The Brereton Diaries*. New York: William Morrow, 1946.
Butcher, Harry C. *My Three Years with Eisenhower*. New York: Simon and Schuster, 1946.
Caldwell, Donald L. *JG 26*. New York: Orion Books, 1991.
Carell, Paul. *Invasion — They're Coming*. New York: E. P. Dutton, 1963.
Chandler, Alfred D., Jr. ed. *The Papers of Dwight David Eisenhower*. Baltimore: The Johns Hopkins University Press, 1970.
Churchill, Winston S. *Closing the Ring*. Boston: Houghton Mifflin, 1951.
_____. *The Hinge of Fate*. Boston: Houghton Mifflin, 1950.
Coffey, Thomas M. *HAP*. New York: Viking Press, 1982.
_____. *Iron Eagle: The Turbulent Life of General Curtis Le May*. New York: Crown Publishers, 1986.
Cole, Hugh M. *The U.S. Army in World War II: The Lorraine Campaign*. Washington, D.C.: Center for Military History, 1950.
Collier, Basil. *The Battle of the V-Weapons, 1944–1945*. New York: William Morrow, 1965.
Collier, Richard. *Ten Thousand Eyes*. New York: E. P. Dutton, 1958.
Collins, J. Lawton. *Lightning Joe*. Baton Rouge, La.: Louisiana State Univ. Press, 1979.
Copp, Dewitt S. *A Few Great Captains*. Garden City, N.Y.: Doubleday, 1980.
Craven, W. F. and J. L. Cate, eds. *The Army Air Forces in World War II*. Chicago: Univ. of Chicago Press, 1948.
_____. *Plans and Early Operations, January 1939–August 1942*, Vol. 1 of *The Army Air Forces in World War II*.
_____. *Europe: TORCH to POINTBLANK, August 1942 to December 1943*. Vol. 2 of *The Army Air Forces in World War II*. Chicago: The Univ. of Chicago Press, 1949.

_____. *Europe: ARGUMENT to V-E Day, January 1944 to May 1945.* Vol. 3 of *The Army Air Forces in World War II.* Chicago: The Univ. of Chicago Press, 1951.
_____. *Men and Planes.* The Univ. of Chicago Press, 1951.
Davis, Albert, ed. *56th Fighter Group in World War II.* Washington, D.C.: Infantry Journal Press, 1948.
Davis, Richard C., *Carl A. Spaatz and the Air War in Europe* Washington, D.C.: Center for Air Force History, 1993.
de Gaulle, Charles. *Unity: 1942–44.* Vol. 2 of *War Memoirs of Charles de Gaulle.* N.p., 1959.
Delmar, Sefton. *The Counterfeit Spy.* New York: Harper and Row, 1971.
De Seversky, Alexander. *Victory through Air Power.* New York: Simon and Schuster, 1942.
Devon Francis. *Flak Bait.* New York: Duell, Sloan & Pearce, 1948.
Doolittle, James H. *I Could Never Be So Lucky Again.* New York: Bantam Books, 1991.
Douhet, Giulio. *The Command of the Sky.* New York: Coward-McCann, 1942.
Eden, Anthony. *The Reckoning.* Boston: Houghton Mifflin, 1965.
Eisenhower, Dwight D. *At Ease.* Garden City, N.Y.: Doubleday, 1967.
_____. *Crusade in Europe.* Garden City, N.Y.: Doubleday, 1948.
Ellis, John. *Brute Force.* New York: Viking, 1990.
Ethell, Jeffrey. *Mustang.* London: Janes's, 1981.
Farago, Ladislas. *Burn After Reading.* New York: Walker, 1961.
Ferrell, Robert H., ed. *Eisenhower Diaries.* New York: W. W. Norton, 1981.
Foot, M. R. D. *S.O.E. in France.* London: Her Majesty's Stationery Office, 1966.
Freeman, Roger A. *B-26 Marauder at War.* New York: Charles Scribner's Sons, 1979.
Fry, Garry L. and Jeffrey L. Ethell. *Escort to Berlin.* New York: Arco Publishing, 1980.
Galland, Adolf. *The First and the Last: The Rise and Fall of the German Fighter Forces, 1938–1945.* New York: Henry Holt, 1954.
Gavin, James M. *On to Berlin.* New York: Viking Press, 1978.
Gilbert, Martin. *Winston S. Churchill: Road to Victory, 1941–1945.* Boston: Houghton Mifflin, 1986.
Glines, Carroll V. *Jimmy Doolittle.* New York: Harper and Brothers, 1949.
Godfrey, John T. *The Look of Eagles.* New York: Random House, 1958.
Goralski, Robert and Russel W. Freiburg. *Oil and War: How the Deadly Struggle for Fuel in World War II Meant Victory or Defeat.* New York: William Morrow, 1987.
Gruenhagen, Robert W. *Mustang: The Story of the P-51 Fighter.* Rev. ed. New York: Arco Publishing, 1976.
Hamilton, Nigel. *Master of the Battlefield.* New York: McGraw-Hill, 1983.
Hansell, Haywood S., Jr. *The Air Plan That Defeated Hitler.* Atlanta, Ga.: Higgins-McArthur/Longino and Porter, 1972.
Harker, Ronald J. *The Engines Were Rolls-Royce.* New York: Macmillan Publishing, 1979.
Harris, Arthur. *Bomber Offensive.* New York: Macmillan Publishing, 1947.
Harrison, Gordon A. *The U.S. Army in World War II: Cross-Channel Attack.* Washington, D.C.: Office of the Chief of Military History, 1951.
Hastings, Max. *OVERLORD.* New York: Simon and Schuster, 1984.
Healy, Allan, *The 467th Bombardment Group, September 1943–June 1945.* Privately printed, 1947; reprint, 1980. North Tonawanda, N.Y.: Enterprise Printing, 1980.
Hess, William N. *P-47 Thunderbolt at War.* Garden City, N.Y.: Doubleday, 1977.
Hewitt, Robert L. *Workhorse of the Western Front.* Washington, D.C.: Infantry Journal Press, 1946.
Hinsley, F. H. *British Intelligence in the Second World War.* New York: Cambridge Univ. Press, 1988.
Howard, James H. *The Roar of the Tiger.* New York: Orion Books, 1991.
Jackson, Robert. *The Secret Squadrons.* London: Robson Books, 1983.
Johnson, Charles. *History of the Hell Hawks.* Anaheim, Calif.: Southcoast Typesetting, 1975.
Johnson, J. E. *Wing Leader.* New York: Ballantine Books, 1957.
Jones, R. V. *The Wizard War.* New York: Coward, McCann and Geoghegan, 1978.
Kantor, MacKinlay. *Mission with Le May.* Garden City, N.Y.: Doubleday, 1965.

Kimball, Warren F., ed. *Churchill and Roosevelt, the Complete Correspondence*. Princeton, N.J.: Princeton Univ. Press, 1984.
Kingston-McCloughry, E. J. *The Direction of War*. New York: Frederick A. Praeger, 1955.
Knight, Frida. *The French Resistance*. London: Lawrence and Wishart, 1975.
Kozaczuk, Wladyslaw. *ENIGMA*. Frederick, Md.: University Publications of America, 1984.
Liddell-Hart, B. H. *The Rommel Papers*. London: Collins, 1953.
Lindbergh, Charles A. *The Wartime Journals of Charles A. Lindbergh*. New York: Harcourt Brace Jovanovich, 1970.
McFarland, Stephen L. and Wesley P. Newton. *To Command the Sky*. Washington, D.C.: Smithsonian Institution Press, 1991.
Macmillan, Harold. *War Diaries*. New York: St. Martin's Press, 1984.
Messinger, Charles. *Bomber Harris*. New York: St. Martin's Press, 1984.
Michie, Allan A. *The Air Offensive against Germany*. New York: Henry Holt, 1943.
Middlebrook, Martin and Chris Everitt. *The Bomber Command War Diaries*. New York: Viking Penguin, 1985.
Mierzejewski, Alfred C., *The Collapse of the German War Economy, 1944–1945*. Chapel Hill, N.C.: The Univ. of North Carolina Press, 1988.
Morgan, Kay Summersby. *Past Forgetting*. New York: Simon and Schuster, 1975.
Mortensen, Daniel. *A Pattern for Joint Operations: World War II Close Air Support North Africa*. Washington, D.C.: Office of Air Force History and U.S. Center of Military History, 1987.
Murray, Williamson. *Strategy for Defeat*. Maxwell AFB, Al: Air University Press, 1983.
Officers of the Regiment. *History of the 120th Infantry Regiment*. Washington, D.C.: Infantry Journal Press, 1945.
OMAHA Beachhead. Washington, D.C.: Historical Division of the War Department, September 20, 1945.
Parton, James. *Air Force Spoken Here*. Bethesda, Md.: Adler Adler, 1986.
Patton, George S., Jr. *Was as I Knew It*. Boston: Houghton Mifflin, 1947.
Pogue, Forrest. *Ordeal and Hope*. Vol. 3 of *George C. Marshall*. New York: Viking Press, 1966.
_____. *The U.S. Army in World War II: The Supreme Command*. Washington, D.C.: Office of the Chief of Military History, Department of the Army, 1954.
Puryear, Edgar F., Jr. *Stars in Flight*. Novato, Calif. Presidio Press, 1981.
Richards, Dennis. *Portal of Hungerford*. London: William Heinemann, 1977.
Rings, Werner. *Life with the Enemy*. Garden City, N.Y.: Doubleday, 1982.
Rostow, W. W. *Pre-Invasion Bombing Strategy*. Austin: Univ. of Texas Press, 1981.
Rust, Ken C. and William N. Hess. *The Slybird Group*. Fallbrook, Calif.: Aero Publishers, 1968.
Sallagar, F. M. *Operation STRANGLE (Italy, Spring 1944): A Case Study of Tactical Air Interdiction*. Santa Monica, Calif.: Rand, February 1972.
Schlaefer, Ronald and S. D. Heron. *Development of Aircraft Engines and Fuels*. Boston: Harvard Univ. Graduate School of Business Administration, 1950.
Shulman, Milton. *Defeat in the West*. New York: E. P. Dutton, 1948.
Slessor, Sir John. *The Central Blue*. London: Cassell, 1956.
Strong, Kenneth. *Intelligence at the Top*. New York: Doubleday, 1969.
Taylor, John M. *General Maxwell Taylor: The Sword and the Pen*. New York: Doubleday, 1989.
Tedder, Sir Arthur. *Air Power in War*. London: Hoddard and Stoughton, 1948.
_____. *With Prejudice*. Boston: Little, Brown, 1966.
Thomas, Lowell and Edward Jablonski. *Doolittle*. Garden City, N.Y.: Doubleday, 1976.
Webster, Charles and Noble Frankland. *The Strategic Air Offensive against Germany, 1939–1945*. 4 vols. London: Her Majesty's Stationery Office, 1961.
Wedemeyer, Albert C. *Wedemeyer Reports*. New York: Henry Holt, 1958.
Ziegler, Junior G. *Bridgebusters*. New York: Gannis and Harris, 1949.
Zimmerman, Bodo. *The Fatal Decisions*. Ed. Seymour Freiden and William Richardson. New York: William Sloan Associates, 1956.
Zuckerman, Sir Solly. *From Apes to Warlords*. London: Hamish Hamilton, 1978.
_____. *Scientists and War*. London: Hamish Hamilton, 1966.

Index

Acheres 99
Aerial gunnery 22, 24
Air Defence of Great Britain 52
Air Forces *see* specific division
Air-ground Cooperation: AAF policies 87–88; armored column cover 124, 141; Arnold 84; discord 87, 88, 141; Edwards' 84; enmity 7, 9, 11; Quesada 124; Weyland 143
Air Ministry (UK) 112
Air supremacy: AAF policy 88; AEAF 53; F. Anderson 89; benefits 61, 131, 135; "Big Week" 65; Eaker 28; Eisenhower 98; Overlord 5; P-51 39–50; Pointblank 59–68; RAF 66; Spaatz 53, 55; transportation campaign 58; weather 145
Air War Doctrine 12, 35, 88
Air War Plans 12, 19, 20
Airborne forces 115–117
Aircraft equipment 24, 85
Aircraft modification 23, 62, 83
Aircraft obsolescence 24
Aircraft types, U.S.: A-20 107; B-17 20, 22, 49; B-24 20, 22, 30, 62; B-26 56; C-47 89, 115; P-40 45; *see also* BG-322; P-38 aircraft; P-47 aircraft; P-51 aircraft
Airfields 66–68, 83, 113, 135, 171
Allied Expeditionary Air Forces: Arnold 52, 148; bridges 108–110, 145; Butler 52, 55–56; invasion 123; Eisenhower 6, 148; escort fighters 53, Leigh-Mallory 6, 14–15, 52, 53, 148; medium bombers 56, 57; P-51 54; Quesada 160; RAF 14; Spaatz 52, 53, 55; staff report (US) 161; terminated 148; track cuts 162; transportation campaign 71; Vandenberg 55, 124, 148
Allison engine 37, 40
Amiens 95, 156
Anderson, Maj. Gen. Frederick 35, 53, 57, 74
Anderson, Brig. Gen. S. E. 107, 111, 122
Angers 99
Anti-aircraft Artillery: 22, 23, 65, 84, 102, 104–106, 110, 111, 128, 135, 145, 170, 174
Appeasement 69
Argentan 99
Argument *see* Pointblank
Armies: First Allied Airborne 145; Second Army (UK) 116; Third Army 143–145; *see also* First Army

Armored Column Cover 85, 142–143
Army Air Corps 8, 84
Army Air Forces: Evaluation Board 161–164; Headquarters 33, 49, 52, 62, 84, 88; Proving Ground Command 47, 50, 103; Pursuit Boards 30, 84
Army Field Manual, FM 100–20 8
Army Groups: 12th Army Group 143, 196; 21st Army Group (UK) 73, 109, 137
Arnold, Gen. H. H.: AEAF 52, 148; B-24 62; Brereton 84, 90; directives 59, 84, 136; drop-tanks 32–33; Eighth Air Force 25, 31, 33; Eisenhower 78, 147, 148; German Air Force 59, 126; gunners' claims 25; Hopkins 44; long-range fighters 46; Lovett 46; Marshall 11, 87; Normandy 126; P-51 43–44; Portal 28; RAF 28, 126; Roosevelt 44; strategic bombing 147; tours of combat duty 60; USSBS 169; V-weapons 103
Atlee, Clement 96
Aulnoye 94, 156
Avranches 143

Bayerlein, Maj. Gen. Fritz 131, 141
Bearings 28, 64
Beaugency 145
Berlin 64
BG-322 aircraft 56; bomber escort 28; bomb loads 107; bridges 110; characteristics 56; Cherbourg 128; Doolittle 56; Ijmuidan 56; Loire 121; Oissel 111; tactical radius 121; Utah Beach 121
"Big Week" *see* Pointblank
Bishops' Appeal 96
Blainville 98
Blakeslee, Col. Donald 67–68
Blois 120
Bocage 135
Bomb loads 20, 85, 107, 124
Bomb releases 83
Bomber: escort 26, 28, 64; formations 21–22, 61–62, 107
Bombing Analysis Unit 156–159
Bombsights 23
Bottomley, Air Vice Marshal Norman 148
Bourges 113

205

Bradley, Gen. Omar: AAF 136; air support 88, 123; artillery 170; Cobra 139–141, 174; First Army 123; Quesada 123; 12th Army Group 143
Brereton, Lt. Gen. Lewis: Arnold 84, 90; bridges 110; First Allied Airborne Army 145; medium bombers 57, 107; Ninth Air Force 13, 90; Omaha Beach 123; P-51 54–55; road blocks 118, 126; tactical research 89; V-weapons 170
Bridges *see* Interdiction
Brüx 102
Butler, Maj. Gen. William 52, 56

Cabell, Brig. Gen. Charles 78, 82, 96, 175
Caen 99, 118, 137
Call, Col. Lance 103, 109
Carpet Bombing *see* Cobra
Casablanca Conference 26–27
Châlons-sur-Marne 98
Chambly 98
Chartres 121
Cherbourg 115, 128–129
Cherwell, Lord 96, 109
Chokepoints *see* Road Blocks
Churchill, Sir Winston S.: Casablanca Conference 26; civilian deaths 94–95, 101; de Gaulle 99–101; droptanks 30; Eighth Air Force 23–24; Eisenhower 15, 94; Harris 15; Leigh-Mallory 14; Portal 24, 30; RAF 26, 94; Roosevelt 100–101; Spaatz, 9; Tedder 14; transportation campaign 73, 94, 101
Chief of the Imperial General Staff 73, 77
Cinq Mars 121
Civilian Casualties 81, 82, 95–97, 101
Cobra: aborted 139; Bradley 139, 173–174; carpet bombing 139–141; Doolittle 173; evaluated 172–174; Leigh-Mallory 137–139; Zuckerman 137
Collins, Maj. Gen. J. Lawton 128, 139, 140, 142
Combined Bomber Offensive *see* Pointblank
Combined Chiefs of Staff 5, 87, 94, 147
Commands *see* specific command
Committee of Operations Analysts 27
Compiègne 156
Conflans-Ste. Honorine 111
Corps: V Corps 116; VII Corps 116, 128, 140–142
Cotentin Peninsula 128
Coutances 99, 118, 119, 121
Creil 156
Crossbow *see* V-weapons

De Gaulle, Gen. Charles 99–101
DeSeversky, A. 24, 84
Dive Bombing *see* Fighter Bombers
Divisions: 82nd Airborne 115–116; 101st Airborne 115–116; 2nd Armored 142; 4th Infantry 116; 30th Infantry 140; Panzer Lehr (Ger.) 133; 2nd SS Panzer (Ger.) 133; 17th SS Panzer (Ger.) 133
Doolittle, Maj. Gen. James: aces 106; B-24 61; B-26 56; bridges 120, 121; Cobra 173; Eighth Air Force 9; fighters 63; P-38 37; radar 74; Spaatz 61; transportation campaign 73; warnings to civilians 118; weather 61; *see also* Eighth Air Force

Droptanks 31–33, 64
Duncan, Maj. Glenn 85–86
Duxford 40, 43

Eagle Squadrons 67
Eaker, Lt. Gen. Ira: AAF headquarters 10; Arnold 34, 36, 37; background 22; Casablanca conference 26; criticism 25; diversions 26; droptanks 32, 33; Eighth Air Force 21, 34, 50; fighter escort 26; Hunter 34–36; MAAF 9, 76; medium bombers 56; RAF 22, 71; strategic bombing 21; tours of combat duty 60
Eden, Anthony 96
Edwards, Maj. Gen. Idwal 84
Eglin AFB 38, 50, 103
Eighth Air Force: air supremacy 5, 28, 66; airfields 171; bombers 20; bombsights 23; bridges 119; Churchill 23–24; commanders 35–36; Cobra 139–140; criticism 24–25; invasion 118, 128; diversions 26; droptanks 31–33; escort 35; fighters 29–51; growth 19–51; gunnery 22; Hansell 49; leaflets 118; LeMay 22, 33; losses 28; oil 113; ORS 21; policies 21; Rouen 21; submarine pens 22; transportation campaign 98; weather 22
VIII Bomber Comand: F. Anderson 35; Eaker 21; gunnery 22; LeMay 22; Rouen 21; submarine pens 22; weather 22; *see also* Eighth Air Force
VIII Fighter Command: air supremacy 64–67; Cobra 139; criticism 33–35; droptanks 31–33; Hunter 29, 34–35; invasion 119, 128; Kepner 35, 51, 63; *see also* Eighth Air Force
Eisenhower, Gen. Dwight D.: airborne operations 115; Butler 56; Churchill 15, 94; Cobra 137; commanders 21, 37, 58; Leigh-Mallory 14–15, 55, 118, 137, 148; Marshall 14, 17, 147; Oil Campaign 80–82; Overlord 5; Pointblank 55; Portal 15, 77; Quesada 128; road blocks 118; Spaatz 5–11, 53, 71, 81; Tedder 5, 15, 71, 81; transportation campaign 71, 75, 79, 81, 94, 153–154; USSTAF 53, 59; V-weapons 170–171
Encounter 175
Enemy Objectives Unit: agents 101; bridges 161; CBO 71; German troop moves 162; interdiction 161; Overlord air plan 101; track cuts 77; transportation campaign 73, 75, 155
Engineers 58, 89, 124, 129, 136
Enigma 66

Field Manual 100-20 88
Fifteenth Air Force 10, 59, 102
Fighter-bomber: airfields 68, 106, 171–172; Blakeslee 68; bridges 109–111, 160; Cherbourg 128; Cobra 138, 140; dive bombers 84; Duncan 85–86; effectiveness 107; EOU 161; flak 145; Godfrey 106; missions 44, 84; Normandy 117, 124–126; radar 123; tactics 110; track cuts 121; train attacks 167; Wymond 86
Fighters: aces 100; droptanks 31–33; Eaker 25, 34, 63–65, 76; effectiveness 62–64, 64–65; escort 26, 28, 30, 35, 64; Hunter 31, 32, 34, 46; ORS 23; problems 29–51; sweeps 31, 55; tactical radius 65

First Army: air support 123–126; Bocage 135; Bradley 88, 123; Cherbourg 128–129; Cobra 140
France: de Gaulle 99–101; Koenig 101; Resistance 101, 131, 163; road blocks 98–99; Roosevelt 99
Freeman, Air Chief Marshal Wilfred 32
Friedrichshafen 98

Galland, Gen. Adolf 64, 65, 130–131
Gavin, Brig. Gen. James 117
German Air Force: air supremacy 5, 66–67, 82, 88; Arnold 126; attrition 64–66; Eaker 28; fighter tactics 63–64, 130; fuel shortage 102, 114; intelligence 89, 127; invasion 118, 130, 169
Ghent 94, 156
Giles, Lt. Gen. Barney 46–47, 51
Gliders 115
Godfrey, Capt. John 113
Goering, Reichsmarschall Hermann 64
Grenoble 98, 148
Ground attack: Army policies 87–88; Arnold 84, 87; Duncan 85–86; GAF 127; German troops 127, 131; Normandy 87, 117, 124; Kindleberger 156; P-47 66–68; pilots 85; Quesada 87, 123, 124; Rommel 134; training 58, 123; USSTAF 134; weather 146; Weyland 143; Wymond 86–87
Groups: 322nd Bomb Group 56–57; 467th Bomb Group 120–121; 4th Fighter Group 29, 68, 106, 128; 55th Fighter Group 38; 78th Fighter Group 30; 353rd Fighter Group 85, 86; 354th Fighter Group 49; 365th Fighter Group 86–87, 103–104, 110–111; 366th Fighter Group 112; 373rd Fighter Group 112; 67th Tactical Reconnaissance Group 83
Gunnery 22, 24, 26, 36, 50
Gunsights 46, 50

Hansell, Brig. Gen. H. S., Jr. 22, 23, 49
Harker, R. 40–41
Harriman, W. Averell 26, 42
Harris, Air Chief Marshal Arthur: character 15; Eisenhower 148; oil campaign 80, 103; Overlord 15; Portal 15; submarines 26; Tedder 15, 16; transportation campaign 74, 77
Hitchcock, Margaret 43
Hitchcock, Thomas: Arnold 43, 45; fighter production 44–45; gunsights 46; Harriman 42; Hopkins 44; Hunter 46; killed 89; Lovett 43; P-51 40–46; E. Roosevelt 43; F.D. Roosevelt 44; Winant 42
Hoeffner, Col. Hans 165–166
Hopkins, Harry 26, 42, 49
Hunter, Brig. Gen. Frank: Arnold 33, 34; droptanks 31, 32; Eaker 34, 36; Eighth Fighter Command 34; Hitchcock 46; P-47 34; relief 35; World War I 33

Ijmuidan 56
Intelligence: Arnold 127; British sources 89, 96, 127; GAF 83, 89, 127; JIC 127; oil campaign 127; Spaatz 114; transportation campaign 95; 12th Army Group 166; V-weapons 103; *see also* Ultra

Interdiction: AAF Evaluation Board 161, 163–164; AAF doctrine 70, 88; goals 77; AEAF 71, 108, 161; agenda 78; bomb fuses 112; Brereton 118, 126; bridges 74, 109, 110–113, 119–121, 160, 163, 167; Eisenhower 155; handbook 161; Leigh-Mallory 71, 155; locomotives 163; Ninth Air Force 156, 163; Quesada 160; railroad traffic 163; rings 35, 75, 119; road blocks 171; SHAEF 113; Spaatz 81, 84; Tedder 96, 155; track cuts 89, 121, 162, 163; trains 113; Zuckerman 71, 76, 176
Italy 76, 86, 176

Jettisonable tanks *see* Droptanks
Johnson, Wing Cmdr. J. E. 66
Joint Chiefs of Staff 7, 11, 87
Joint Intelligence Committee 127

Kepner, Maj. Gen. William: background 35; Eighth Fighter Command 51; gunsights 50; Normandy 135; P-38 38; P-47 62, 63; P-51 54–55; Giles 51
Kindleberger, Maj. Charles P. 156, 175–176
Kindelberger, J. H. 44–45
Kluge, FM Gunther von 143, 165
Koenig, Gen. Joseph 101

Lancaster 40, 93
Landing fields, advanced 58
Laon 94, 127
Leaflets 94, 113, 118
Leavenworth 136
Leigh-Mallory, Air Chief Marshall Trafford: AEAF 6 14, 52; airborne losses 115; air supremacy 53; ambiguous status 12, 14; Brereton 55; bridges 108–109; COBRA 134, 137, 139; death 148; Eisenhower 14–15, 148; mediums 56; P-47 54–55; P-51 54–55; personality 52–53; Portal 56; record 148; road blocks 118; Smith 14; Spaatz 53–55; Spitfire 28; Tedder 15, 52; transportation campaign 74, 155, 158
Leipzig 113
Le Manoir 111
Le Mans 93, 95
LeMay, Brig. Gen. Curtis 22, 33
Leuna 102
Lille 93, 156
Lindbergh, Charles A. 45
Lisieux 99, 118
Lockheed Aircraft Co. *see* P-38 aircraft
Loire River 119–121, 156, 158–161
Long-Range Escort Fighters: AAF doctrine 28, 30; Arnold 464; Churchill 30; Giles 46; Lovett 46, 54; Pointblank 65; Portal 28, 30; *see also* P-38 aircraft; P-47 aircraft; P-51 aircraft.
London 75, 170
Lovett, Asst. Sec. of War Robert: background 43; gunsights 46; Hitchcock 43–44, 49; long-range fighters 43, 44, 46; P-51 54–55
Luftflotte 6, 130
Lützkendorf 102

MacArthur, Gen. Douglas 13
McNair, Lt. Gen. Lesley 140

Maisons-Lafitte 111, 121
Malines 98
Mantes-Gassicourt 110, 111
Marshall, Gen. George: Combined Chief of Staff 5; Arnold 11, 87; bombers 147; command appointments 14; Eisenhower-Portal agreement 17; Combined Chief of Staff directive 147
Martin Marauder *see* B-26 aircraft
Mediterranean Allied Air Forces 9–11, 76, 86
Medium Bomber *see* B-26 aircraft
Merderet River 115
Merseberg 102
Messerschmitt, Willy 171
Meulan 111
Michie, Allan 24
Microwave Early Warning System (MEWS) 123
Middle Wallop 89
Milch, Gen. Feldmarschall Erhard 65, 167
Ministry of Economic Warfare (MEW) 73, 77, 80, 97
Montgomery, Field Marshall Bernard 6, 109, 136
Morgan, Lt. Gen. Frederick 132
Morgenthau, Henry, Jr. 40
Munich 19
Mustang *see* P-51 aircraft

Namur 111
Nantes 120, 121
Neptune *see* Overlord
Night Bombing 26, 93–94
IX Bomber Command: AEAF 56; Anderson, S. E. 107, 111, 121; bombing 107; Brereton 107; bridges 110–111, 112, 121; Cobra 139, 141–142; commended 112; interdiction 121, 162; Loire River 121; size 55; V-weapons 104; *see also* Ninth Air Force
IX Engineer Command 58, 89, 124
IX Fighter Command 13
IX Tactical Air Command: armored column cover, 124; Brereton 90; Cobra 141–142; First Army 90, 123–126; invasion 123–126; Quesada 123, 124; radar 142; track cuts 89, 121, 163; *see also* Ninth Air Force
IX Troop Carrier Command 55, 58, 89, 115–116
XIX Tactical Air Command 90, 143–145, 146
Ninth Air Force: AEAF 52, 148; airfields 88, 171; Arnold 84; Brereton 13; bridges 109; Crossbow 103–104; EOU 162; escort 88; interdiction 156; lessons 126; mediums 107; P-51 54; Pointblank 55; reconnaissance 83; road blocks 171; size 55; supply crisis 145; transportation campaign 98, 156; UK bases 83; USSTAF 55; Utah Beach 121; Vandenberg 145
Normandy 115–123
North American Aviation Co. (NAA) 39, 40, 44, 49; *see also* P-51 aircraft
North African Theater of Operations 26, 30, 88

OBOE *see* Radar
Office of Strategic Services 101; *see also* Enemy Objectives Unit
Oil Campaign: attacks 82, 101–102; Cabell 78; EOU 101; Messerschmitt 171; plan 71, 80, 101–102; production 78; results 80, 102, 114, 169; SHAEF 114; Spaatz 101–103; USSBS 169
Oise River 110
Oissel 111, 121
Omaha Beach 123
Operational Research Sections: AAF Evaluation Board 153, 161; bomber formations 21; bridges 110, 160–161, 112; Eaker 23; road blocks 171; tasks 89; track cuts 89, 162
Orival 160
Orléans 99, 120
Overlord: air supremacy 5, 14, 53, 59–69, 66; Cobra 123–129; commanders 5–17; Harris 15; interdiction 107–114; invasion 83–90; Morgan 132; oil campaign 81–82, 101–103; reconnaissance 83; Spaatz 14, 53–54, 66, transportation campaign 69–82; V-weapons 102–104; *see also* Eisenhower; SHAEF

P-38 aircraft: characteristics 37–38; escort 50; 474th Fighter Group 127; gasoline 39; invasion 117–127; Kepner 38; losses 105; tactical radius 64
P-47 aircraft: bridges 109; characteristics 29, 30–31; dive bombing 85–86; Eighth Fighter Command 29; escort 50; ground attack 66–67, 85, 86; Hunter 34–35; losses 105; modifications 51, 83; Ninth Air Force 54–55; Normandy 124; pilots' opinions 62; range 83–84, 102; 365th Fighter Group 103–104
P-51 aircraft: air supremacy 66; AAF 40; breakdowns 88; bridges 112; British 39; characteristics 39–40, 47; Eighth Air Force 54–55, 83; escort 59; gasoline 47; Giles 46–49; Hitchcock 40–43, 53; Kepner 51; losses 66; NAA 39, 44–45; Rolls-Royce 40–42; tactical radius 64; Winant 40, 49, 75
Packard Motor Co. 40, 45, 49
Pantelleria 69
Panzer Lehr *see* Divisions
Paris 112
Pas-de-Calais 109, 112, 113
Pathfinder operations 93
Patton, Lt. Gen. George: flanks 143; fuel shortage 145; interdiction 145; Third Army 143–145; Weyland 102
Périers 134, 138
Pershing, Gen. John 7
Pétain, Marshal Henri 96
Ploesti 102
Pointblank: "Big Week" 64–65; CBO 13, 53, 59, 102; endangered 26, 59; evaluated 171; plan 71–72; timing 13
Poissy 111
Polish mathematicians 65–66; *see also* Ultra
Pontaubault 121
Portal, MRAF Sir Charles: Arnold 28; Casablanca Conference 26; Churchill 24, 30; civilians 94; Eighth Air Force 23, 24; Eisenhower 15, 77, 79; Harris 15; medium bombers 57; oil campaign 80; Spaatz 9, 60; Spitfire 28; strategic bombing 59, 148; Tedder 7 77; transportation campaign 78, 79–81; USSTAF 95

Poznan 113
Pratt and Whitney engine 30, 1
Proving Ground Command 11, 38, 103
Proximity fuse 29, 170

Quesada, Maj. Gen. Elwood: AEAF 148; armored column cover 142; Bradley 123; bridges 160; Eisenhower 128; ground attack 87, 124; Ninth Tactical Air Command 13; track cuts 90; 354th Fighter Group 49; *see also* IX Tactical Air Command

Radar 61, 74, 98, 104, 123, 170
Railroads: anti-invasion 75; cargo 113, centers 70–71; Hoeffner 165–167; Italy 76–77; Leigh-Mallory 158; MEW 97; RAF 98–99; Resistance 132, 133; SHAEF 97; Tedder 95; track cuts 89; traffic 157, 163; trains 113; *see also* Transportation Campaign
Reconnaissance: air campaigns 153; Bocage 135; bridges 113; Cobra 141: invasion 117; Ninth Tactical Air Command 58; Overlord 83; 67th Tactical Air Command Reconnaissance Group 83; V-weapons 103, 170
Regensburg 28
Regiments: 120th Infantry 140
Das Reich *see* Divisions, 2nd SS Panzer
Republic Aviation Co. 29, 85; *see also* P-47 aircraft
Resistance: Allied bombing 95; de Gaulle 99–101; evaluations 163; invasion 121, 131–133; 2nd SS Panzer Div. 133; losses 132
Rickenbacker, Capt. Edward 43
Ridgeway, Maj. Gen. Matthew 117
Rockets, 28, 29, 49, 83; *see also* V-Weapons
Rolls-Royce 40, 43–44, 49
Rommel, Field Marshall Erwin 127, 134
Roosevelt, Eleanor 43
Roosevelt, Pres. Franklin D.: AAF 19; Arnold 44; air war plans 19–20; Churchill 101; de Gaulle 99–101; Eisenhower 5; Hopkins 42; Overlord 5; P-51 44; Spaatz 9; transportation campaign 101; USSBS 169; Winant 42
Rose, Brig. Gen. Maurice 142
Rostow, Maj. W. W. 161, 176
Rouen: bridges 109–110, 111, 112; Joan of Arc 99; Pétain 96; rail center bombed 21
Royal Air Force: air supremacy 66; Arnold 127; Bomber Command 13, 93–94, 98, 117; bridges 109; carpet bombing 137; Cherbourg 128; coast artillery 117; Eaker 32; Fighter Command 66; oil campaign 103; radar 104; Saumur 119; SHAEF 82; transportation campaign 98–99; Trappes 93, 150; V-weapons 103
Ruhr 103
Romania 13, 102
Rundstedt, Field Marshall Gerd von 101, 165

Sabotage 132–133
St. Gilles 142
St. Lô 118, 138–140
St. Omer 86
Ste.-Mère-Église 115

Salerno 5
Sarreguemines 98
Saumur 99, 119
Schweinfurt 28
Second Tactical Air Force, (RAF) 52, 117
Seine River: BAU 160; bridges 108–113, 131, 158–160; Mantes-Gassi-court 110; Ninth Air Force 156; Ninth Bomber Command 111–112; Quesada 160; SHAEF 158; Vernon bridge 109–110
SHAEF *see* Supreme Headquarters Allied Expeditionary Forces
Sicily 176
Sinclair, Sir A. 26
Slessor, Air Chief Marshal John 76
Smith, Brig. Gen. Frederick, Jr. 109
Smith, Lt. Gen. W. B. 9, 14
Sorou 113
Spaatz, Lt. Gen. Carl: air supremacy 14, 53–54, 66; Army commanders 136; Arnold 8, 59, 61, 62, 136, 148; authority 13, 60; B-24 62; bombing errors 174; bridges 83, 109, 130; Brereton 54, 58, 59; carpet bombing 134; character 11, 12; civilians 82; Doolittle 61–62; Eaker 10–11, 59–60; Eisenhower 8, 11, 14, 53–55, 71, 80, 102, 147; fighters 63; ground attack 55; Leigh-Mallory 53, 54, 56, 118, 134; Lovett 54; medium bombers 56–57; oil campaign 78, 79–80, 101–102; 169; P-51 54–55; Pointblank 53, 59–68; Portal 60; RAF 147–148; road blocks 98; staff 11; strategic bombing 13, 59, 148; Tedder 9, 15, 16, 77–81; combat tours 60; transportation campaign 71, 79–80; Ultra 66; V-weapons 58, 103; weather 61
Special Operations Executive 101, 132
Speer, Reichsminister Albert 102, 169, 170
Spitfire 28, 66
Stimson, Sec. of War H. L. 43, 169
Strategic Bombing: AWPD-1 19–20; AWPD-42 19–20; CCS 147–148; criticized 24, 29; defined 8, 13–14; oil 102; proposed 20; RAF 23; targets 13, 22, 27–28, 102; theory 21; *see also* Pointblank
Submarines 22, 28
Summersby, Kay 12
Supercharger 31
Supreme Headquarters Allied Expeditionary Forces: air priorities 94; authority 15, 82; BAU reports 156–159; bridges 158; G-2 reports 113, 114, 155; interdiction 71; railroads 157; Resistance 101, 132; strategic air forces 14–15, 53, 147, 158; transportation campaign 97–98; Zuckerman 157
Synthetic Fuels *see* Oil Campaign

Tactial Air Commands *see* Commands
Tactical Air Operations *see* Ground Attack
Tactical Radius 5, 13, 20, 121
Taylor, Maj. Gen. Maxwell 115
Tedder, Air Chief Marshal Arthur: BAU 156; bridges 108; carpet bombing 137; civilian deaths 95–96; critics 77; Harris 27; interdiction 75–76, 96–97; Leigh-Mallory 15, 52–53, 118;

Montgomery 186; Overlord 5; road blocks 118; SHAEF 15; Spaatz 9, 16, 79; transportation campaign 71, 72, 78, 79, 95, 96, 99, 154–155; V-weapons 103; Zuckerman 69, 156
Tergnier 94, 95
Third U. S. Army *see* Armies
Thunderbolt *see* P-47 aircraft
Tours 98, 120–121
Track Cuts *see* Railroads
Transportation Campaign: AAF Evaluation Board 163–164, 168; AAF opposition 70; attacks 74, 93–99; BAU 157–158; Churchill 73, 94, 101; civilian deaths 73, 94; criticisms 71, 73–78; ends 113; Eisenhower 71, 94, 153; EOU 177; evaluations 153–155, 157–158, 163, 167; French reactions 101; goals 71; Hoeffner 165–166; Italy 76–77; Kindleberger 175–176; Leigh-Mallory 158; locomotives 166; Ninth Air Force report 156–157; plan 70–72; RAF 98–99; results 95, 98–99, 113, 145; Roosevelt 101; SHAEF 97, 113; targets 70, 93; Tedder 71, 72, 78, 95, 96, 99; timing 77; 12th Army Group 166; Zuckerman 72, 74, 157–158
Trappes 93, 156
Troop Carrier Command *see* Commands
Troyes 98
Trucks 113, 145
Tutow 113
Typhoon 104, 128

Ultra 65–66, 89, 95, 102, 127
United States Embassy 43, 75
United States Strategic Air Forces: airfield campaigns 172; air supremacy 65–67; Combined Chief of Staff 147; invasion 117; mission 13; oil campaign 78–80, 80, 102, 113, 114, 169; SHAEF 71, 82, 147–148; Spaatz 6, 13, 59–67; Third Army 143–145; transportation campaign 78, 98, 101; *see also* Eighth Air Force; Fifteenth Air Force; Pointblank
United States Strategic Bombing Survey 169, 171
Utah Beach 115, 121
Uxbridge 90

Valenciennes 95
Valogne 170
Vandenberg, Lt. Gen. Hoyt 56, 123, 140, 145
Vernon 109–110, 158, 161
Villers Bocage 118
Vire 99, 118, 131
V-Weapons: AAF Proving Ground Command 103; Arnold 103; attacked 108, 113; Crossbow 102; Eighth Air Force 103; Eisenhower 170–171; 467th Bomber Group 120–121; London 170; Ninth Bomber Command 58; reconnaissance 103; Spaatz 102; threat 12, 13; 365th Fighter Group 87, 103

War Cabinet (UK) 73, 94–95
War Department *see* Arnold, Lovett; Marshall, Stimson.
Weather 22, 61, 71, 75, 163, 145
West Point (USMA) 7
Weyland, Maj. Gen. Otto 143–145, 148
Williams, Maj. Gen. Paul 89
Winant, Ambassador John 42, 49, 75
Wright Brothers 7–8
Wymond, Maj. Gilbert 86–87

Zuckerman, Solly: AEAF 69; BAU 156–157; Cobra 137–138; Hoeffner 167; Italy 77, 176; Kindleberger 176; Rostow 176; Tedder 69–70, 76, 77, 156–157; *see also* Transportation Campaign

www.ingramcontent.com/pod-product-compliance
Ingram Content Group UK Ltd.
Pitfield, Milton Keynes, MK11 3LW, UK
UKHW050529150426
5217IPUK00026B/1857